Share the of those who have been there . . .
Adult sons and daughters speak out about their challenges in
Recovering from the Loss of a Parent

"After a month or so, everyone in my office took it for granted I was fine again. I would get so angry at everyone's indifference . . . I couldn't accept that the world was going on as if everything was the same, when it wasn't the same at all . . . "

"I was somewhat relieved when it was over but wondered if I could have done anything different. I always thought that perhaps I should have paid more attention to her. Maybe I should have gotten her to the hospital sooner. I always wondered if there was something else I could have said or done that would have helped."

"I became convinced that I had cancer and that I was going to die of it as my mother had done. I went to a doctor who reassured me I did not have cancer. What, then, was wrong with me? I was a man looking for a disease. I felt so guilty for some of the things that happened before my mother's death that I had to kill myself with a disease. I wanted punishment."

"It does get better. Now I can't really remember how it was the first year, but I guess time takes care of that. At the moment, it seems to me that it was another lifetime ago—and another person's life."

RECOVERING FROM THE LOSS OF A PARENT

KATHERINE FAIR DONNELLY

BERKLEY BOOKS, NEW YORK

Material from *Concerning Death: A Practical Guide for the Living* by Earl Grollman, © 1974 by Earl A. Grollman, Beacon Press, Boston, 1974, used by permission of The Beacon Press.

"Mother's Day Again: Wish She Were Here" by Walter Kaner, Copyright © 1986 by New York News, Inc. Reprinted by permission.

Material from the *Bereavement Support Program Training Manual* by Karen Arfin, copyright © 1991 by Karen Arfin and reprinted with her permission.

"Recollections: I Remember What They Looked Like" appeared in *Thanatos* magazine and is reprinted here by permission of the author, Katherine Fair Donnelly.

Material from *Living with an Empty Chair* by Roberta Temes reprinted here by permission of Irvington Publishers, Inc. Copyright © 1984 by Roberta Temes.

"A Nursing Home Trauma" appeared in *Thanatos* magazine and is reprinted here by permission of the author, Katherine Fair Donnelly. Copyright © 1991 by Katherine Fair Donnelly.

RECOVERING FROM THE LOSS OF A PARENT

A Berkley Book / published by arrangement with
the author

PRINTING HISTORY
Dodd, Mead & Company edition published 1987
Berkley edition / September 1993

ISBN: 0-425-13916-6

A BERKLEY BOOK ® TM 757,375
Berkley Books are published by The Berkley Publishing Group,
200 Madison Avenue, New York, New York 10016.
The name "BERKLEY" and the "B" logo
are trademarks belonging to Berkley Publishing Corporation.

PRINTED IN THE UNITED STATES OF AMERICA

10 9 8 7 6 5 4 3 2 1

This book is dedicated in loving memory to:

Rose Fair
and
Claire Donnelly

Contents

PART ONE
Experiences of Bereaved Adult Children

PART TWO
Helping Hands

Acknowledgments

I want to thank Ruth Hannon for her invaluable help and careful reading of the manuscript, as well as for her enthusiastic encouragement and friendship.

My thanks to Hillary Cige, Senior Editor of The Berkley Publishing Group, for her insight and helpful suggestions.

I am appreciative of those individuals who took the time to listen to or read all or portions of the book. These include: Dr. Roberta Temes, Athena Drewes, Kenneth Banschick, Ann Magid, and Margaret McAllister.

Most of all, grateful thanks and appreciation to the bereaved adult sons and daughters who participated in this book in a warm outpouring of compassion and sharing, and who have permitted the use of their real names. They are:

Charles (Chuck) F. Akerland, Karen Arfin, John H. Donnelly, Harry Finnegan, Hilary Friedman, Edgar J. Gintz, Max Glauben, Edith E. (Peggy) Griffiths, Walter Kaner, Vivian Kessler, Beth Landau, Sandra Levine, Andrea Fodor Litkei, Margaret McAllister, Ellen Martin, Marjorie Martin, David K. Meagher, Philip Musmacker, Andrew M. Rezin, Carol Richardson, Mary Stellakis, Edward Steudtner, Lisa Strahs-Lorenc, Alex Tanous, E. Joan Urbas, Paul Vento, and Gia Williams.

For others who requested confidentiality and privacy, this wish has been respected and those names and locales or other identifying factors have been changed.

SPECIAL THANKS:

To my husband, John, for his caring, help, and guidance.

To my beloved brother, Jerry Fair, who died too soon, my everlasting love and appreciation for his support, his caring, and his pride in the work I do.

And to whoever handed out brothers and sisters, my eternal gratitude—mine are the greatest: Fannie, Trudy, Al, Sam, and Zetta. They have always been there to help.

Introduction

The death of a parent isn't something that happens to only a few people. Unless we predecease both of them, the death of a parent happens to all of us at some time in our lives.

Although it is normal for bereaved adult children to mourn the death of a parent, many cannot face the sometimes overwhelming process of grief. When mourning goes awry, the rest of life suffers. Grief doesn't disappear simply because it is denied or not recognized. If we don't face up to the pain, the guilt, and the anger, those feelings can immobilize us for years. Suppressed emotions can erupt later—at any time.

Often adult sons and daughters don't know which way to turn because they don't understand or recognize their problems as being related to grief. How many times do we hear the pleas, "I feel so lonely. . . . I can't understand these bouts of crying. . . . I don't know why I'm fighting with everybody. . . . I haven't been successful. . . . I have these incredible anxieties." When traced back, these problems may have started after the death of a parent, grief specialists tell us. "Something bad" is happening to them and they don't know what to do about it. They may suffer from a host of symptoms. Because of delayed mourning, or of being "stuck" in a particular stage of grief, hidden problems can emerge down the road.

A son or daughter whose parent has been dead a

few months, a year, five years, or longer, may run into stop signs along the highway of mourning, with no other direction to guide him or her. For many, the loss is so painful they are able to endure the strong emotions of grief for only brief periods, suppressing them from time to time so as not to be overwhelmed. The adult child may take a long stride forward only to suffer a seeming setback in his or her mourning, a situation similar to the childhood game of Simon Says, when we would take two or more steps forward only to take one or two steps backward.

Human pain is like that—apportioning itself so we are not buried in one huge landslide. Given the respite from an all-encompassing pain, we are able to move toward the final steps to survival: acceptance, forgiveness, and hope.

Important as it is to understand that adult children want explanations for what is happening to them, it is equally important to offer solutions. They will ask, "What is the answer to my problem?" or "How can I help myself?" or "What can I do?" Here we are touching very deep emotional chords, but when sons and daughters have the opportunity to identify with symptoms and problems experienced by other adult children, they can say, "Yes, my parent died and my whole life changed; maybe that does affect me." Although the reader may not relate to every story in this book, there is a common thread—the death of a parent. And just as there is a common thread in the loss, so is there a common thread in the recovering. Bereaved sons and daughters will be able to select what is best for them, what is most comfortable. Just as no two people are alike, no devastations are alike and no recoveries are alike. When bereaved sons and daughters were asked why the impact of the death of a parent was so great, most stressed the long-lasting aspects as well as the uniqueness of the parent-child relationship:

"When you lose your parents, you lose someone you can never replace. You can remarry and you can have many spouses, but you can only have one mother and one father," says a thirty-one-year-old son.

"Even though I'm married and have children, and my husband loves me dearly, when my father died I knew there would never again be anyone who loved me the way my father did," states a thirty-eight-year-old daughter.

"After your parents die, you are suddenly faced with the fact that *you* are the adult in your family now. Up to then, you were still somebody's baby. Now, you're nobody's baby," said a twenty-nine-year-old daughter.

"My father loved me unconditionally. No matter what I did, he would still love me. How many people are going to make allowances for your faults and your mistakes in life the way a parent will?" comments a twenty-four-year-old daughter.

"When Father's Day rolled around, and my father wasn't here, I was shocked with the realization that I was now the 'father' in our family that everyone was looking to for answers," said a bereaved son of twenty-nine.

"Yes, I am a grown woman, supposedly an adult and on my own. But, I always knew I could turn to my mother or my father if I had a problem. Now, with their deaths, I have no one who will care about me the way they did. When my mother died this year, I felt adrift, as if I had suddenly been put into a canoe all by myself to pull the oars. I was responsible for myself getting to safety, to a shore where I would have to face the world alone," said a forty-one-year-old daughter.

There is no golden wand that will wave sons and daughters past the grief of the loss of a parent without attendant sadness. But relief is achieved when adult children can ventilate their sorrow, their remorse. Pent-up feelings of guilt, anger, and resentment can be spoken aloud—to a trusted friend or relative, a clergyperson, a family doctor, a counselor, or at support groups in the presence of those who have suffered the same pain. In fact, the bereaved can avail themselves of several means of aid simultaneously.

As one daughter said, "You can blame other people or curse at God, but that doesn't help. You can ask yourself, 'Why?' and you won't get an answer. But when you are able to talk about your feelings, the initial, severe anger, guilt, and depression lessens. Eventually time does heal. When you learn how others feel, what they did, how they handled their grief, then there is tremendous comfort and hope."

That spirit of hope is offered by the adult children who have come forward to share their experiences in the belief that their routes to recovery will help others carry on with their lives after the loss of a parent.

Their stories are woven throughout these pages, all people like you and me—a teacher, a business executive, a dentist, a housewife, a barber, an auto repair mechanic, a secretary, a pharmacist—all expressing honestly and openly their own confrontations with death and grief. They tell where they are today and what they went through to get there.

By giving examples of their own lives, they show others how to survive, how to cope with the loneliness and depression, the guilt and the anger, how to handle difficulties with siblings, a surviving parent, friends, and coworkers. And they show how to accept that there will always be some sad moments, especially on certain anniversaries or special days. These personal testimonies of men and women who have lived through the problems they describe show

how they managed to overcome them.

If you find you are unable to find a way to help yourself, write to me at the address shown below. I will do my utmost to put you in touch with others who may have found a solution to the problems you have encountered. The message of this book is to offer hope—to know there is indeed a light at the end of the tunnel. It is there, and you can find it. You can survive—if you choose to survive.

Katherine Fair Donnelly, Author
c/o The Berkley Publishing Group
200 Madison Avenue
New York, New York 10016

In Memoriam

Fathers:

Isidor Arkind
Gustav Joseph Akerland, Jr.
Al Arfin
Abe Baum
John H. Donnelly, Sr.
Charles J. Drewes
Isidor Fair
Jerry Fair
Nandor Fodor
Gerald Friedman
Mose Gappelberg
Max Gintz
Isaac Glauben
Samuel Glauben
John Griffiths
Nathan Gross
Louis Halpern
Philip Kaner
Sidney Landau
Jacob Levine
Irving Loiterman
Alexander McAllister
Robert Martin
Philip J. Meagher
John Rezin
Ernest Richardson
Sigmund Strahs
Thomas Tanous
Salvatore Vento
David Wildman
William Young
Samuel Zomper

Mothers:

Ida Mayberry Akerland
Sophie Arkind
Angelina Drekolias
Rose Gappelberg
Helen Gintz
Faiga Glauben
Haya Ruhel Glauben
Alice Atherton Griffiths
Helena Grain
Helen Gross
Ida Cohen Kaner
Ellen Martin
Esther V. Meagher
Mary Moran
Violet Musmacker
Anna Rezin
Blanche Richardson
Elsie Steudtner
Adele Strahs
Ann Alice Tanous
Bessie Gorman Young
Sarah Zomper

RECOVERING FROM THE LOSS OF A PARENT

⌒ PART ONE

Experiences of Bereaved Adult Children

> Death's sting is two-pronged and in the apportionment of the suffering, the survivor takes the brunt.
>
> *Arnold Toynbee*

CHAPTER 1

A Parent Dies

Each of the sons and daughters who appear in this chapter has experienced the anguish of losing a beloved mother or father. As we move on in the book, we will read more about the ways they coped with their grief. But first, the bereaved set the scene and tell us what happened to change their lives so dramatically.

Twenty-one-year-old Phil Musmacker was living 2,000 miles from his mother when he learned of her death. Not only was he a long way from home, but he had just recently been released by the police after having been held for possession of a gun. Phil's troubles with the law began when his girlfriend was harassed by two thugs who were attempting to break into the apartment Phil shared with her. Soon after, he purchased a gun for their protection—a precaution not uncommon in Texas towns.

Because Phil had been brutally treated by the arresting officers, all charges against him were dropped. Following his release, Phil was anxious to return home to see his mother, but a lack of money made this impossible. He was working to earn the transportation fare when a long-distance phone call announced his mother's death. The trauma of not having been at her bedside was a forerunner of intense guilt feelings and remorse. It was years before Phil was able to face up to his grief.

Two years prior to his mother's death, Phil had run away from his hometown, from an overwhelming hospital scene, and from a mother who, wracked with cancer, had dwindled from 235 to 105 pounds. At his mother's pleading, Phil had been giving her injections of the painkiller Demerol in ever-increasing amounts and was tormented that he might overdose and kill her. Added to this was anger with his father, brothers, and sisters who were of little help or comfort. The emotional burden had at last become unbearable and Phil had escaped to Texas with his girlfriend.

In the above story, a young man is tortured by guilt for what he sees as neglect, and by anger at events and at those who could have helped but had failed, he felt, to do so. The following anecdote concerns a young woman whose sense of loss at the death of her father is so overwhelming that she thinks it will be with her for the remainder of her life.

But there is hope for both these people, for hope never dies. Different as their stories are, they both tell of deep suffering, as indeed do all the stories that follow.

On a Sunday afternoon in March, Beth Landau was visiting a friend and so was not at home to receive her mother's urgent phone call. Mrs. Landau had tragic news for her daughter—the girl's father, age sixty-four, had died of a heart attack while playing tennis. The grief-stricken mother finally succeeded in reaching family friends who said they expected to see Beth that evening. "Don't tell her about her father's death," urged Mrs. Landau. "It will be better if she learns about it when she comes here."

While Mrs. Landau was still on the telephone, Beth arrived at the friends' home and took the call. She heard her mother's strained voice saying, "Daddy's not well, Beth. Please come home." The young woman's friends drove her to the Landau home. Although everyone in the car, except Beth, knew of Mr. Landau's death, they all remained silent. When Beth entered the house, she wondered at the presence of a number of her parents' friends but was totally unprepared for her mother's news. In an upstairs bedroom, Beth learned from her mother that her father was dead.

"My knees turned to water," Beth recalls, "and I just collapsed. What followed was an awful night, for the news had come as a shock. My father had suffered a heart attack many years before, but recently he had been in very good shape. Now he was dead and it seemed that a part of me was missing—a feeling that is still with me. I've had a very rough time coping with his death, with the fact that I will never see him again, and with the change it has brought about in all of our lives."

Marjorie and Ellen Martin, twin sisters, were thirty-one years old at the time of their father's death, their mother having died when the girls were eighteen. Robert Martin had long been in poor health and had alternated between a stationary home respirator and a portable machine that he used on his rare trips to the doctor. Mr. Martin suffered from severe emphysema, made worse by a lung condition that permitted him to use only one quarter of his breathing capacity. After his wife's death, Marjorie and Ellen took care of their father's needs.

One evening Ellen became ill and Marjorie accompanied her to the doctor. "We were gone about two hours," Marjorie recounts. "While we were away, robbers broke into the apartment and were apparently angered that there was so little worth stealing. Besides destroying the whole place, they pulled the plug out of our father's respirator. It was coldly and deliberately done, as the plug was high and not easy to reach. It was quite obvious that it had been intentionally unplugged. Those people murdered our father when they pulled that plug."

Mr. Martin was unable to call for help once the respirator had been disconnected, for his lungs rapidly filled with fluid. He became lightheaded and collapsed before he could reach the telephone.

When Marjorie and her sister returned and found their father almost unconscious, they quickly called for an ambulance. Mr. Martin was rushed to a hospital, where he died shortly thereafter. As their father was in no condition to describe the robbers, the police had little to help them solve the crime. To this date, the perpetrators have not been apprehended.

Above we have read how two sisters suffered from the shock of finding their father gasping for breath and dying. In the next story, we learn how a son suffered from the trauma of identifying his father's body. Each of these bereaved children—the two daughters and the son—is still haunted by horrible memories of a beloved father's death.

Salvatore Vento was lying on a slab in the morgue when his twenty-seven-year-old son, Paul, was called in to identify him. "That was a nightmare," Paul remembers. "I wouldn't go through such an experience again for anything. They tell you they are going to show the body through a window and that you'll see only the face—nothing more. That's not true. They bring you right inside, right to where the slabs are, and you identify the corpse. None of the bodies are very pretty. They don't fix them up the way an undertaker does, and they don't prepare you for what you're going to see. The bodies are covered with a butcher's paper—like the paper used for wrapping meat in a butcher shop—not with a cloth of any kind. It was horrible. My father's face was full of blood. It's something that gave me nightmares, and I still see him. In fact, maybe my son and I are crazy, but we feel that somebody is walking around the house, all these years later. We hear noises. We see shadows going by. We think this is my father walking around and that he is looking over our shoulder."

Paul was at home when he learned of his father's death. "He had been found on the street. The police came to our house and told us that he was dead and that his body was at Bellevue Morgue. They said he had died of a fatty liver and that the pancreas had burst. Although my father had been in the hospital several times over the years, he had recently been in very good spirits. He was only fifty-three. So when we were first notified and I got in touch with our relatives, my uncles said, 'It's probably a mistake, it's not your father.' My wife also felt that way. But I thought to myself, 'Very seldom does the police department make a mistake like that.' So I ran up to my mother's to take care of her."

While Paul Vento accepted the news of his father's death when he received the phone call advising him of the tragedy, this isn't always the case with bereaved children. In the next two accounts, we will learn about the reactions of daughters who refused to believe the callers.

When the doctor phoned Carol Richardson at work to tell her that her mother had died, the young woman didn't believe it and just went on working. The doctor sensed that the shock was so great that his news had not sunk in. He made a second call, but this time he asked for Carol's boss. "I was called inside," Carol said, "and they asked me if I understood what had happened. 'What happened? Nothing happened.' I was very nonchalant and uncomprehending. It took a while for me to understand and absorb that something *had* happened and that my mother had really died."

Carol tells about the effect on her: "My mother's death was totally devastating. Although she had cancer of the colon, she had not been sick very long. We learned in October that she had cancer and by December she was dead. My mother was fifty-one at the time and I was twenty-one. I certainly was not ready to lose my mother."

Carol explains that while it is very difficult to lose a parent, one never wants to see a person suffering with cancer, or to continue in that suffering. "You more or less look forward to her death to take her out of her misery, even though it's very hard for you. I always feel it would have been more difficult to see my mother linger on with the disease."

After her mother died, Carol continued living with her father and was with him until his death seven years later. While her mother's illness lasted three months, her father's illnesses went on for years. "He was in and out of hospitals. He had cancer of the prostate and diabetes, and there were other complications.

"My father felt that he wasn't useful anymore. I tried to tell him this was not so, but he just wanted to die and be with his wife. That's all he kept saying toward the end. When my father passed away, he had completely given up. It was a very draining experience to visit him and be told, 'I don't want to be here.' It was especially difficult for me at the time of his death because I had just come out of the hospital myself, after minor surgery. So physically and mentally, his illness was a terrible strain. Then after he had died, I realized that I was nobody's baby anymore. I was my own baby."

When Alexander McAllister died in May 1984, his daughter Margaret was twenty-two. She recalls the weeks and months prior to his death: "In the last year of my father's life, I watched him deteriorate steadily until he became another person. He was no longer able to do anything. He couldn't even stand at the sink to shave. He couldn't wash his own back or take a shower, for the steam would make his heart palpitate too much. He couldn't walk more than a block without taking twenty minutes to rest. In the last few months, he walked with a cane. He hated what he had become, and I am convinced he wanted out of that life. My mother and I told him, 'This time you're going into the hospital and you're going to get better. When you come out, everything will be fine.' But I think he knew we were just hoping, because he cried that morning. He wasn't afraid of many things, but I think he was afraid of hospitals, and he cried because he didn't want to cause problems for anyone. The night before, he had said to my mother, 'Jeannie, I don't feel well.' So we were both very concerned. The next day, my mother was unable to get off from work, so I took my father to the hospital.

"Because the doctor who had been taking care of my father had moved away, Dad changed doctors. To make things worse, my father's roommate in the hospital didn't like noise, especially the sounds coming from the hall, and he had gotten up and closed the door, which created a panic situation for my father. In his last few months, my father was terrified of having his air supply cut off. Later, the nurse told us he had gotten up and tried to open the door, but it was stuck. 'He began to pull it, working himself up into a state,' she said. The hospital called to advise us that although they had planned to release him, they were not going to let him go because his blood pressure had soared. In addition, due to the treatment that had been given him for edema, he had lost water so rapidly that his metabolism was out of control. As a result, the doctors said they wanted to keep him in the hospital one more day.

"Before I left my father, I had helped him sit up in the bed to a comfortable position. He had asked for soda, which I got, as well as some books. He seemed fine. When my mother came, we went out to have some lunch. It had been a long day for her. When we returned to the hospital, the nurses told us that there was nothing more we could do. My father was very sleepy, so we went home. Later in the day, my mother tried to call his room but got no answer. That wasn't unusual, though. Whenever he felt better, he liked to wander the hall because he felt caged up in his room. But instinct told my mother this was not the case now. 'Something is wrong,' she said. With that, she called the switchboard but was transferred to someone else, and then to still another person. A little voice inside of me started to scream.

"I heard my mother say, 'You're not trying to tell me my husband died, are you?' Then I heard her cry out. I ran to the phone and a spokesman for the hospital was on the other end. I said to him, 'What happened? My father was fine when we left.' He told me my father had a heart attack and was just too weak to survive. I went through the gamut of emotions at that point. First, I was enraged that we were told this news on the phone. It was so cold. I also felt the hospital must have been remiss and had made a mistake. It wasn't my father who had died, and they were calling the wrong family."

While the daughters in the above stories were unable to accept the news of their parent's death, another daughter had a premonition that something was amiss with her father. Peggy Griffiths was on a train on her way home from college for the Labor Day weekend. While she was riding between Philadelphia and Newark, she had a strong feeling that something was terribly wrong with her father. "I was very apprehensive and couldn't understand what I was feeling while on the train. But when I got home, I understood well enough. My mother told me that my father had been getting up to get dressed for breakfast when suddenly he sat back on the bed and collapsed. He died of a massive cerebral hemorrhage." It was instantaneous and totally unexpected. When Peggy entered the apartment, her father's body was still in the bedroom. "My mother was waiting for the doctor to come," she says when speaking of that time. "Not realizing that my father was dead, she had called the doorman of the building to send for medical help. A doctor who lived in a neighboring apartment walked in shortly after I arrived. He went into the bedroom, examined my father, and told us he was dead. I have always been grateful that I was with my mother at that moment."

Fifteen years later, on her eightieth birthday, Peggy's mother fell and broke her hip. "The doctor explained to me that her bones were brittle and that this had caused her fall. Even though I was with her at the time, I wasn't able to catch her and break her fall." That night, Peggy brought her mother to the hospital, where she was operated on two days later. Over the next few weeks, Mrs. Griffiths made good progress and was even learning to walk again.

"It was such a great feeling to see my mother walking and moving," says Peggy, "and I was looking forward to bringing her home. But then bed pneumonia set in. That last week was a tough one with the doctors doing everything they could to save her life, but because of her age, my mother didn't respond to the antibiotics, and she died on February 4th. I knew that the Good Lord was calling her home, and she knew it, too. While I understood and accepted it, I still was in a state of shock. No matter how old your parent is, you are not prepared for that loss, and my grief was great."

The loss of a parent does not always evoke much sympathy but, as many sons and daughters attest, it can be extremely traumatic. One such son was John Donnelly, whose mother tried to shield her twenty-five-year-old son from the pain of witnessing her death from cancer. She was adamant in her wishes that his visits be limited, and the hospital staff went along with her. She insisted that her son be permitted to see her only after her blood transfusions, for it was then she looked her best. When she was propped up in bed, she presented a hopeful picture to John each time he visited her. "My mother is looking better," he would think.

But on December 6th, John decided to visit his mother unannounced. "I went to her regular spot in the hospital, but she wasn't there. When I asked where she was, the nurse, without thinking, said, 'Oh, she's out on the porch.' And there I went, expecting to see my mother sitting up in a chair, but what I saw was unbelievable. She was going into her pre-death period and I began to scream. Two nurses and a doctor I didn't know came running and they gave me smelling salts. They reprimanded me, saying, 'She can hear you. How can you do this?' 'But,' I moaned, 'I didn't know, I didn't know.' Then they asked, 'Who are you?' When I told them I was her son, they said, 'Her son? Didn't anyone tell you?' But no one had told me. For the first time I had seen her before she had been given the blood and when she wasn't propped up."

John finally summoned enough courage to return

to the porch. "It struck me for the first time that my mother was about to die, and I was so grief-stricken that I just couldn't let her go. I kept pulling her back to consciousness and talking to her. I kept holding her and telling her what a beautiful day it was, with tears streaming down my face. She kept on drifting into a coma and I could see her eyes would roll back, but I continued to talk to her, holding her hand, and saying, 'No, Mother, you can't go.' And she would all of a sudden catch herself. That went on for an hour or so.

"Finally, a nurse came and said, 'I think you should let your mother go to sleep.' But I was in total shock and terrified that if she went to sleep she would never wake up. My fears were well grounded. She didn't wake up."

In years to come, John was to agonize over his inability to ease his mother's dying but he later came to understand that just being there had been important, that his mother had sensed his presence and acknowledged it by struggling to live. He realized that that is what she wanted him to do: to live. So he set out to find ways to do so.

It is difficult to know which is more traumatic to a surviving child—being told beforehand about a decision to commit suicide or not being told at all. Chuck Akerland experienced both. When he was ten years old, living in Bangkok, Thailand, he had no idea that his sixteen-year-old brother would kill himself by jumping off the roof of a building. Much later, when Chuck was twenty-two, his father, the mayor of a small city in Maryland, committed suicide by shooting himself. Some months earlier, the father had telephoned Chuck, who was then living in another city and state, to say that he felt inclined to take his life.

In recalling this incident, Chuck said, "He told me

he was depressed because the city's budget was a mess. He felt he would be held accountable for the problem even though he had inherited it." Chuck was numbed by the phone call. "I didn't know what to say." Concerned, Chuck asked his father to call him before taking such an action.

Chuck was away for a portion of the weekend when his father shot himself. The grieving son has no way of knowing if his dad had tried to reach him. For a while, this troubled Chuck, but he later realized that he could not have changed his father's suicidal decision, that he, Chuck, was not responsible for the suicide, and that the choice was not his, but his father's.

"My father did not die instantly, but lingered on for four days in a coma. The police had come and knocked on my door and told me to call home. When I learned what happened, I immediately left for Maryland."

There were distinct differences between his brother's death and his father's. When Chuck's brother died, the family was living in a foreign country. While Chuck's parents had friends nearby to help them, Chuck felt alone and scared. "When my dad died in Maryland, there were neighbors and friends who were actually taking care of us," Chuck recalls. "Also, my father remained alive for a time, whereas my brother died instantly. With my father, there was something to hope for in the days before he died, and our friends and neighbors rallied round."

Chuck remembers crying after his father's death. "I felt permission to do this, being in my own home with boyhood friends who had come to see me. In addition, my favorite aunt was there to strengthen the support network." Chuck also remembers screaming and crying even before his father died, whereas when his brother died, he was far from home, isolated, and had no one with whom to cry.

His sense of being alone there, of having no relatives or friends to support him in his grief, was overwhelming. Chuck reflects: "When my father died, I had been through such a death before when my brother took his life."

Mary Stellakis, in her mid-fifties, was working in Greece when she received a call from a local nursing home that her mother had suffered a heart attack. "I ran like a crazy woman into the street, but found the way to the nursing home blocked by young people who were protesting the killing of students by the police. There were no cabs available, and I was half out of my mind trying to get to my mother. When I frantically begged a young motorist to help me, he graciously said, 'Get in,' and drove around the traffic. After zigzagging every which way, he finally got me to a spot where I could pick up a taxi.

"In the cab, I began to think back to the time when I had separated from my husband and had sought a new life across the Atlantic. On my many return trips to the United States, I had tried to get Mom to come to live with me. Greece was her native country. But she wouldn't leave her other children and her grandchildren. Each time, I'd leave her with a heavy heart.

"Then, out of the blue, my mother asked me to take her back to Greece. She was seventy-nine and suffered from diabetes, circulatory problems, and heart disorders, and because of her age and illness, she was carried onto the plane in a wheelchair. At Athens Airport we were met by her sister whom she had left as a girl some sixty years before. Mom was bedridden and, as I had to work, friends found a nursing home for her. I visited her every day after work, and would stay to tuck her in and kiss her good night. Now suddenly here I was in a taxi rushing to her bedside, not knowing if I would get there in time."

When Mary arrived at the nursing home, she

learned that a doctor had been giving her mother oxygen and injections for the last four hours. "He arranged for a room at a private clinic and phoned the Greek Red Cross for an ambulance. I felt numb, but listened attentively when the doctor told me the diagnosis was pulmonary edema. Struggling with my feelings, I rode with Mom in the ambulance.

"All that night I stayed in her room, constantly listening to make sure she was breathing. Four days later, her breathing became so labored that a cardiologist was called in. But Mom didn't wait for him. She stopped breathing and I closed her eyes. I couldn't believe my beloved mother was gone."

While Mary Stellakis was able to ride with her mother en route to the hospital, Eddie Gintz had to ride in a car behind the speeding ambulance which rushed his father away. "When my father suffered a heart attack, my mother went along in the ambulance where the paramedics were trying to revive him. My sister and I rode in the car behind them, and I'll never forget the shrieking ambulance siren. I'll never forget that sound. Now every time I hear an ambulance, that picture comes back to me." When he arrived at the hospital, Eddie was overwhelmed at the scene before him.

"Pandemonium broke loose at the hospital when a Code Blue was called. I watched as machinery and people whizzed by to my father's room. It seemed as if the whole hospital was rushing there. They tried everything to revive him but to no avail. It was over very fast. That scene is something I will never forget; it sticks in my mind."

Eddie, who was forty-five when his father died, recalls the impact of his mother's death years later. "My father's death was sudden. There was no time to prepare. With my mother, we had a siege for a whole year. We were living in New York, but my mother was in Florida, where she was suffering from cancer. My wife and I went to Florida to be with her for a while. After we returned to New York, we got an urgent call to return to Florida. So down we went and no sooner did we get back to New York when we had to rush back to Florida again. This happened repeatedly and for many, many months. Finally, there was a last call."

The sudden death of a parent is especially devastating to adult children. There is nothing that can prepare them for this. A parent who has died from a catastrophic illness has had long-standing care by family, doctors, or nurses. The son or daughter of a parent who dies without warning not only suffers the anguish of losing a loved one, but the loss of the ability to do anything to ease the parent's dying. One such daughter, Lisa Strahs-Lorenc, tells of her sense of vulnerability and of the psychological impact of her father's sudden death.

"I was at home and it was two o'clock in the morning when the telephone rang. And I can tell you that if today the phone were to ring at two o'clock in the morning, I would probably go out of my mind."

The phone call that Lisa received at that early hour was from Canada, where her parents were vacationing. When Lisa answered, she was still groggy with sleep. But as soon as she heard her mother's voice, Lisa knew something was wrong. Something was *very* wrong—her father was in a Toronto hospital emergency room after suffering a massive coronary attack.

Lisa's mother had wanted to wait till daylight before disturbing her daughter, but she had been told by the emergency room nurse that the situation was critical. The nurse suggested that she get in touch with her daughter at once.

Today Lisa recalls: "My mother was alone in a foreign country, in Canada. Of course, my husband and I were shocked beyond belief, for my father had been the healthiest person in the world. He had never had any kind of problem physically and he was a young man by today's standards, only in his fifties. We just couldn't believe he was in a hospital and dying. At once we rushed to the airport and took the first flight out at five in the morning. But when we reached the emergency room, my father had already died."

Lisa was struck by the fact that her biological mother had died a sudden death, too. "She died instantly after being hit by a car when she was twenty-eight and pregnant. So I have had two parents who died quite suddenly. I do have a mother who adopted me when I was four and a half, and as far as I am concerned, she is my mother. She is the only mother I remember. But I no longer have a biological link to living parents."

Another type of shock hit Kathleen Riley, who had entered a convent at eighteen. Fifteen years later, at thirty-three, she left it. But when Kathleen returned home, she found her father dying of a brain tumor.

This news was a heavy blow to Kathleen and left her reeling. "I wanted to say, 'Hey! Wait a minute. I'm trying to deal with a death of my own—the fifteen years that I was in the convent. And now I have to deal with my father's death?' "

It began one night when Kathleen's mother and father were watching television. "My mother noticed that he seemed to have an attack of some kind. As he spoke, he used words that didn't make any sense. At first my mother thought it might have something to do with his heart. But after cardiograms and a visit to a heart specialist, he was given a clean bill of health. However, he continued to have these 'attacks' and would feel lightheaded, but then the spell would pass. He said repeatedly that there was a taste of almonds in his mouth. Those were the first words he used to describe his experience."

The family continued to be frustrated when no diagnosis could be made. "We took him to three different doctors and none of them could diagnose my father's trouble. My sister thought it might be TIA [transient ischemic attack], and that not enough oxygen was reaching the brain, which would indicate a failure in a function of the heart. Although the doctors didn't rule out TIA, they thought my father's illness had other causes. That was in March.

"Then things began to seesaw," Kathleen went on. "My father would be without his worrisome symptoms for a while and then he would have another attack. This went on for three months and then he started to get terrible headaches. Finally, through my sister, who is a nurse, we took him for a CAT scan in July, and it was then the brain tumor was discovered. My father lived eight months after that."

The hardest thing for Kathleen during this rocky period was being unable to talk to her father about his illness. "My mother was adamant about not telling him the cause of his illness. He was a very private person, and she felt that he needed to be the strong one. So she pretended, right up until he died, that she didn't know he had cancer." Kathleen went along with the pretense, but it troubled her. She knew her father was an intelligent man. "He was technologically oriented and he even commented, when he saw the X rays, that they showed unusual spots.

"Eventually, he had to go for radiation treatment. Now everyone knows that such treatments mean cancer. But he never asked. He never questioned, and I think he did that for my mother. He was a very protective type of husband. My mother certainly is a capable person, but he was always very concerned about her."

Kathleen's pretending came to an end when her

father died—on the day after her thirty-fourth birthday.

We now hear from a bereaved son who also could not celebrate birthdays. As a teenager, Max Glauben wasn't riding a bicycle down Main Street. Nor was he on drugs or alcohol. He wasn't able to go to the movies or play baseball or watch television or go to the corner drugstore for a soda.

On a sunny afternoon in May 1943, Max had to grow up fast. German troopers put him in a boxcar headed for a concentration camp in Majdanek, Poland. Along with Max went his father, mother, and younger brother. Because they were selected as laborers, Max and his father were cordoned off in a separate area. The last, long look of the tiny figure of his mother growing smaller and smaller in the distance is one thing Max will always remember. She was ultimately killed in the gas chambers with his brother.

Max and his father were put on a heavy work regime. "Often the guards would try to show us what would happen if we did not work harder. They would come and take one of the men, beat him and whip him in front of us. But I was a hothead, and when the Germans came over to me and said something derogatory, I would spit in their faces or raise my hand to hit them. My father pleaded with me, saying that the one thing that would endanger my life was my temper. So all through the years that I was in the camp, I kept seeing my father's face and always controlled my temper so that no one would kill me for losing it."

Shortly after their arrival at the concentration camp, three people escaped. "The guards took as punishment thirty of the men and laid them on the ground in a U-shape—ten, ten, and ten—with their faces down. They threatened to set an example by killing them. My father was one of those thirty prisoners. As he was pulled away, his eyes sought mine as if to say, 'Remember, don't lose your temper,' and I remained silent. He had made me promise that even if they came to take him one day to beat him, that I was to control my anger.

"The next morning, we were put out for reveille. There were about twelve or fourteen pairs of boots and shoes standing where the men had stood on previous mornings, but the men were not there. The guards had found two of the three people who had escaped, and so they let the remainder of the thirty people who had been lying on the ground return to the camp. But the other twelve or fourteen did not return—they had been killed. The rumor was that one or two were shot, but the rest were tortured and beaten to death during the night.

"I spoke to two of the survivors to learn how my father had died. 'Because we were lying face down, we couldn't very well move. If we made the slightest motion, they would harm us.' One man told me he thought my father had asked to go to the bathroom and as he was going, one of the guards pretended he was trying to escape and shot him. The other man I spoke to thought my father was beaten just for asking to go. He said they hit my father on the head with the butt of their rifles until he was unconscious. Whichever account was correct, my father was dead and his boots were all that remained."

Max was horrified. He was all alone in a concentration camp, with no father, no relatives, but the picture of his father's boots was emblazoned on his memory. Equally imprinted was the look on his father's face pleading with him to contain his temper. Max kept his word to his father to remain silent and to fight for the survival he knew was his father's last hope, but the suppressed anger of maintaining that silence took its toll. At age fifteen, Max was an adult.

CHAPTER 2

The Emotions of Grief

Numbness . . . Shock . . . Denial . . . Anger . . .
Panic . . . Yearning . . . Fear . . . Hopelessness . . .
Helplessness . . . Rage . . . Searching . . . Guilt . . .
Depression . . . Craziness . . . Disorganization . . .
Refocusing . . . Acceptance . . . Recovering . . .

There are many emotional responses that bereaved daughters and sons may experience in their
grief. These responses may be erratic and at times
confusing and frightening to the adult child, but
whatever an individual's response may be, the fact
remains that it is painful to grieve for a dead parent.
Often those sons and daughters who hide their feelings or run away from them suffer greatly and may
never get over their grief. What they do not know or
understand is that their feelings of loneliness or sadness, of hopelessness or helplessness, of anger or
guilt, of depression or "craziness" are all perfectly
normal feelings.

Rabbi Earl Grollman, a giant in the field of bereavement help, says, "Some people [who have suffered a loss] will refuse to think about death at all;
others will think about nothing else. Some will ve-
hemently protest; others will quietly resign themselves to the reality. Some will curse God; others will
console themselves in a future world-to-come. Some

will be disorganized; others will effectively reshape their lives. Some will cry hysterically; others will remain outwardly impassive and emotionless; while still others may even laugh. Some will deify the deceased; others will be angry at the dead person for leaving them alone and abandoned. Some will blame themselves for the death; others will project the guilt upon the physician, the clergyman, or another member of the family. Reactions to death are varied and contradictory; they are neither prescribed nor are they predictable."

In the early days of grief, adult children often find it difficult to comprehend that a parent has truly died. They look for some way out of accepting the death, thinking "Maybe it was a mistake. Someone is going to call and say it isn't so." They may think they are having nightmares and that when they awake in the morning, this awful thing will not really have happened. One daughter recalls: "I was in my mother's house that morning and just a few hours later my sister called to say our mother had died of a heart attack. I still can't believe it. I remember her hugging me and the wonderful smell of her perfume. It seems that I'm having a bad dream and that my mother is going to come and wake me up and tell me this didn't happen."

The death of a parent affects everyone—some more than others. A younger son or daughter may be more dependent upon the dead parent for clothing, housing, food, money, and emotional needs than his or her older siblings. When you are twenty-five and your forty-five-year-old mother dies, you ask, "Why did she have to die? She was so young." Older children will feel the tragic loss, but can say that the parent lived a long and fruitful life. "The intensity of the grief and the time needed to recover depend on how emotionally dependent the child was on the deceased parent," says Dr. Roberta Temes, Clinical Assistant Professor of Psychiatry, Downstate Medical School, and author of *Living with an Empty Chair*.

"Many mature adults grieve for a 'normal' period and go on to lead well-adjusted lives," Dr. Temes maintains, "whereas a twenty-two-year-old college student in the dormitory or an eighty-two-year-old in a nursing home may still be dealing with unresolved grief."

Athena Drewes and her husband, Jim Bridges, psychotherapists in Orange County, New York, have found that delayed mourning and unresolved grief are more common than one would expect. "Most people don't realize how long the mourning process can last," Drewes explains. "For many it takes up to three years, with the hardest being the first year with birthdays, holidays, and anniversary dates to be passed through. For those bereaved sons and daughters who have not worked through their grief, or who get stuck in any of the stages along the way, difficulties emerge with interpersonal relationships—such as not wanting to get emotionally close for fear of losing another important person, and reawakening the past loss. Physical ailments, ulcers, problems dealing with stress, depression, sleep disturbances, fears, and phobias may surface, which are usually treated as unrelated to the bereaved person's grief."

After the death of a parent, adult children go through various stages of bereavement. Although they may not experience all the stages, most bereaved sons and daughters go through some of them—but not necessarily in the same order. In the early stages of grief, the mourner experiences a psychological earthquake—shock and numbness at the turn of events in his or her life. This is usually followed by denial, a disbelief that the terrible tragedy has really happened. Next may come anger—anger at God, at the doctors or nurses in the hospital, anger at the disease, anger at other members of the family, and even anger at the deceased.

The first stage of bereavement begins at the moment of death and lasts for many weeks or months, according to Dr. Temes. It includes the shock of the death and its temporary denial. The next phase, she indicates, is that of disorganization. It is at this point, when the numbness has passed and the full impact of the death is felt, that the bereaved go through the emotions of yearning, anger, fear, and guilt. The adult child may be yearning for his parent. "Feelings of anxiety and panic rise when the realization hits home that a reunion is impossible. The son or daughter may become angry that he or she has been abandoned by a loved one," Dr. Temes states.

Andrew Rezin, twenty-five years old, felt that sense of abandonment when both his parents died within twenty-two months of each other. He has this to say of his experience: " 'Why me?' I thought. 'What did I do to have this happen to me? Why have they left me?' I was angry at anyone and everyone." This stage of anger may rapidly be followed by feelings of guilt. One daughter, whose mother died after a long illness, felt guilty at her sigh of relief. Another daughter had guilt pangs because she was not able to say goodbye to her father when he was killed in a car accident. A son felt guilty because he had had a fight with his father just prior to the death.

It is appropriate to feel a sense of relief simultaneously with sorrow. It is normal to experience the feeling of being free of the physical burdens imposed by caring for a dying person. Also, it is normal for parents and children to share all kinds of human experiences, including yelling, laughing, screaming, arguing, and a host of other activities that may later create guilt. Furthermore, it is normal to think we should or could have done something that might have altered circumstances.

Bereaved sons and daughters may say, "I should have taken them for medicine . . . I should have gotten the doctor earlier . . . I should have gone to see them more often . . . I should have moved in with them,'" indicates Roslyn Marcus, Bereavement Director of Transition Bereavement Program in Centerport, New York. Marcus also explains that at the other end of the pole are the surviving children who did all of those things and then go into "I *shouldn't* have." In groups, sons and daughters often complain, "I *shouldn't* have taken my mother to live with me. I *shouldn't* have taken her out of her home. I *shouldn't* have argued with my father." Counselors use both of those positions—the *shoulds* and the *shouldn'ts*—to help people see how powerless they are.

That powerlessness plays a very large role in all deaths. What the bereaved try to do is invest themselves with the power to change events—"I should have done *this* so that *that* would have happened"— and "they play that over and over again in their own minds so they can explore it," says Marcus. We are normal human beings, capable of love as well as anger and resentment. We are not all-powerful and cannot wave a magic wand to do away with people or to bring them back. Guilt feelings need to be expressed to acknowledge on a conscious level that the death did not occur because of anything we did or did not do or say.

A man whose grief was mixed with anger tells his story below: "After my mother died, I found myself unable to communicate with other family members or former friends. I was angry at most of these people. They hadn't come to see my mother when she began radiation therapy, for they were afraid of what they would see or hear. When her hair began to fall out, and she lost weight, and she was in pain, no one came. They only came at the beginning of her hospital stay, brought a bunch of flowers, and figured that they had done their duty. My mother sensed their fear and apprehension, and I was angry that she had to feel rejection on top of everything else she was enduring.

"At the funeral, these same people came and sobbed, and again felt they had done their duty. I was enraged. The anger was preventing me from functioning. I didn't want to get up in the morning. I didn't feel like brushing my teeth. I didn't have a desire to make breakfast or get dressed. Finally, my aunt insisted that I needed to face my anger, but to do this I should go to someone specifically experienced in grief counseling. A friend recommended a therapist to her, and my aunt drove me to his office. If I hadn't gone, I think I would have destroyed myself with anger."

This son realized the need to talk about the things he thought about, things he was afraid about, angry about. *Talking to the right person is the real key to recovering.* The most basic need of a grieving person is to have someone nearby to listen, to share in the pain, and to care, be it a close friend, a relative, a coworker, a clergyperson, a counselor, a therapist.

Emily Marlin, former president of NYAMFT, the New York division of American Association for Marriage and Family Therapy, explains what happens after the initial stage of grief: "A son or daughter who has lost a parent may experience a letdown when they begin to face the fact that the loved one is really gone. The bereaved may also experience a sense of being alone, and find friends are no longer as accessible as they were in the early weeks and months after the death. This period can be one of bewilderment and physical apathy. The grieving son or daughter will see the dead parent in a restaurant or walking in the street." This stage of grief can last a long time, therapists agree.

A bereaved daughter shares her foray into the outside world: "Everybody seemed so busy with every-day activities. My neighbor was painting his fence. My best friend was participating in an art exhibit. At work, everyone was occupied with their jobs. Everything appeared to be so normal. But nothing seemed normal to me. It was like I was living in a world that spoke a different language and I was lost in it. The funeral was three months ago, but everyone seems to think things are fine. But they are not fine. How can everything seem so normal when you have lost someone you love? I resented their 'normalcy.' "

For some individuals, resentment is taken out on those nearest them. This may offer a temporary sense of relief. In other instances when we think we are starting to move ahead in our grief, a small incident can set us off again and evoke a memory that causes us pain: a kitchen timer that the dead parent can no longer hear, an old shirt, or a holiday . . . an anniversary . . . our parent's birthday . . . our own birthdays.

One son was twenty-eight when his father died of a heart attack at forty-nine. Years later, as the son entered his forties, he began to develop severe anxieties about the age of forty-nine. "I felt very nervous about it and wondered if I was going to make it to forty-nine. My great fear was that I would die at the same age as my father." On every birthday, he found himself vulnerable. Whenever he saw advertisements for birthday sales or for anything to do with birthdays, he became anxious about his own mortality because of his father's early death. "My wife suggested I join a group at our church that helped in bereavement and loss. There were about ten of us, with different types of losses. But the feelings we were experiencing were similar. The group helped me to see that I was not alone in thinking these thoughts or in being afraid of reaching forty-nine. Then, when I did have my birthday, I felt very good about passing that 'birthday syndrome.' "

Modern medicine places great importance on the causes of our parents' deaths, and it stresses that heredity is a vital factor in one's physical makeup. When we go for a checkup because of a chest pain or other symptoms, the doctor asks if our parents had a related illness. The age of death becomes a spotlighted issue—and something we are bound to think about because of the way we are conditioned. After the death of one of your parents, you may occasionally have such thoughts, but it is not something out of the ordinary—it is quite *normal*. If you cannot cope with the disturbing thoughts or if fears overwhelm you, then it's time to seek professional help because such thoughts or fears may be so deep-seated that you cannot deal with them on your own.

Anne Rosberger, psychotherapist and Executive Director of the Bereavement and Loss Center of New York, cautions that acute depression may set in around the first anniversary of a death because many bereaved carry about with them an unconscious timetable that allows only one year for mourning. All people have their own individual clocks, their own individual calendars when it comes to grief. Grieving may take months or years. It is not a disease. It is not an unnatural function. It is a natural and necessary process in bereavement.

The grief counselor does not help one to forget the pain, Ms. Rosberger notes, but rather helps the person to realize it. One of the ironies, she states, is that when the bereaved seem to cope well during the initial period of numbness, everyone concludes they no longer need help. By the time the numbness wears off, friends and relatives may be emotionally unavailable at the very time they are needed most. Even the most sympathetic relatives and friends become impatient if a bereaved person fails to "snap out of it" within a few months. We are brought face to face with the knowledge that moving through our grief can be a lonely experience.

An adult son or daughter who has lost a parent suffers and grieves in his or her own way. Grief cannot be measured or compared, yet we find many such people saying, "My pain is greater than that of others because my parent died suddenly . . . because my father was so young . . . because my mother withered away before my eyes . . . because my father committed suicide . . . because my mother was drowned and we never found the body . . . because . . . because . . . " It's like playing a game of one-upmanship with "See, I am more handicapped than you—my pain is greater." But often adult children who ask the question, "Is grief more painful in some than in others?" are simply seeking some explanation for their own pain, thinking no one else could be feeling such anguish.

While there may be differences in the horror of the tragedy, grief is grief. And no matter what the age of the parent or how the death occurred, the pain for the surviving adult son or daughter can be devastating.

A differing opinion on the stages of grief is offered by Dr. David Meagher, Professor of Health Sciences and Director of the Thanatology Program at Brooklyn College, New York. "I don't believe there are stages of grief or bereavement," he says. "I don't like the concept of stages. It creates an inflexible process by which everyone must fit into the pattern or is determined to be atypical or abnormal.

"We can't put people into stages. There are emotional, behavioral, and attitudinal responses—anger, depression, denial, acceptance, shock, reorganization. My approach is that we have to take a look at the nature of the relationship and understand those idiosyncratic aspects of that relationship and make a model—whatever model will fit that individual or those individual survivors. We can sense or know that in a general way death, even in an expected situation, is never planned for. All of a sudden there is a hole in our life, a disruption. There is something missing now that will touch everything else in our lives. Our task is to start putting things together again, to put our life back to where it was. Or at least to fill that hole. We should remember the deceased, and realize that we are the result of that relationship, no matter how good or bad. When we accept that, we will be able to engage in new relationships, knowing that we can suffer a loss and survive."

There can be many indicators that the bereaved are getting better. One is the recollection of happy occasions together. Then, too, recovery is on the way if the dead parent is not the last thought in the bereaved ones' minds before falling asleep and if it is not always their first thought upon awakening in the morning. They may think or say, "I slept through the night," or "When I got up my mother wasn't in my thoughts for the first time." When sleep patterns, energy, appetite, and other interests quietly reenter our lives, the final step to recovery is taken—acceptance.

We see the measurement of recovery when the bereaved emerge from the "I don't care about anything" attitude that calls every day "lousy," and their sense of listlessness has disappeared. Trivial things become significant again. There is a return to plan making: "I want to do this" or "Let's go there." When bereaved children become future-oriented instead of past-oriented, they are well on the road to recovery.

It is important for sons and daughters to understand that recovering doesn't mean they have to forget. Nor does it mean they may not have occasional setbacks. Anniversary reactions* are normal. While there may be many good days, there may also be

*See Chapter 8.

some difficult ones. Time allows people to ventilate their emotions, and those bad days will occur with less frequency. Some sons and daughters feel extended bereavement is necessary as a tribute to the deceased parent. Often they believe the longer they grieve, the longer they are symbolizing their love. But this is an impairment to recovery. Parents will always be missed but no one has to serve a lifetime sentence to prove it.

To sum up, there are many different feelings bereaved children experience in the grief process, and each person's temperament and makeup determine those emotions. Athena Drewes expresses the poignant view that many adult children come to realize: *"When a parent dies, suddenly life becomes our responsibility."*

☙ CHAPTER 3

This Can't Be True

- David was at a business conference in another city when he received word that his mother had died. "But she can't be dead," he insisted. "I didn't even have a chance to say good-bye."

- When Jim was nineteen, he was told that his father had been killed in an auto accident. The shock was so great that he burst into hysterical laughter, refusing to believe it.

- As forty-one-year-old Rose was being led from her mother's coffin, she began to scream, "Mama! Mama! Don't leave me. I'll be all alone. This can't be happening. You can't be dead."

- After George buried his mother, he kept searching for her everywhere—even in his dreams.

- Florence's brother called to tell her that their father had died of a massive heart attack, but Florence insisted her father should be rushed to the hospital to be revived. Even though her brother kept repeating for a half hour that their father was really dead, Florence would not believe him.

When an adult child learns that a parent has died, the first response is generally one of shock and disbelief. People expect their parents to live forever. This denial period can last from one or two days to six months or longer. It is during this time that guilt can plague children who suffer because they don't "feel" anything and haven't been able to accept the death. Often, the adult child can't cry until well after the funeral. One daughter describes her reaction: "I was so numb after my mother's death that I didn't cry, not then, not for weeks and months afterward. But when my birthday arrived, I felt a hollowness in the pit of my stomach. Every year my mother was the first to phone me in the morning to wish me a happy birthday. When I realized that she wasn't going to call me on this birthday, I broke into hysterical weeping. I couldn't control the sobs."

A common behavior pattern evoked by the death of a parent is the child's searching for the departed. The search can take the form of hallucinations, dreams, or actual looking from room to room. During this period, bereaved sons and daughters often go through daily activities thinking they see the dead parent sitting on a bus or walking in the street. This denial stage is not only common, but normal—and will be experienced by almost all adult children who lose a parent. "It becomes serious only if the denial continues for an extended time and there is no acceptance of the death," states Dr. Roberta Temes.

For the week following her mother's funeral, Joan Urbas, in her mid-forties, kept going back to her mother's apartment where she then made the bed, putting on new sheets and fresh pillowcases. She even laid out her mother's robe, saying, "I think I'll keep the slippers and the robe here just as if Mother has gone out and will soon return." Joan changed the sheets several times that week, making the bed ready.

A short time before this, when Joan's mother had come home from the hospital, she seemed to be in good health. She was able to get around and go outdoors. At that time Joan wanted her mother to stay with her for a while, but the older woman, insisting she could take care of herself, had returned to her own home. Joan promised either to call or to visit her mother every day, even though they lived an hour apart by car.

During the week between Christmas and New Year's, Joan and her family were busy with holiday activities, and Joan was also involved in preparations for returning to the elementary school where she was principal. She called her mother on the Saturday morning in the holiday week, but there was no answer. Joan assumed that her mother was out shopping. She surmised, "Mother must be feeling better and went to the store to pick up some groceries."

Joan called again on Sunday morning. When she received no answer, Joan believed her mother had returned to her habit of going out to buy the Sunday newspaper. "I thought I would call her very early Monday morning as it was a busy holiday time and we all had too much to do. Nevertheless, I should have called her again that day, and now I've got all kinds of guilt feelings.

"When I called Monday morning and still didn't get an answer, I became worried. Calling my mother's neighbor, I asked him to investigate. When he went to my mother's apartment and could get no answer to his knocks and rings, he obtained a passkey and discovered her body. He at once called me to say my mother was dead," Joan recalls.

In a state of shock, Joan vaguely remembers making the long drive to her mother's apartment. When she arrived, she went into her mother's bedroom alone and saw the body on the bed. Still in shock, she called the police. While waiting for them, Joan sat across from her mother. Suddenly, she saw that the body was "blowing up." Joan gasped in astonishment. Later, the funeral director explained that the phenomenon was caused by internal gases. But the vision of her mother's lifeless body suddenly moving reinforced the feeling that none of this was real—that her mother was still living.

The police soon arrived with a medical examiner who pronounced the mother dead, her death being the result of a massive stroke. Later, the funeral directors suggested a closed coffin. "I was very grateful to them for that suggestion and for all the help they gave us. I had not wanted an open coffin for my mother. I wanted people to remember her as she was when she was alive. So I put on a table near the coffin pictures of Mother at different stages in her life, in all of which she looked well and happy."

When Hilary Friedman was twenty-one, her father died at age forty-six of chronic kidney failure. He had been a successful lawyer who had been forced by illness to stop working. During the last four years of his life, he was in and out of hospitals, and Hilary, watching her father deteriorate after the strenuous usage of dialysis, had felt drained. On the day of the funeral, she was "totally out of it," unable to express her grief or to cry. "It was as if I were somewhere else and this was not really happening. Many people attended the unveiling of the gravestone a year later, and that helped ease the pain, but there was still a numbness. I just couldn't believe my father was dead."

Kathleen Riley was heartbroken that she had not spent more time with her father when he was well. After his death from a brain tumor, she was stricken with memories of his illness and subsequent death. "It all happened too fast for me. During the fifteen years I was in the convent, I had of course not lived at home, although I visited my parents from time to time. But the visits were short and lacking in the intimacy that one gets from sharing meals and daily chores. Now, after two years, I seem to block out all the details, such as the kind of medication my father took and that kind of thing. I just can't accept it. It's too painful."

After reflecting on her life after the death of her father, Kathleen now says, "Sometimes I think I haven't processed the death at all yet. I feel ashamed to admit this, for my sisters, on the other hand, dealt directly with it. They were angry . . . at the disease . . . at God. I haven't been able to deal with it the way they did. But then, they weren't going through the drastic change in their own lives that I was after I left the convent. And they were not living at home with my mother and father the way I was while he was dying."

When Margaret McAllister learned of her father's death, she couldn't accept it. "I didn't believe it was my father who had died. I kept thinking the nurses had misplaced him. I told myself, 'The hospital spokesperson who had talked to us on the phone obviously didn't realize that a mistake had been made; that the dead man was this other person. In their confusion, they thought it was my father.' I went to the hospital by myself because my mother couldn't handle it. When I arrived, the nurses told me to go and pick up his things. In my mind I envisioned that a hospital staff member would show me a black suit and I would then say, 'My father came in here wearing a brown suit. This couldn't possibly be my father's.' But the suit he wore was with all his other belongings—the radio he had brought in, his books, his other clothes, pills he was taking, and things like that.

"Despite this, I still convinced myself it was not my father who had died. The staff had simply moved him to another room and put someone else in his room. They just forgot to move my father's clothes and things at the same time. I continued to think that this other man had died and they were giving us my father's belongings by mistake.

"I couldn't accept his death until the first night of the wake. I was determined I was going to walk into the funeral parlor and there was going to be a man lying in the coffin and I would turn around to my mother and say, 'Who the hell is this? This is not my father.' Then I would march straight to the hospital and say, 'Excuse me. There is a man lying in a coffin and it's *not* my father!'

"When I walked into the room, it was such a shock when I finally saw it was my father in the coffin. I thought to myself, 'Well, there's no more denying it now, because there he is.'

"I think what helped my mother and me in a lot of ways was the kindness of the funeral director. We went to Neufeld's and the man who took care of us was the nicest person at a time like that. This may sound macabre, but my father looked wonderful. He looked so peaceful, as if he could sit right up and tell us he felt better now than he had in the last two years. Up to then I had loathed wakes. But I could understand now how important they would be in removing pressures from the family. I know that seeing him helped my mother and me, and it made us feel good to see so many people coming to pay tribute to my father."

Margaret added, "So many times funeral directors are stereotyped as 'grim reapers' dressed in black clothes who size people up for coffins. In reality, they are truly compassionate people who feel for your loss and who wish to help you at such a difficult time. And the artful job they perform to make the deceased look their most presentable and peaceful can do much to allay the fears of a bereaved son or daughter. I think they do a great deal to comfort the family."

In an earlier chapter, we read of the shock John Donnelly experienced when he saw his mother dying after he had been led to believe she was getting better. The result of that shock is seen in John's reaction to the news of his mother's death. On the morning of December 7th, he received a phone call. "It was three o'clock in the morning when I learned my mother had died. I was unable to move. I was in such a state of shock that I couldn't cry. Nor did I cry when I looked at her during the wake that lasted three days. Nor at the funeral service. But when we got to the cemetery and I saw the coffin going into the ground, I couldn't stop crying."

When the funeral was over, John refused to accept that his mother was dead. "I didn't believe she was gone, and for the next year I searched for her face in every crowd I was in, in every room I entered, in every restaurant, every bus, every train, every city. In order to bring her back, I forced myself to dream about her. Before going to bed I'd think to myself, 'I'm going to see my mother. I'm going to dream about my mother.' And not only did I dream of her, but always in a situation where she was helping me. I envisioned her at the age she was when I was a child, protecting me in my teens, always protecting me as I grew older, supportive of me, as she had been when I was young. It wasn't until many years later, after counseling, that I was able to accept her death."

Gia Williams was devastated when she heard the news that her mother, at forty-two, had died of pneumonia. Gia, twenty-five, had not seen her mother for several years. "She lived in one city and I in another," Gia now says, "and we had grown apart for other reasons. So when I heard the news of her death from my grandmother, I was absolutely stunned. I had heard that my mother was ill and receiving treatment for what they called walking pneumonia. But this one afternoon, she apparently felt worse than usual. So she went to bed and didn't wake up. My mother was very young, and it was hard for me to believe she was dead. I was especially sad since I knew I had not resolved the differences between us, and now it was too late. Afterward, I would dream that the two of us were talking and that she was stroking my head or touching it. Those dreams helped me a lot."

The reader will recall having met in Chapter 1 the people in the accounts given below. Here we learn how the death of a loved one affected each in the days and weeks after the death.

Beth Landau couldn't deal with the fact that her father's funeral was going to take place the next day. "I went to Mercy Hospital, where they had brought him. I just felt I needed to talk to someone there. Perhaps I needed a sedative. At any rate, I was given a prescription for Valium. In addition, I wanted to find the doctor who had pronounced my father dead, but in that I was unsuccessful.

"From the hospital I went to Gutterman's, the funeral chapel, where my father's body was to be ready for viewing that afternoon. My mother had decided not to have a formal gathering that evening at the chapel, but I made up my mind to go anyway. There another shock awaited me—my father's name on the door struck me like a blow in the face. The casket was open, and I moved closer to see him. He looked great. As I stood there and spoke to him, I started to cry. I reached out to touch him, but he was cold. I was glad I was alone with him for that time, but I still couldn't believe the whole thing."

On the night Beth learned of her father's death, she

slept with her mother. But she would wake up crying. "My mother was crying, too. It was a very eerie feeling that first night. I was in shock, I suppose. My father had been there that morning, and then that night he was gone. So there was something unreal about the next couple of days. My world seemed upside down. I felt like I was going crazy. His eyeglasses were around and his clothes. I kept looking in his closet. I put on his bathrobe. I just felt terrible.

"The day after he died, I took the car and went into Long Beach to our old house, then to the beach and to the boats where he used to take me. I felt an urge to return to where I was as a child, and I tried to replay every memory I had of him, how he looked, what he said, the parts he played in different events in our lives. It was upsetting, but it was also comforting to me because I felt that if I didn't bring past events to mind, I would forget."

When Peggy Griffiths' father died, she was in her early twenties and two months away from receiving a master's degree at the Wharton School of Business in Philadelphia. She refused to allow herself to think about her father's death. "I was deluged with studies and getting my thesis done," she says. "I just plain buried myself in work so that I didn't have to think about the death of my father. After I graduated and returned to New York, I began to accept that my dad was gone."

Fifteen years later, Peggy's mother died. "Although we had some time to prepare for the blow and even though we knew she could not live long, her death, when it did come, was a horrendous shock." Peggy, who was working at the time, recalls how helpful her employer was. "He knew my mother well, and he had lost his father. So he was well aware of what the loss of a parent meant—each one irreplaceable. Again, my salvation was to keep myself busy and my mind occupied. I knew I could not afford to sit still and dwell on my mother. I didn't want to think about her as being gone."

Peggy's best friend, whose mother had died of cancer, made a request. "Peggy, I want you to do something for me. I want you to put this whole thing about your mother and her illness and death into a closet. And keep it in that closet with the door closed for two years. Just keep it out of your mind and stay as busy as you can. At the end of two years, open the door and take a look at it. You will be able to handle it much better than you can now." Peggy took her friend's advice. "That is exactly what I did. It was difficult, but I did it. And it helped me enormously."

Paul Vento was twenty-seven when his father died. Day after day in the time following his father's death, he cried intermittently. He found it hard to sleep, but when he did drop off, his nightmares awakened him. His feelings were a jumble of anger, hurt, fear, and a sense of abandonment; they even affected his job. As a route salesman, Paul was required to drive. "I had a van and before I would get into it, I used to look inside to see if my father was there. That was the result of my viewing his body at the morgue.

"That experience had left its imprint on me and the image kept coming back. I was afraid to go out of the house, for our imaginations play tricks on us. I was so scared that I kept looking in the van for a good few weeks. I didn't know which was more frightening—remembering the way I had seen him in the morgue or thinking he was hiding in the van. Although I knew I had seen my father dead, I kept thinking he was around."

Carol Richardson was reluctant to go to the hospital when she was notified that her mother had died. Because the twenty-one-year-old Carol was an only child, she had to go to the hospital alone. "It took a while before I could make myself go there, because I knew what I was going to face when I got to the hospital. I decided that the longer I stayed away, the less time I'd have to face that whole scene."

Carol had been to visit her mother that same morning. "She seemed fine and talked to me. She was sitting up and I felt comfortable about leaving her to go to work and take care of a few odd jobs. I had been in the office about an hour when the doctor called to tell me that she had died. At first I didn't believe it, and I just went on doing my work. It was as if I simply had not heard what the doctor said to me."

When Carol mustered up the courage to return to the hospital, she spoke with her mother's doctor. "He was very compassionate, and explained to me what had happened and why she had seemed fairly well earlier in the day. Then I had to get rid of my mother's things at the hospital. As I looked through them, I began to remember how she had wanted me to bring this particular object to the hospital and how she had wanted that one.

"At first, I was going to keep everything, but then I just said to myself, 'No.' I kept only her jewelry, but I put it out of sight. You don't throw jewelry away. But I never wear it. I put it into a safe place and every now and then I go and look at it, and think of her when she was wearing it in her better days."

Carol realized that funeral arrangements had to be made and she was grateful for the help given her by her mother's church. But Carol was walking around as if she were living in a dream. She now describes that time. "From the day of my mother's death to her actual burial, I was so preoccupied with what had to be done as far as funeral arrangements were concerned, that I don't think it really sunk in until perhaps two weeks later. It finally struck me because it was Christmas—the first Christmas she wouldn't be there. *That* was a very difficult situation to deal with."

The last conversation Lisa Strahs-Lorenc had with her father took place when he called from the Canadian hotel where he and his wife were vacationing. He told Lisa what a beautiful place it was and described the next day's activities. "When I heard of his death, my first thought was that I had been unable to say good-bye to him. Oh God, it was as if I were watching myself in a movie. The whole thing seemed impossible—it couldn't be. I had studied Kübler-Ross and I know I went through all the stages. Everything I did, I did automatically—calling the funeral home and trying to figure out how to get the body home.

"One thing I do remember is that the funeral director was very helpful. It was the same one our family had gone to when my grandmother had died and, ironically, also for my biological mother. (See Chapter 1.) The funeral director remembered our family and that made us feel better. Also, he didn't pressure us about anything. I can see where people could be very vulnerable at a time like this and spend a fortune. But this funeral director saw to our needs and helped us with our preferences not to have a gaudy casket and things like that."

After the funeral, Lisa returned to work, and every day she passed the cemetery in her car. "So I stopped and visited the grave each morning, almost as if I were looking for him. I thought it would bring me close to him, but it didn't. Then as time passed, I cut the visits to only once a week and eventually to once a month. Then, I guess I just stopped looking for him."

⌒⋎ CHAPTER 4

Dealing with Anger

Carol Richardson was extremely angry at her mother's death. " 'Why her?' Those were my exact words. She didn't do anything to anybody. Why did she get cancer? She maintained an excellent diet. She didn't have high blood pressure. She took care of herself. She shouldn't have gotten it—and that's how I felt. But the fact remained that she did, and now she was dead, and nothing could be done about it."

Carol would become annoyed if a friend invited her home for a dinner cooked by "my mother," and this happened quite often. "I would tell those people, 'I'm not looking for another mother, and don't invite me so your mother can cook for me.' They were just trying to help, but I didn't appreciate their efforts. Things got to be so bad that on Mother's Day, I didn't want to be around anyone who had a mother."

In time, Carol's anger lessened, but a couple of years passed before it really diminished. "I was hostile toward *anybody's* mother, especially if she tried to be helpful with something, making some such remark as 'Oh, Carol, you don't seem to be dressed warmly enough.' Then I was ready to tell women like that to mind their own business. I was angry very often.

"In the beginning, many people were not aware that Mother had died; these people, whom I saw but once or twice a year, would ask, 'How's Blanche?' And I would reply, 'Don't you know?' And I'd be cross with them for not knowing. I still get angry every now and then. I get angry on holidays if someone says, 'What are you doing this weekend?' And when I reply I'm just going to stay home, they may say, 'Lucky you. Are you going to have a dinner cooked by your mom?' Not knowing. When my foster daughter was much younger, I would sometimes get angry and frustrated that my mother wasn't there to help out, thinking there were many little things she could do so much better than I."

Carol also had to deal with the anger of her father's death. His had been a difficult illness. "It started with an infected toe, but gangrene developed and the doctors had to amputate both legs. He lived on for three years, but a year after the amputations, it was discovered that he had cancer of the prostate. My father felt useless, making it more than a little difficult to transport him back and forth for medical care.

"My father was not a *little* hostile, he was a *lot* hostile. I had a home-care service involved. It was very frustrating because this man, so very active before his illness, just did not accept what was happening to him. Then he developed cataracts. By this time he had been ill for many years and I knew he was nearing his end. But I imagined, remembering my mother's death, that this time I would be prepared for the worst. Or so I thought."

Carol had received many false alarms from people at the hospital who would say, "This is it, get here at once." And so, she gradually became somewhat indifferent to the continued calls that cried wolf. "Each time I would go, fortunately he would be okay. So that last time, when the hospital telephoned me to come, I explained that I had been out of the hospital myself for only two days, and asked if I could send someone else. I was told I had to come.

"I was instructed to stop at the nurse's station, but when I arrived she wasn't there. I went into my father's room and I saw they had called a Code Seven on him, the hospital's signal that a patient's vital signs are dropping. I saw them working on my father, and I was standing there when the doctor said, 'We've lost him.' My first reaction was to take it out on the nurse. She must have had a hard day because she turned on me and brusquely said, 'Look, we lose people every day and I don't want to hear it.' She went on like that and the nurse and I just yelled at each other. I couldn't believe how detached and insensitive those people were.

"After I thought about it, I realized this *was* something they did every day, but you would think they'd have enough consideration to understand that people don't lose a parent every day. I later learned this nurse was dismissed. Although I felt her behavior that day contributed to her dismissal, I really regretted her loss of her job. It was a pity she could not have been a little more sympathetic. Perhaps then my anger would not have been so great and perhaps she would not have responded in the way she did."

After the death of a parent due to a long-term illness, it is not unusual for adult children to vent their anger and frustration at the attending doctors and nurses. One daughter recalls her actions at such a time: "When my father died after a long illness, I was so angry at the doctors and nurses that I accused them of malpractice. I yelled at the top of my voice and threatened to sue them. The next day I wondered if I was losing my mind. Why did I say such things? Now, after many years, I understand that those feelings of anger after the death of a loved one are normal. If only I had known that, I wouldn't have felt so guilty about my anger afterward."

Venting anger at doctors, nurses, and hospital staff is one form of channeling the rage felt at losing a parent. Children also find themselves angry at the departed. John Donnelly did. "I was very angry at my mother for dying when she did. I kept thinking, 'Mother, why did you have to die now? Why couldn't you have waited three or four years if you had to die?' You see, I had stayed in college to please her because it was what she wanted. As her only child, I was reluctant to disappoint her. She was giving me the money to stay in college because she wanted me to become a teacher, something that I myself would never have chosen. I wanted to be a journalist, a foreign correspondent. I wanted to travel, but that was the last thing in the world she wanted, because travel and being a foreign correspondent, too, would take me away from her. The only compromise in that area was that she agreed to my going to an out-of-town college. I wanted to be away from home."

Although John was going to school on the G.I. Bill of Rights after being in the Army for two years, his mother supplemented his income. When his mother died, John's anger surfaced. "I was very angry at her for dying, for deserting me and leaving me stranded to try and get through school by myself. The anger, about which I feel some guilt to this day, was the result of the sacrifice I had made when she was dying. One of the professors at college had nominated me for a Rhodes Scholarship to Oxford University in England. I was ecstatic. Now I'd be able to travel. I could see something of the world—and on a scholarship. New vistas opened before my eyes. My dream was coming true after all. I was walking on Cloud Nine. But my mother's illness precluded my accepting the scholarship and I told my professor I had to turn it down."

Not only did John have to forego the scholarship, he had to give up school entirely. His mother had become ill, and her frequent stays in hospitals required so much money that John had to go to work on a full-time basis. Although he had a stepfather, the mounting bills demanded another income in the family. But John was angry. "I was angry that she had put me in this position. Angry that she had wanted me to go to college and now had left me to sink or swim. And, I was angry at the idea of losing her. I realized later that she had no control over the time of her death."

"Anger at a deceased parent is often experienced by adult children in their twenties and early thirties, more often with an unmarried child, or with those who have had a strong symbiotic relationship with the parent," says psychotherapist Anne Rosberger. "Sometimes we take over for our children and do everything for them. Then they feel unable to pursue life without the parents. 'Why didn't you prepare me to be by myself?' is the question asked by grieving children. Experientially, parents often don't equip their children to take care of themselves, maintaining a protective stance, and they are so busy helping their children avoid mistakes and suffering, they do not see that this is a hindrance to their children; then, when the parent dies, the surviving child expresses the anger at the parent for not preparing them for life alone."

Paul Vento was also angry at his dead parent. After he identified his father's body in the morgue, he had to make all the funeral arrangements, with no help from anyone else. His mother wasn't in any condition to handle it. Paul recalls: "I was angry that my father left me with all the problems. It was an easy way out for him. He left me with the whole mess—and I could no longer go to him for anything. The biggest problem was my mother. Who was going to worry about her, who was going to take care of her? At least if he were alive, he would still be taking care of her. Now it was thrown in my lap. It isn't that I didn't want to take care of my mother, but you feel that way. You feel that anger that he abandoned us, and then later you suffer for it."

Paul believes that his father wished himself to die. "With all the surgery and illnesses he'd had, I think my father was just disgusted and wanted to give up. Let's face it. He was operated on eleven times. He had ulcers, gall bladder, appendicitis, diverticulitis. You name it, he had it. And then his arm had to be operated on several times. There were a million damned things. And his drinking made the illnesses worse. To this day, I think the drinking was his easy way out. As to my anger, I wasn't angry at God or at my mother. I was just angry at my father for leaving."

Kathleen Riley still has a lot of resentment and anger about her father's death. She isn't even sure at whom the anger is directed. "I'm not angry at my mother or the doctors. I know they did everything they could. I think I am angry at *him*—at my father. I know it wasn't his fault and I shouldn't feel that way. But I am just like him. I see myself as he was—a driven person who tries to please everybody—I try to do my job the best I can, I go to work when I don't feel well. And that's the way he was. I resent that he didn't enjoy life more, yet I know he did so, as far as his personality permitted. I don't blame him. I know that a brain tumor isn't caused by a lack of caring for oneself. It just happens. I wasn't angry at God. Yes, I understand that He could have prevented it, but He didn't and I'm not angry at Him. I'm angry that it happened and I'm angry at myself. And I don't deal well with that.

"I've been told by people that I cover up my anger with a nice personality. I smile. I joke around. I try to make it appear that nothing is too much of a problem for me. I have gone for counseling over the years and when I really get down on myself about a lot of things, I go and talk it over with my counselors. I used to pray a lot more than I do now. I know I need something more in my life. I guess I haven't totally coped with my problem and I know that."

The perpetrators who robbed and left Robert Martin to die have never been apprehended. His two daughters, Marjorie and Ellen, experienced varying feelings of anger, bewilderment, terror, grief, and guilt. But most of all, Marjorie and Ellen were angry. Angry at what had occurred, angry at the way it happened. Their immediate reaction was one of bitterness over their father's death. "It was hell that last week to watch him struggling, not being able to breathe, not being able to function at all," Marjorie remembers. "We wondered what kind of vipers could have come and done such a cruel thing to an incapacitated, helpless invalid. What kind of vermin could have left him there to die after deliberately pulling the plug from his respirator?

"What tore at our insides most was that the police never found those criminals. They were never punished for their crime. They murdered our father and they were walking around free as birds. It was one thing to see our house torn apart and ransacked. But it was much worse to see our father gasping for breath because he had no respirator working to help him. I don't think we shall ever completely rid ourselves of that anger. Who could? Could anyone see her father left by robbers to die and not remain scarred? Yes, my sister and I have come a long way. And yes, we have each other. But we should like to see those criminals caught and punished for their callousness to our father."

Marjorie and Ellen's bitterness began to affect their daily lives. "The house went to pot and we didn't care. We threw out almost everything we owned and made no replacements. We felt that if the same perpetrators came back or if other criminals broke in, there would be nothing for them to take except the clothes and the beds."

While visiting her mother at the hospital, thirty-eight-year-old Sandra Ames saw dried food on the front of the sick woman's gown. She also saw that the supper tray had been left almost untouched. Sandra realized that her mother must have attempted to eat the solid foods on the tray, but was unsuccessful. They had dribbled down onto her clothing and dried up.

Sandra was furious. She had been told by the doctors that her mother was to be on a soft diet of such foods as mashed potatoes, Jell-O, ice cream, and liquids. Sandra gave her opinion of this negligence to the nurse on duty. "It had been a long and tiring day for me," she said later, referring to this occasion. "This was one of many trips to and from the hospital I'd had to make over several months, and I was angry. Angry at having to leave the children with a baby-sitter. Angry at being unable to accompany my husband on a recent business trip. Angry at the hospital staff for not providing my mother with food she could eat. Even angry at my mother for not complaining to the nurse about the food."

But Sandra's anger in the days before her mother's death was nothing compared to what it was after her mother died. She accused the nurses of causing her mother's death. "They had not taken care of her the

night she died," said Sandra. "My mother's roommate told me she and my mother both felt intimi-
dated by the night nurse and were afraid to
complain. The woman told me that my mother had
moaned all during that night and said, 'The nurse
just came in and tossed her over on her side like a
sack of potatoes.'"

Sandra's mother had appeared to be in good spirits the day before she died. In fact, she had been sitting up and laughing. Later, Sandra was angry at
herself, thinking: "I should have realized it was the
final surge of energy that a dying person experiences.
The nurses should have sensed this and told us. The
doctors must have known what happens to the dying
as they enter the last moments of life. I believe I just
closed my eyes and wanted her to be better, so I took
her newfound energy to be a sign that she was im-
proving. As a result, I was stunned when the hospital
called me at seven o'clock in the morning to say that
my mother was dead. My first thought was that she
would still be alive if they had taken better care of
her. My anger has subsided, but for a long time I
believed she wouldn't have died if the hospital staff
had seen to her needs. I was convinced of that and I
was bitter."

Another daughter who experienced anger at the
hospital staff was Margaret McAllister. She recalls
two episodes: "I broke into tears when a nurse gave
me my father's belongings. I can describe the con-
tainer in only one way—it looked like a trash bag. I
thought to myself, 'Is this what it came to? Everything thrown into a garbage bag as if he meant nothing?' Because I wanted to look at his things, I asked
if I could have a place to sit. The nurses were very
rude and seemed annoyed at my request. Perhaps
they thought I wanted to see if anything was missing.

If so, they were wrong, for I only wanted to look at each and every article. You know, *this* was my father, but here was all that was left of him. They could at least have had the decency to give me a few minutes before sending me off with a plastic trash bag in my hand."

Margaret recalls that on one occasion she flared up at the doctor. "Soon after we were advised of my father's death, the doctor called. I was very cold to him. He had the misfortune of saying to me that the tone of my voice sounded as if I blamed him. I went crazy. I said to him: 'Blame you? Why would I blame you? I send you my father and you send me back a dead man. Why would I blame you?'

"My mother and I didn't find out until months later that the doctor had been very honest with my father, telling him that he was going to die; that his body was shutting down piece by piece. Another doctor who had treated my father also told us that was so. I believe my father chose not to tell this to us because he felt we would find the news too hard to take.

"But I was still angry. I had to have someone to blame. When I couldn't blame the doctors anymore, I began to blame my father. How *dare* he die on me? My thoughts were: 'How dare you die before I could tell you everything I wanted? How dare you die before I knew you better?' "

Lisa Strahs-Lorenc was beside herself with anger at her aunts, uncles, and other relatives after the death of her father. A few months later, Lisa and her mother were invited to a Thanksgiving dinner at one of their homes, but a wall of silence seemed to surround the table. This infuriated Lisa. "Not one of my relatives talked about my father. In the past, he had always been the center of attention, telling jokes and talking, but now the relatives wanted to block out their memories of him, or maybe they were afraid of what my reaction would be and that they couldn't handle *that*. Whatever the reason, not one of them mentioned his name. This made me so angry that I walked out of the house, terribly upset. Later my mother said, 'Look, they can't cope with it any more than we can. It's very hard for them, too.' And I said, 'But it's worse this way. It's as if he never existed. How could they not speak his name once during the whole day?' "

Andrew Rezin was twenty-five when his father died six years ago. He was angry and could not understand his father's death. "Why did this have to happen? Why did he have to die? Why did he leave me when I was just trying to build a really close relationship with him and my mother? I had just become engaged, and soon I would be leaving the house. I was heartbroken at this loss of someone whom I had looked forward to having, not only as a father, but also as a friend. Why had he died? Then my emotions, my anger took over. I withdrew and didn't want to see other people.

"The next year, after I was married, my mother gave us the family dining-room set. A month later she died. I would come home from work and see that dining-room set and be so furious that my parents weren't sitting at it that I would pick up a chair and throw it. I knew then that my anger was getting out of control. I discussed this problem with a friend who had seen a TV program featuring Anne Rosberger of the Bereavement and Loss Center in New York. I got in touch with her and she has been of enormous help to me. Weekly visits have helped me and my marriage."

Patricia Tremont's mother had been in and out of the hospital for treatment of phlebitis, hardening of the arteries, and related problems. Patricia and her husband had scheduled a trip to Mexico, but were reluctant to leave. "I was afraid I might not be home if anything happened to my mother," Patricia said. "But I didn't want to disappoint my husband either, as it was our twentieth wedding anniversary celebration." Patricia's brother urged the couple to adhere to their plans.

Three days after they left, the seventy-one-year-old mother was put back into the hospital for complications. When Patricia called her brother and learned of this, she wanted to fly home, but was told the situation was not serious. But several calls to her family did not allay Patricia's fears, and she and her husband decided to cut their trip short. When she reached the airport late on Thursday evening, she called her brother. "I'll go directly to the hospital," she said. But the brother insisted this was unnecessary; their mother had enjoyed a very good day, and seemed to be in excellent spirits.

" 'She's probably sleeping and it's a long drive for you,' my brother said. 'So go home. Get some rest and come to the hospital in the morning.' " So Patricia, tired, nervous, and exhausted from a rushed trip, went home. But Friday morning at six o'clock, the phone rang. Her mother had died in the night. Today Patricia says, "At first I was angry at my brother who had discouraged me from visiting the hospital. On the other hand, I knew he was trying to save me wear and tear. Nevertheless, I had not been able to say good-bye to my mother and for that I am still angry."

During his mother's illness, Phil Musmacker began to develop a rage against the world. His father was of little help, for he was both belligerent and alcoholic. Because of his bouts with alcoholism, Mr. Musmacker visited his wife only periodically in the hospital. "When my father was sober," Phil says, "he was kind and gentle. But when he was drunk, he was abusive both physically and verbally to me and my mother. So it was better that he didn't go to the hospital." Phil felt that his brothers and sisters also avoided their responsibilities. "At the time, I felt they were avoiding the situation."

Phil's anger extended to the doctors. "I would ask them what I could do to help my mother's condition, but they could give me no answers." This anger, which was intensified after his mother's death, led Phil to the abuse of drugs and alcohol. He felt trapped. He knew his mother was dying and he sought ways to alleviate his own pain.

Tom Andrews was usually a patient person, immune to the small annoyances that bother most of us. But after his mother died in a drowning accident, thirty-one-year-old Tom found that almost any little thing would irritate him. Things like having to wait in line at a supermarket or at a gasoline station would arouse his anger and he would engage in an argument. At home, he was impossible to live with. His wife, Polly, tells of the change. "If anyone had ever told me Tom would lose his temper this way and have fights with people, or that he would become tyrannical and argumentative at home, I would have said they were talking about someone else, not my Tom. But that is exactly what happened. He got into a fist-fight with a neighbor who asked to borrow our lawn mower. He was going to punch the man for asking to borrow anything when he knew that Tom's mother had died. But Tom's mother had died three months before, and the neighbor probably felt the mourning period was over. Tom argued with the mailman and the druggist. One day after he missed his train by a hairsbreadth, I was afraid he was going to have a stroke. I had driven him to the station and knew we were running late, but I thought he would make it. When he didn't, he came out to the car to wait for the next train. He fell into the seat utterly spent and I was really frightened that he might have a heart attack.

"I was growing increasingly worried about him and sought out a therapist who was familiar with grief problems. Tom agreed to go and it has helped him very much. Tom and his mother were very close, but his anger seemed directed at his mother, too, for leaving him. Her body was never found and this almost destroyed Tom. Since he has been seeing this psychotherapist, the anger has subsided and he seems to have regained some of his strength, both physically and mentally."

Dr. Roberta Temes tells us that often symptoms during the middle phase of mourning can closely resemble some symptoms of mental illness. "The difference, of course," she says, "is that indications of mental illness do not spontaneously and permanently disappear, while indications of grief will eradicate themselves as the mourning process is completed." She continues: "If you were not mentally ill prior to the death of your loved one, you will recover from bereavement and regain your ability to function. Recovery from grief is enhanced and hastened if you are able to experience the temporary, but necessary, irrational feelings and thoughts which are normal during mourning."*

*Temes, Roberta, *Living with an Empty Chair*. New York: Irvington Publishers Inc., 1984.

🦢 CHAPTER 5

Guilt Trips

Dan Sutherland, forty-two, moped around day after day. "I would go out for a walk and suddenly not know where I was. I would look around and wonder how I got there. I knew I was suffering a reaction to my father's death. When they had found him slumped over in the street, he was rushed to the hospital, a victim of a hit-and-run driver. He never regained consciousness and died three days later.

"He had been staying with my sister and needed careful watching, for he suffered from Alzheimer's disease. Whenever she had to go out, one of her neighbors came to sit with him, but on that day the neighbor was ill. Ordinarily, my sister would have done without some groceries she needed, rather than leave my father alone. But he was undressed and in bed, and she planned to be gone but a few minutes. Those few minutes cost my father his life. Unfortunately, he got up, opened the door, and wandered out into the street where he was struck by the car."

Now Dan says, "I feel so guilty. I wish I had taken more time to be with him, but I couldn't bear watching him deteriorate. He had been such a strong man, with such a sharp mind. I went to see him about once a week. I traveled a lot and was out of town at least one week of every month. So when I was home, I always had a dozen chores to catch up on—mowing the lawn, fixing the faucet, going to the dentist—and there wasn't a lot of time left for visiting my father. But deep in my heart, I knew I didn't want to see him. He didn't know who I was half the time. It was such a draining experience and I had to steel myself for every visit."

For a long time, Dan struggled with the "if onlies." "If only I had been a better son. If only I had visited him more often. If only I had called my sister that day, I would have learned the neighbor was sick. Then I could have gone and stayed with him until my sister returned. My sister thought I was out of town, so she didn't call me. But I should have let her know my plans had changed. If I could just make it up to him somehow. I feel so rotten. I feel so guilty."

On a leisurely honeymoon trip, Cynthia Carter and her husband were driving to various places in the United States with no particular destination in mind. Because of the couple's haphazard travels, Cynthia could not be reached when her mother, age fifty, died suddenly of a heart attack.

"I didn't get the news until after the funeral," Cynthia reflects. "Not only wasn't I with my mother when she died, I also missed the funeral. Filled with guilt and remorse, I couldn't believe that I wouldn't know when my own mother died. How could I be in such a state of bliss as not to know that something was wrong? How could it be that my mother was stricken and I wouldn't sense it? We had always been very close."

For a long time, Cynthia had a fear of traveling anywhere. "I wouldn't even get into a car to go shopping or to visit my family. I associated driving with my absence from my mother when she died. I suppose I was punishing myself by refusing to get into a car. Or perhaps I was afraid that someone else would die and no one would be able to get in touch with me. I still felt guilty about being away when my mother died. Now, even if I go to the corner drugstore, I tell everyone where I'm going."

Dr. David Meagher, a counselor and consultant in death and dying, lost both of his parents. At the time of his father's death, David, age thirty, was teaching in New York City, while his father was living in upstate New York. His dad had been ill with cancer and cardiovascular disease. Of this period, David says, "After my father died, I became very concerned with the way I was reacting to his death. While my father was in the hospital, I didn't get up to see him very often. Later, after his death, I began to feel guilty. 'Had I visited him often enough? When I did visit, had I stayed long enough?' I wasn't happy with what I had or hadn't done. I began to question my feelings, and decided to take some steps to understand them better."

Following his mother's recent death, David was not tormented by guilt feelings. He had a closer relationship with his mother than he'd had with his father. "There are still times when I have a tremendous urge to pick up the phone and call her at the times I would call her when she was alive. Also, there are things she did for me in the way of my writing. For example, she acted as unofficial editor. In everything I wrote, she corrected my grammar. She did this for my doctoral dissertation, for my book, and for articles that were for publication. Today when I am writing, I have a tremendous urge to send her the manuscript."

Marjorie and Ellen Martin were consumed with their guilt after their father's death—Ellen because while he lived, she had been in and out of the hospital for a year and believed this had caused him anxiety and worry. She regretted being away that year because it was time that she couldn't devote to her father. Marjorie had guilt feelings about leaving her invalid father alone so much of the time. She had spent every day going to the hospital during her sister's illness. "I felt not enough of my time was given over to my father. I would go to the hospital after work and stay there until seven P.M. Because I never got home before eight or nine o'clock at night, I would give my father a late dinner and put him to bed. Then, by midnight or so I would fall into bed myself.

"We both felt miserable that our father was defenseless when the robbers came and we were not there to help him. We wondered if we had been there if it would have happened."

Gia Williams not only mourned the death of her mother, she also mourned the relationship they had never had. "I felt bad about that. We could have been really good friends, but somehow we missed that. But with the type of pain that I have suffered—pain at not having her with me—I have turned that suffering around and made good of it. I find I can relate to many young people who have problems with their parents. I often talk to them and suggest how they can get along with their parents. And sometimes I meet the parents themselves. In other words, I have grown to the point of minimizing my own problems by thinking of someone else's, and by giving more of myself to others."

Surviving adult children often bemoan the lack of a good relationship with the parent who has died. The loss of the parent is compounded by mourning for the wished-for relationship. Sons and daughters grieve over what they didn't have and now can never have.

In other instances, surviving children may have enjoyed a warm relationship with the parent but may have quarreled with that parent prior to the death. Guilt feelings take over because the quarrels cannot be undone.

Beth Landau was one such daughter. After her father's sudden death, Beth struggled with her feelings of guilt. "My father and I had enjoyed a wonderful relationship. But just before he died we had had an argument. This caused a feeling of guilt at the beginning, but then I realized he would have forgiven me. I imagine that is why I decided to write something to read at the unveiling [of the tombstone] at the cemetery and that something was the things I had never told him."

Guilt after the loss of a parent can take many forms. John Donnelly was certain he had been part of the cause of his mother's death. His guilt was so severe that he sought help. In discussing the problem with his therapist, John was able to release much of the guilt he had felt before and after his mother's death. "For many, many years when my mother was still alive and I was living at home, she would often remind me how horrible it was for her after my birth, physically. I remember when I was young, I asked why I didn't have any brothers or sisters. My mother told me mine was a very difficult birth with forceps, that the doctor tore her to get me out, and that kind of thing. She had refused to go to a hospital because her father had gone into a hospital and never came out. So she insisted on having her baby at home.

"Perhaps my mother wanted to explain to me why having another child was out of the question for her because of the difficulties she experienced at my birth. But I always felt guilty that she had such a rough time with my birth."

An uncle of John's, upon learning what had been

told the boy about his birth, tried to ease his guilt and anguish. "You know, your mother loved to exaggerate pain; she would build up the slightest little thing just to get attention." John figured that since this was his mother's brother talking, he must have known his sister; perhaps she really was exaggerating the birth story. "I noticed that when my mother had a toothache, she made such a thing of it that one would think the world was coming to an end. But perhaps the trauma and pain of my birth caused her to anticipate pain in any sort of health-related situation, such as a tooth.

"Even though I listened to what my uncle told me, I still felt guilty at times. That is why, when she developed cancer of the cervix, I carried the weight of wondering if the problems she had with my birth were in any way responsible for her illness. After she died, that guilt became so intense that I just couldn't take it. So I went to my doctor, who recommended that I see a therapist. In talking to her, she said, 'If your mother had wanted that tear or rip repaired, corrective surgery was a very minor thing in later years. There should have been no problem. Your mother's fear of doctors and hospitals prevented her from properly attending to her medical needs, and you were in no way responsible for her illness or her death.'"

Edward Steudtner, who was thirty-five when his mother died, wept after her death, struggling with the pangs of guilt that engulfed him. "My mother's death was unexpected. She had been in the hospital the week before, supposedly with a GI problem and a heart problem connected. But everything seemed to be stabilized and she was released from the hospital. When that happens, you and your family assume that you're okay. I live in California. My mother lived in New York. So it wasn't a question of just a run around the corner to visit my mother.

"When my mother got out of the hospital, at first she spent some time with my sister Joan who lives on Long Island. I really wish she had stayed for a while and I'm a little resentful that Joan didn't insist my mother remain longer. I know Mom probably said, 'No, I'd rather go home,' but I think at some point the younger ones have to take over and say, 'No, you will not go home because you are not ready to be alone.' But she overruled Joan and she did go home and she did pass away.

"I think I blame myself in a way. Every year my mother came out to California to see us, but this past year, she was having eye surgery, so deep down I didn't want her to come out. My wife had had difficulties getting along with my mother when she stayed at our house for five or six weeks at a time. You know how it can be with a mother-in-law. So I let my wife talk me out of having my mother visit us this past year. Instead, we planned to go East for a visit next year. Mom died in between."

A friend of Edward's urged him not to feel guilty or be too hard on himself. "These are normal feelings," his friend stressed. "The best thing you can do is to say to yourself what you would say to your best friend. And that is 'Think of the number of times in past years you had your mother visit you in California, even though it was hard on you and your wife.' And didn't you give up five or six weeks of your own life so she could be there with you and enjoy time with you? Even though it might have inconvenienced your wife, you both spent a great deal of time with your mother when she visited you."

The friend continued: "Look at how far away you were. It was hard to do more for her when you lived three thousand miles away. The reality is that your mother knew you loved her, and you knew she loved you. The distance didn't sever the cord of love. So now it's time to say, 'She died in her own home where she wanted to be.' Now it's time to say, 'I forgive myself because I know I tried very hard in those previous years to have her with us in California.' So for the one time you missed out, I don't think you should be penalized and I think you should forgive yourself. I'm sure your mother does."

Andrew Rezin also suffered guilt pangs. "I was very depressed. I felt a great deal of guilt. I had been out late Saturday night with my friends, so that when my mother's screams for help woke me, I was coming out of a deep sleep. My father was just lying there, not moving. It was like a bad dream. I went over to him and tried to pump his chest—to do something to revive him. But it was all unreal, and anyway I wasn't sure about what to do in this kind of emergency.

"How many people know what to do when they find someone dying? I had never thought of my father as being seriously ill. But, when we were cleaning out his things after he died, I discovered nitroglycerin pills that had been prescribed for him; apparently he had been taking them. But I never knew it, and was very much surprised when I found them. Later, I would dream about hearing my mother screaming and running to help my father, and I would be miserable, thinking that perhaps I hadn't done enough to help him."

Although Andrew's mother had called for an ambulance, his father was already dead. "It wasn't long before two police officers came to the house. Then we spent dreary hours waiting for the medical examiner to come—and thinking about my father's body lying there. I had to notify my married sister and brother, who were living in homes of their own. When my brother-in-law heard my voice, he knew something had happened. I could barely speak; my throat was clogged and tears were choking me.

"It was hard to say anything, swallowing every word I was trying to get out. It's hard enough to be in shock and at the same time try to tell another person what has caused that shock. Somehow I got out the words that described my father's death from a stroke. But I felt a lot of guilt. What did I do wrong that he had to die? I didn't really understand why he died. My therapist helped me a lot in dealing with those first few minutes after finding my father."

When Tom Andrews heard that his mother was going on a boating trip, he felt uneasy. His parents were separated and now his mother was seeing another man whose great interests were boats and fishing. Mrs. Andrews had invited Tom and his wife to go along, but they could not do so, and Tom tells how he tried to talk his mother out of going, too. "The guy was ten years younger than my mother and I didn't like him. I thought he was a gigolo. When my mother asked me to go, I declined because I didn't want to be in his presence. I just used an excuse about having to look at a new car, but I was uneasy about her going and had a premonition something was not right. I told myself that the 'premonition' grew out of my resentment of the guy.

"But it was more than that. A storm came up, the boat capsized, and my mother's body was lost at sea. To this day, I keep seeing images of sharks and other fish eating her, and wondering if she was screaming with no one to hear her. My friends try to tell me she probably drowned right away. Her boyfriend drowned, too. I even feel guilty about that. I keep saying to myself, 'If only I had gone, as she wanted me to, perhaps she wouldn't be dead. Perhaps I could have done something to prevent the boat from going over.'"

Tom also feels guilty for being angry at his mother for dying. "I know I shouldn't be angry at her, but I am. I had told her not to hook up with that guy, but she did. And because she did, she's no longer alive."

After her father died, Margaret McAllister was left with tremendous guilt. "I kept envisioning the day of my father's death—over and over again in my mind. I kept asking myself, 'Why weren't you more demanding at the hospital? Why didn't you insist that he be moved to the coronary care unit, especially since he was having trouble breathing?' I kept thinking, 'I should have done this or I should have done that.' In addition, there was my guilt for never having told him the things I wanted to tell him.

"I felt my father never knew how much I loved him. Later, I talked to a friend about this. I couldn't talk to my mother. I was afraid I would add to her burden, for I knew she was going through her own hardship after his death. And it's strange, my guilt was such that I was afraid if I told her about all the guilty feelings I was having that she would get angry with me and say, 'Well, if it was that important, why didn't you tell him what you were thinking?' Sometimes she used to say to me that I should tell him more of how I felt, or what I thought.

"I didn't always put my true feelings into words. I was much more verbal with my mother than with my father. My mother felt guilty, too. She felt guilty that the last night she and my father talked on the phone, she forgot to say 'I love you.' He had said it. He always said 'I love you.' Now, in retrospect, we wish we had that night back to say it.

"A friend of mine gave me a poem that read something like this: 'If I had known that last time we were together would be the last time I would ever see you,

I would have looked at you more closely. I would have listened more carefully to what you had to say. I would have said to you all the things I ever wanted to tell you.' "

🐦 CHAPTER 6

The Caretaker Syndrome

For the last two years of her mother's life, Sandra Ames took care of the sick woman's every need. When her mother had doctor's appointments, Sandra not only drove her, she also waited for her and then took her home. Sandra took care of getting prescriptions and other medical items for her mother from the druggist.

When her mother was hospitalized, Sandra spent her lunch hours driving to and from work daily in order to visit her. After her mother left the hospital, Sandra literally turned part of her home into a hospital room. She provided a special bed that could be cranked up to elevate her mother's feet. She rented a commode chair, a Walkerette, and a wheelchair. She had a special telephone system installed and put in switches that automatically turned lights on and off.

Her mother's deteriorating health took a heavy toll on Sandra. At work she was jittery, wept for little reason, and couldn't concentrate. "I don't know how much more I can take of this," she thought. "I feel like a bouncing ball. One minute I'm asleep and the next minute my mother is crying out for me to help her. My nerves are shot and my patience has a short fuse." In most instances when her mother called, Sandra would get out of bed and go to her mother immediately. But there were other times when she felt like screaming, and became angry because her mother complained constantly. On those occasions, Sandra paced herself and tried to control her exasperation before going to her mother. During one of her mother's more trying moments, she said to Sandra, "I am in such pain that I wish I could die." Exhausted, Sandra had run out of patience. She retorted sharply, "Well, if you want to die, then go ahead and die, but if you want to live, you must help yourself." After her mother's death, this statement was to haunt Sandra. "I can't forgive myself for saying that if she wanted to die she should go ahead and die."

Despite the heroic sacrifices she had made and the help she had given to her mother, Sandra had difficulty dealing with her guilt, especially the guilt of wishing her mother wasn't ill. She had resented her mother for complaining so much and for not being more aware of her daily and insistent demands. "But then after she died, I wished she was there to make them. The memories haunt me. I see my mother sitting in the chair watching TV. I can't enter the ground floor of the house without thinking of her because that is where she spent so much of her time."

Now, when Sandra comes home from work, she feels a great sadness engulf her and tears well up in her eyes. She has a sense of uneasiness because her mother is no longer there to greet her. "The house seems so empty without her. My husband and children come home later in the day from school and work. But I was always the first to come home and my mother was always there. Now when I walk in, I look at the empty house and feel depressed."

• • •

Harry Finnegan, fifty-six, lived with his elderly mother who had been a robust woman with no serious illnesses until she was in her seventies. Her doctors then determined that she needed a pacemaker. Not only one, but ultimately five pacemakers! His mother stayed indoors most of the time, venturing out only for a stroll with her son. Harry had to watch his mother constantly to be sure her pulse didn't weaken, a weak pulse being an indication that a new pacemaker was required. His mother wore her pacemakers for thirteen years and was a good patient, aside from minor complaints about aches and pains. Harry was devoted to his mother and saw to her every need. He did the food shopping, took care of the laundry, prepared meals, accompanied his mother to the doctor when needed, and, in general, kept up her morale. He joked and watched television comedy programs, enjoyed seeing her laugh, and was proud of his spirited mother.

This good climate was interrupted one day when Harry heard a loud crash in the living room. He rushed in to discover a bird had flown in through an open window and had collided with a nearby chair. Harry's first concern was the effect the bird would have on his mother, for she was very superstitious. "She used to tell a lot of stories, and I know one of them told that finding a bird was an omen. I knew a lot of people believed it meant a death, and I knew it had an effect on my mother."

Six weeks later, Harry's mother died. "We may never know the psychological effect the bird had on her condition. She began to go downhill after that. She didn't die from her pacemaker, but from general deterioration," Harry recalls.

The last four months of his mother's life were very hard on Harry. "So many extra things were required for her care, things like cleaning her bedpan, helping to wash her, changing her sheets. I did all this, but it was a strain. Gradually I came to know the end was near. I had been in the Medics in the Army, and I sensed she didn't have much time left.

"The last night my mother was home, I telephoned an emergency doctor. After he examined my mother, I asked him if she was going to die—her blood pressure was down so low. He said no, but I didn't believe him. Later, she became dehydrated and I gave her ginger ale. Suddenly, she complained that she was feeling cold. I put a heating pad around her body to warm her. She lapsed into heavy breathing, and I called the 911 emergency number to get an ambulance. They came right up to the apartment and told me she was not good. As they lifted her to take her out of the apartment, she let out a scream. I winced when I heard it because they were not gentle in picking her up in the bed sheet. The next morning she was dead.

"My brother was with me at the hospital, but he didn't want to go in to see her body, although he had literally saved my mother's life many years before. He was at our apartment and had one foot out the front door when he heard a thud. He decided to go back in and found my mother collapsed on the bathroom floor. The pacemaker had failed and he rushed her to the hospital. But this time, he just couldn't see my mother dead. So I went in. I felt I owed it to her, I guess. And also you think crazy things. You want to make sure it was she and not somebody else.

"I was somewhat relieved when it was over but wondered if I could have done anything different. I always thought that perhaps I should have given her different medicine, or that I should have paid more attention to her. Maybe I should have gotten her to the hospital sooner. She didn't eat, but in that I couldn't force her. I always wondered if there was something else I could have said or done that would have helped."

Even in the end, there was no one to take care of his mother except himself. "When I went to my mother's bedside in the hospital after she died, they had failed to close her eyes."

In reminiscing about his mother, Harry remembers the happy times they shared. He also remembers the last year of her life when she was failing. "And, strangely enough, I guess it was God's will for me to be there those last four months to help her. My company went out of business so that I was able to be with her all day long while she was dying. So I guess it was meant to be for me to be there with her."

Charlene Stevens was forty-eight when her elderly mother died. She tells about her lingering guilt for foisting a hearing aid on her mother. "I used to argue with my mother about getting a hearing aid until a friend called me aside. She cautioned that my mother might think we felt she was becoming senile. I was floored, but I decided to temporarily shelve the subject. As time went on, I became very exasperated at having to repeat every other sentence or shouting when the phone or doorbell rang and she didn't hear it. When we would be talking, she would nod her head up and down and smile. Then there would be a lull in the conversation because she wasn't really hearing what we were saying. But she was ashamed to say she couldn't hear. To her, a hearing aid was out of the question because she felt others would perceive it as her deterioration."

As things got worse with the shouting, Charlene became adamant and insisted her mother get a hearing aid. "We had heard so many good reports of how hearing aids had improved people's lives, and made it possible for them to enjoy so many things they could not before. But Mother was never happy with hers. And now I feel depressed that I made her get something that caused her such misery. She hated that contraption on her ear. Every time the television or radio blasts something loud now, I think of that damned hearing aid and I cry. My friends tell me I'm foolish and that given time she would have become adjusted to its benefits, but I still wish I hadn't pushed her so hard to get it."

Alice Figura became very close to her father during the last nine months of his life. His doctor had told Alice that her father was suffering from terminal cancer of the lung. "The news couldn't have come at a worse time for I had just broken up with my husband. I have been living in Michigan and my father was in Chicago. I was torn about whether to continue in the job I had. Finally, deciding I wanted to be where my father was so that I could take care of him, I picked up and moved back to Chicago. It wasn't easy. I had very little money to fall back on and actually sold some of my personal jewelry to make sure I'd have enough."

Alice, who was forty-two at that time, took over her father's nursing care and tried to make him as comfortable as possible. Rather than leave her father in the hospital, she chose to care for him at home. In order to do so, she supplemented her income by doing typing work at home for a local real estate firm. While her father was still mobile, Alice saw to it that he took a walk every day, and on sunny days she would accompany him to nearby parks where he liked to play checkers with friends he met there. Often Alice packed a light lunch to take along.

When it became too difficult for her father to move, and he became unable to leave the house, Alice read to him, talked to him about the things he liked to do, and at other times she just sat quietly. "I wanted him to know I was there, but that he didn't have to push himself to talk or listen. I just wanted to ease his pain somehow." Shortly thereafter, her father returned to the hospital. "He was racked with pain and it was terrible for him and for me. Once it was so bad I went into the bathroom and threw up. When it was over, I was guilty at the sense of relief I felt."

Alice's two brothers lived in Oregon. One attended the funeral, the other did not. "Joe and Charlie were as different as day and night. Joe came to the funeral because he wanted to see what was going on with my father's will. Charlie was a semi-invalid himself, and I knew that while he wanted to come, he couldn't make the trip because of his health. He felt very bad about it, I know. But Joe was a different story. It wasn't two days after my father was in his grave when Joe wanted to know what he was entitled to from my father's property and his belongings. It really left such a bad taste in my mouth for my brother. Here I was hoping it would bring us closer together and instead it drove us farther apart."

After her father's death, Alice found it difficult to grieve. Even though she had done so much for her father, she felt she might have done more. Before his illness, the relationship between father and daughter had been a distant one. Her father had remarried, but his wife had died four years earlier. Alice had seen her father on special occasions. Now, after his death, although they had become very close for the last nine months, Alice regretted all the lost years prior to her father's illness. "Although I've gone back to work and am trying to rebuild my life, that great sense of regret—that I could have been closer to him in previous years—remains. I guess the thing I have to learn to live with is that what is done cannot be undone."

Dr. David Meagher explains how to help those who have the "caretaker syndrome." "Such people were wishing their mother or father would go, and now

THE CARETAKER SYNDROME 77

that parent has died. So the children are feeling great guilt because there may have been something they should or could have done, but didn't do. I have had a number of situations like that. The first thing I try to get them to focus on is what they did—or didn't do—was not so unusual or wrong. When we are in such a situation, it is natural to feel that we are being locked in, that we are losing time and being forced to do things that we might not want to do or continue to do. This is a natural response. If I can get such people to begin to see that there was nothing really sinful in their handling of the situation, and that whatever they felt had nothing to do with the death of the parent, the guilt is easier to deal with."

Feeling some element of guilt is a normal reaction to grief. Even when totally unjustified, the questions of "Maybe if I had done this" or "If only I had done that" arise. It is unusual for guilt *not* to be present in some form or another after the death of a loved one. It is also a normal and natural reaction to be tired and worn out from exhausting trips to and from hospitals or nursing homes—every lunchtime, every evening, every Saturday, all day Sunday. Marriages often skate on thin ice because of the demand. The home is neglected and children go unsupervised. It is natural that there would be some resentment against the cause of these strains—the ill parent.

Then that person dies; at the moment of death, there may be an immediate sense of relief that it is "over"; again, this is natural. Later, when the guilt feelings set in, bereaved sons and daughters are urged to equate those feelings with the time and effort put into taking care of the parent before he or she died. As one daughter suggests, "After all, we did the best we could, and we are only human. We're just human beings and we are not all-wise and all-powerful. It is important to understand that our parents were not, either. They were just as human as we are, and they made mistakes just as we do. But we also do the best we can. We have to remember that we did the best we could. We have to let those who have died rest in peace and allow ourselves to have peace, knowing that we did everything we could for our parent."

❧ CHAPTER 7

Signs of Bereavement

When Beth Landau's dreams became overly disturbing, she sought explanations from a therapist. "My sleep has not been good throughout the year since my father died. Once I dreamt that I heard his voice. The therapist said it was normal for a person who mourns to have a dream in which the dead person talks to you. The voice usually sounds far off, like a long-distance phone call from Africa."

Beth became quite disturbed after she had another dream in which she gave birth to a baby who was born dead. "I was very upset. I visualized myself in the delivery room and the whole thing. My therapist explained that the feelings I was experiencing in the dream had their source in dead emotions and in exhaustion. She added that the 'so-called' baby was dead because I was having bad and mournful thoughts."

Another dream that emanated from her grief was equally upsetting. "I dreamed I couldn't return to the house where I grew up, for it had been demolished or burned down. I took it as meaning that my childhood and youth were over." Facing reality—awake or asleep—doesn't come with a built-in guarantee that there will be no more pain.

After work, Beth would go home and leaf through

photographs of her father as a paratrooper, and study the paraphernalia and memoirs of earlier times. "I read letters he wrote to me when I was in college, and I would sit there and cry. I kept to myself more than I had done before. I also gained twenty pounds after he died—something that would not have made him happy. When I began to try to cope with his loss, I gave myself completely to any grief I felt. I totally went with the mourning."

The above daughter is an example of what bereavement counselors call "normal grief." The following two anecdotes of sons who had continuing difficulties after the deaths of their mothers are more indicative of pathological grief. In both instances, their life-styles changed dramatically. Both of these men turned to alcohol to escape the reality of the deaths.

Immediately after his mother's death, John Donnelly's life took a drastic turn. "Before my mother died I had been a very regimented person. For the six years I spent earning my degrees on a scholarship, I kept regular hours, going to bed at 11 P.M. and rising at 7:00 A.M. My waking hours were given largely to school and to study. Although I spent some time socializing and dating, everything still had an order to it.

"But when my mother died, my life turned topsy-turvy. I started to drink, but in a strange way—strange in that I didn't know with whom to be or how to drown the horrible reality of her death. So it was cocktail lounges in the afternoon, bars and clubs in the evenings until I was so numb I would pass out and someone would have to take me home. I had done some light drinking before then, but nothing like this. When I was in the Army, I hated beer but I drank it because all the guys would go over to the canteen and drink beer. At that time, too, I made the nightclub circuit as soon as I discovered what girls were like, and I wanted to impress them by taking them to glamorous places. I was past eighteen, and I would order a Scotch or a Tom Collins. But you never got drunk from one Scotch. And you never got drunk from a Tom Collins because it had mostly soda and lemon juice, with just a little gin added."

John's complete swing to heavy drinking rose from the idea that imbibing was the thing to do. "I didn't realize I was drinking to forget—I thought I was drinking to be alive." His life-style became the exact reverse of anything he had formerly been accustomed to. "I began living at night and sleeping all day. I would lose jobs. I spent all my money. I just didn't care about anything except forgetting my mother's death."

At one of the cocktail lounges, John met a woman who was much older than he was. In need of a mother figure, he continued the relationship for several months. "She reminded me of my mother. When I lost my scarf, she bought me one. She was concerned if I didn't feel good. She looked a lot like my mother and I needed someone to be with who understood. I would say she was about forty-five, my mother's age, a divorcée who had a son almost my age. I didn't realize it, but she was an alcoholic. She had been in and out of hospitals, and her husband had divorced her because of her drinking.

"Even as we were drinking, I was thinking she was drinking too much. She would get to the point where she would fall on the ground and start screaming. She wouldn't let anyone pick her up. It was just terrible. But I put up with it because I was so desperate for a mother. When I met her after work, the first thing she had on her mind was a drink. This shocked me at first. What I wanted to do was go to dinner, or to a movie, or to someplace where we could dance, with a drink to finish off the evening. But she would insist on having a drink right away. And she would gulp it down. Even at my worst, I would nurture a drink for a long period of time. Because I didn't drink to get drunk. I thought drinking would help relieve my pain. When it didn't, I stopped drinking and stopped seeing the alcoholic substitute mother."

But stopping the alcohol took a toll on John. He became caught up with hypochondria. When he was drinking, he didn't think of illness. When he stopped, he did. Soon he was ridden with guilt feelings about his mother's death. He had lost a lot of weight and was run down.

"I became convinced that I had cancer and that I was going to die of it as my mother had done. I went to a doctor who was very sympathetic. After examinations and tests, she reassured me I did not have cancer. At first, she thought I was having a normal reaction to my mother's death. But as it continued she realized this was not the case. For example, I would say I thought I had cancer of the rectum, so she would examine that. Perfect. I would go for about a month and then I would return convinced I had cancer of the lips. She would examine them. Nothing. I would go for another three or four weeks and then it would be the throat. Finally she told me there was absolutely nothing wrong with me physically other than being run down. She then suggested I see a psychoanalyst."

John's reaction to his doctor's suggestion was one of disdain. "I thought she was crazy. I didn't need any psychoanalysis. That was the last thing in the world I needed. I had no problems." John's physical symptoms persisted in his mind for more than a year. "Even though the doctor had gotten me angry, I kept on going to see her because I thought cancer was breaking out all over. I was despondent when she told me there was nothing wrong.

"After I was definitely told I did not have cancer, I developed a tremendous thirst. That seemed to point to diabetes; perhaps that was my problem. I went through all sorts of tests, but they proved negative. What, then, was wrong with me? I was a man looking for a disease."

Saddled with this heavy burden of guilt, John felt he had to die. "I felt so guilty for some of the things that had happened before my mother's death that I had to kill myself with a disease. I had to die, and with a disease that was slow and painful. In other words, I was never afraid of a heart attack or a stroke. I wanted punishment."

But John's punishment came in a different form. It was not through cancer or diabetes. It was the death of the grandmother he loved. "I collapsed completely then. I couldn't go to see her at the wake. I couldn't go to the funeral."

A secondary loss often has a devastating impact on the bereaved son or daughter. John's grandmother had been a bulwark for him when he was young, an unflagging source of love and attention. Now his rock had been dislodged, and he could no longer face the world of the living.

"I started to read a book I had enjoyed as a child, Breasted's *History of Egypt*, a classic. In my elementary-school days, I had read the book for fun because I wanted to be an archaeologist. Now I was reading it be cause Egypt was the land of the dead."

John's roommate tried to pull him out of his depression by throwing a party. "One of the girls was asking the various guests what each one did and what they wanted to do with his life. Then she turned to me and said, 'What do you want to do, John?' I replied, 'I want to live in a tomb wrapped like a mummy.' Everybody laughed, but it wasn't a joke. I meant it."

John's depression reached its lowest point when

two or three years later he couldn't rise from a chair. Try as he might, he couldn't pull himself upward and so he held tight to the arms of the chair until he was able to move again. "I realized then that I was in a serious state and I went back to the doctor. In the office, I began to sob. Then, getting control of myself, I said to her, 'You know, this is the first time that I've cried in almost two years.' She said she realized that and told me she had made an appointment for me with a psychiatrist."

After Phil Musmacker's mother died, he went into a tailspin—one that nearly wrecked his life. His drinking increased. He lost jobs because of drunkenness. He began taking drugs. During that time, he married and fathered a baby, but he still grieved over the death of his mother and his inability to be with her when she died. He would lock himself in his room and brood. He didn't want anything to do with the baby. He couldn't face all the problems of his present situation, especially the unpaid bills. Even though he had some money, he feared that if he paid the bills, there would be nothing left to pay for his drug and liquor habits.

One night he went into a blackout that lasted nineteen hours. During that time, he destroyed all the furniture in the house, beat up his wife, and tore into neighbors who came to stop him. When police were summoned, he resisted arrest and landed in jail.

After her father's death, Lisa Strahs-Lorenc became afraid that she was going to die suddenly of an accident or mortal illness. "Part of this was tied to my mother's death in an accident and since my father's sudden death from a heart attack. My fear of dying continued for a few months. Perhaps that's why I became so obsessed with changing my way of life. I felt that time was going to run out on me and that I had better do everything I wanted to do right now. The issue of mortality came up at meetings of the HEAL group I attended. Everyone there suffered from some loss. The name of the group was *H*elp *E*ase *A L*oss. And that is what it did—helped ease our losses."

Lisa joined HEAL in September. Her father had died in May. "I wasn't ready for help immediately. I rushed back to work as if I wanted to make everything normal again. I tried to say, 'It will be all right,' but it wasn't all right. I was just trying to get things back to some kind of normalcy but it was clear that nothing was normal again. In fact, everything, my whole perspective on life had changed. I was getting angry at the least little thing. If someone made even a mild comment to me about, for example, a misscheduling of appointments, I would get off the phone filled with resentment. I would say, 'That's not important.' My perspective on what was important and what wasn't had changed completely. Now nothing at all seemed important. I thought I would never laugh again or be happy. I thought I would never enjoy the sun or the earth. Joining HEAL was the best thing I could have done. At its meetings, I began to share my feelings with others. I learned that I wasn't alone in those negative and depressing thoughts."

Six months after the death of Hilary Friedman's father, her cat died. The secondary loss had a devastating effect. She says of it, "When my cat died, I mourned deeply. That was a grief and a pain that I didn't have to share with anyone. This was *my* cat. We had another cat, but this one was mine. It was a grief I could feel and a pain I could cry about." This time, Hilary could express herself more openly because it was *her* cat, whereas after her father's death, although she mourned, she had to share her grief with her mother's pain and her brother's. Hilary didn't suffer more from the loss of her cat than from the loss of her father, obviously, but this was different—she had lost something of her own and did not have to share her grief with others. "But even then, there was a numbness. There was always a numbness."

Hilary had thoughts of going to join her cat and her father. She then realized that her emotional state was bad, and she decided to go to a bereavement support group for help. "I felt I wanted to emulate my father and my cat. It was a real feeling of blackness, like going to sleep and not bothering to wake up. When I opened my eyes, there was no color in my life. I was hurting so much. And there was no one. My mother was grieving. My brother was in another state. Most of my friends were away at school. So there was a real feeling of isolation. It was like sitting Shiva [the Jewish ritual of mourning] during the first week of mourning—the mirrors are all covered up in the house, so you don't see yourself. But people who are present give you an assurance that you are on *this side*. I imagine that is what I needed more of, to be reassured that I was on this side. So I went to the bereavement group where I was helped by being with others who had suffered a loss."

After his father's death, Paul Vento began to hit the bottle. His daily alcoholic intake went up to a quart of whiskey, and each day he smoked four packs of cigarettes. "I drank a little before my father died, but never that much. I more or less picked up where he had left off, it seemed." Paul didn't mourn for his father right away. But months later, he began to realize that his father wasn't around any longer. "I used to go to him whenever something was wrong, and he always came up with answers to help me. Now he was gone, and I thought, 'Where are you going to go now for advice?' I think everyone needs someone to talk things over with. Of course, there was my mother, but how much could she do? She was grieving herself. I just ran away from it all and took to the bottle."

In an attempt to combat the alcohol, which was his problem for ten years, Paul went to AA meetings. "You can go to a hundred meetings at AA, but if you don't really want to give up alcohol, forget it. I only went to three or four meetings. You can go to a million meetings and see a hundred thousand doctors, but if you're not ready, you're not going to quit. I stopped going for another reason, too. I got disgusted because I saw young girls who were telling how they would sell their bodies for drink. I was thinking how I would feel if my daughter had to sell her body just for drugs or drink. So I didn't go to the meetings anymore. AA is a great movement, but I just wasn't ready to face myself and my problem."

Paul didn't ever think of going for professional help because he never thought of himself as a drunk. "You figure if you buy top shelf and don't live in the Bowery like a bum, you're not a drunk. This is not true. People think that if they are able to pay for their own drinks they are not drunks. They only think they are drunks when they don't buy their drinks and have to panhandle for them. I know quite a lot of guys like that. One fellow who began drinking about the same time as I did was caught walking around with no clothes on. His union put him in a detoxification ward. Today he is a counselor at AA. He is retired and helps teach about the dangers of alcohol."

One day Paul decided he wasn't going to drink anymore. That was six years ago and he hasn't had a drink since. "You just sit down and say, 'Look at all the money I've made and where did it go? For booze and cigarettes. If my wife didn't work, we'd starve to death. And where the hell are you really going? You're only going to end up bad, and you're dragging everybody else down with you.' So I said to myself, 'To hell with it. I'm going to stop drinking.' And I did. As I said, you have to mean it."

Paul believes his underlying problem was that there was nobody to talk to, no one to comfort him or cry with him after his father's death. "There was nobody. Nobody. I swear to God. I think that was one of the reasons I drank to the extent I did. Eventually, you have to become your own man. You are no longer a child and you can't use that as a cop out. You begin to realize that you have responsibilities as an adult. I guess that is what allowed me to start dealing with the alcohol. Drinking doesn't make things better—it makes them worse."

When Andrew Rezin's mother died, his twenty-seventh birthday was just around the corner. His friends realized how difficult that was going to be for him. "They tried to cheer me and help me get through the day. I was really surprised and shocked when they had huge helium balloons sent to me, but those balloons helped take the bitter edge off the day. I had been very despondent thinking about first my father being gone and now my mother. This was my first birthday without both of my parents, and I had a lot of depression. I thought I was going crazy, for I had so many anxieties. I felt very lonely. Since my parents died, my whole life had changed."

Andrew became abusive. He began to drink. His pain was such he could not bear to see anything that had belonged to his parents. He couldn't concentrate at work. Sleep was unbearable because he would dream of his father. He would envision the whole death scene again. "In the beginning, I would dream of what had happened to him, seeing him lying there, with me trying to revive him. Then I would dream of the burial, and become physically ill, with stomach pain and cramps. My eyes would well up with water, but I wouldn't let my emotions show."

Later Andrew's emotions caught up with him— and then they began to emerge in a great swelling of rage. Rage at being left alone. Rage at not having his parents with him. Rage because he didn't have the answer to "Why?" When the emotional burden grew too heavy and he began to hurl objects and throw things at home, Andrew knew he had to do something. "I figured a counselor would be the one to help me."

Sandra Ames had always had a fair share of worries, but after her mother's death she seemed to be worrying about anything and everything. "When I came into the house, I would look around for my mother, although I knew she wasn't here, but I would still look—almost as if it would make me feel better to know I had acknowledged her, even though she was dead. I didn't know how to explain this to anyone. I couldn't describe my feelings to my friends or my family. I felt disloyal—and almost like I was neglecting to say 'hello' to the 'presence' that remained, to that part of her that would always be with me. I thought I was paying homage to her memory by looking for her. After a few weeks, I stopped, because I didn't want to become a neurotic or a slave to such feelings. But I had developed a habit of worrying about everything."

When the weather forecast predicted rain, Sandra worried that the house might be flooded, that there might be a tornado, that there might be thunder, that the house might be struck by lightning. If the weather was sunny, she worried that she might get sunstroke. Her thoughts were preoccupied with fears that something bad would happen to her, her family, or her home.

At work, Sandra had no patience with customers whose telephone inquiries seemed to her trivial, and her replies to them were curt. Her fellow employees commented on her change in personality. Before her mother's death, she had been a considerate worker, kind, and had a good sense of humor. Now she was short-tempered and resentful. Anxious for her friend, a coworker told Sandra their boss thought her manner often abrasive, but was making allowances because of her mother's death.

"I was ready to walk out at first, but my friend calmed me down and helped me to think things through. She took me out for coffee and explained that I was really taking my anger out on the wrong people. She told me about a group that met in a nearby church, all of whose members had lost a loved one. I decided to call and see what was involved, but before the first meeting I was scared to death. Probably that was the root of my problem—I was not so much scared *to* death, as scared *of* death."

We have seen in some of the stories above how many adult children stop functioning well and no longer can do the things they did, either in the house or at work, following the death of a parent. One such bereaved daughter underwent a radical change in her lifestyle after the loss of her mother. Therapists agree that when this happens, it is a sign of pathological grief and the son or daughter experiencing this behavior should seek professional help.

Before her mother's death, Cynthia Carter had never taken medication. She so truly believed in the efficacy of natural healing and health foods that she wouldn't even take an aspirin. However, her mother's death changed all that. "I couldn't sleep," she now says. "It got to the point where I was walking the floor at night, in a state of great agitation. But during the day it was a different story. I would drag around the house, extremely depressed. This no-sleep-at-night-and-no-sleep-at-day routine began to take its toll of me and my marriage. I couldn't make breakfast. I didn't feel like taking a shower. I refused to go out of the house to shop. I wouldn't sew a button on my husband's shirt. I didn't feel like having sex, and I knew my husband was getting more disgusted by the minute. But I didn't know what to do. It seemed like I was in a fog. I just didn't want anything. Nothing. Zero."

When Cynthia fainted one morning, her husband, concerned that she was not only physically harming herself but that she was becoming mentally deranged from grief and lack of sleep, forced her to go to a doctor. Cynthia tells about her visit: "The doctor prescribed sleeping tablets for the night and a tranquilizer for the day. So for the first time in my life I took medication. In the beginning, the sleeping tablets worked and I would sleep most of the night. Because the tranquilizer had a calming effect during the day, my mental outlook improved. Although I again became interested in my home again, I noticed that I needed to continue use of both pills to maintain my equilibrium."

After two months, Cynthia was no longer sleeping through the night. She increased her dosage, from one to two pills. However, when she awoke in the morning, she felt as if she had a hangover. "I began to feel that sense of hopelessness returning. I went back to the doctor, and he changed the medication to a different kind of sleeping tablet. He told me to increase the tranquilizer from two a day to three per day. I continued on this 'drug path' for six more months. At the end of that time my nerves were so frayed that I went to an outpatient group of a rehabilitation center. For the first time since my mother's death I felt I had a chance to make it back, and I was given hope. There were people there who had also suffered losses."

ↄ CHAPTER 8

The Trauma of Holidays and Anniversaries

Some adult children find that they may do well for many months or a year and then find they are incapacitated by grief at holidays or during days surrounding the anniversary of the death, according to psychotherapist Dr. Roberta Temes. "Such anniversary reactions are normal."

On the first New Year's Day after her father's death, Beth Landau became very despondent. She had suddenly realized that she had to face a "new year" without him, and she began to wonder what she had to look forward to in the coming months. As she ruminated over the previous year, her sadness deepened.

"I had made brunch plans with some girlfriends for New Year's Day, but while I was getting dressed, I began to sob uncontrollably. It seemed that nothing had triggered the attack. I called my friend and told her I was very upset. She asked why, and I replied that I had been thinking about my father. My friends insisted that I not remain home alone. 'Come to brunch and spend the day with us. You'll feel better.' In the end, I went along with them, but I sat at the table wearing sunglasses. However, as the day wore on, things became easier for me."

While some children can't bear the thought of going to the cemetery, or they block out the date of the loved one's death, others find these things make them feel better. Beth relates her thoughts on this subject: "I go to the cemetery on every special day and I feel good about being there. My grandparents are buried in the same plot. I was very close to them, too. Before the anniversary of the day my father died, I said to my sister, 'Let's go to the cemetery. I'd like to write a little something and say it out loud to Daddy. And maybe it would be nice if you did that, too, or if Mommy did.' But it was something she couldn't face, and she said, 'I don't want to deal with *that*.' But I'm going to do it whether they stand there and listen or not. I think it will make me feel better and kind of catch up the year that I lost with him."

Beth's doctor indicated that these were normal emotions for a grieving daughter. The idea of a new year not shared by her father shocked the young woman into the realization that she would be facing a year without him. She became frightened at what the weeks and months of that year would bring, and to her fears was added a sense of aloneness that grew out of the thought of being without her father. Fortunately, her friends were sensitive to her needs, and created an environment for Beth that would pull her out of the doldrums.

When Christmas came, Carol Richardson wanted to go to the cemetery to place flowers on her mother's grave, but very bad weather made travel impossible. Instead, she volunteered to work on Christmas Day. "I decided to treat it as just another day, in the belief that working would keep me from thinking of my mother. That's how I coped with it the first year. By Christmas of the next year, holidays were still difficult, but I did go to the cemetery and found the visit comforting. On other holidays and anniversaries we went to St. Maarten. My father had been born there, and his family provided a supportive network, making sure we were kept busy during our visits. In this we were lucky because our trips to St. Maarten took us away from our own home and into another country. That helped a lot."

Peggy Griffiths presents us with another example of how the Christmas holiday was handled after her father's death. Her family gathered at their mother's home in Poughkeepsie, but Peggy confesses, "It was pretty tough on all of us. We did not have a Christmas tree because my father had died the previous Labor Day weekend, and we were still grieving. Nevertheless, we had a real Christmas dinner, with relatives in to visit, and the day passed quickly.

"After that first Christmas, the wound began to heal gently and gradually. However, my mother and I realized that we had to keep busy, and we pursued that goal with zeal. Meanwhile, we tried not to dwell on the grieving, much as we had loved my father. To keep his memory fresh, however, we sent, in his name, flowers to the church on holidays and special occasions. Above all, we tried desperately to avoid all public expressions of grief that would embarrass others."

The holiday that was hardest for Paul Vento to endure was Father's Day. Paul himself was a father, and the realization that he was now the male head of the family was, to him, frightening. "It really floored me to think that I was the central figure on Father's Day," he says. "There I was in my twenties already being given the job of man of the family. I was upset to even think about it, and on that day I missed my father even more than usual. Father's Day and his birthday were days when he should still be here. They were times when I could go to him, ask his advice, and talk things over with him. My wife and children and myself used to go to my parents' house to celebrate Father's Day, but last year my mother came to my house. It was a complete reversal, and I knew that every Father's Day from now on would be focused on me. It was scary in many ways, and I felt the pressure of my father not being here even more."

Lisa Strahs-Lorenc was faced with Father's Day only two weeks after her father died. He had bought tickets for the entire family to attend some sports events, and Lisa had insisted that everyone spend the day as her father had planned. "He had wanted to go to these games and he had wanted us all to be together for Father's Day. It was something he would have enjoyed. So we went. Neither my husband nor my mother wanted to go. They thought I was crazy. But I was determined to do the things my father had planned for that day. And that's the way we dealt with that difficult Father's Day—doing everything we thought he wanted us to do."

Then came December and the Hanukkah holiday. "Fred and I went to my mother's, and tried to celebrate the holiday there, but it was very traumatic for all of us. There had always been the four of us and now there was only three of us present. My mother and father and Fred and I often did things together. During the eight years of our marriage, the four of us spent weekends together, and took trips together, too. We were such a close-knit foursome that it hurt when there were only three of us at Hanukkah because someone was missing. My father was missing—and his absence was glaring. We tried not to think about the fact that he would be missing from every other holiday we would try to celebrate."

As in the case of Beth Landau earlier in this chapter, Lisa wanted to write something on the anniversary of her father's death. She felt comforted at the unveiling as she read a memorial she had written to him. "That was my process of grieving," she now says. "I believe that the more you take part in that grieving, the more you feel you are doing something for yourself and for the departed."

John Donnelly's mother died on December 7th—the anniversary of Pearl Harbor Day. Her birthday fell on another special date—Groundhog Day, February 2nd. "Even if I wanted to forget those days, the newspapers and the television and radio were reminding us about them. For years, I dreaded December 7th. It was nothing I could ever forget because I knew where I was on Pearl Harbor Day and I also knew where I was on the December 7th that my mother died.

"I would work up to the anniversary day and suddenly I would develop the symptoms of a cold or a sore throat or some other ailment. Or I would get a pain in my stomach and think I had stomach cancer. For many years thereafter, when that date would approach, I would have to prepare myself. Now, today, all these years later, maybe on December 5th, I will have some unpleasant thoughts and may not know why. Then I will suddenly realize that December 7th is around the corner and I will say, 'Oh, that's it.' I didn't have as much trouble with Groundhog Day. Because my mother's birthday was very close to mine, I would try to remember some good things about her. I recalled that she used to say I was the best birthday present she could have received, for her birthday followed mine by two days."

For John, his first Christmas without his mother was extremely traumatic, coming as it did less than three weeks after her death. "My mother always had a big Christmas," he recalls. "Since I was the youngest of my cousins, she had the party at our house on Christmas Eve and she would give everybody gifts. After she died, I bought presents for everyone, spending three or four hundred dollars—and that was a lot of money then. I bought gifts for my aunt, my uncles, and for my grandmother.

"On Christmas Day, I brought them all these gifts, but they were in mourning. They had no Christmas tree or other holiday decorations. They had just wanted to see me for Christmas, especially my grandmother, and when I gave them the gifts, they were shocked. They had not bought me anything because they had not expected anything so soon after my mother's death. But I didn't want her to be dead. I wanted things to be as they had been in the past. Somehow I had it in my mind that bringing presents would make this Christmas like all those Christmases of the past.

"Instead, everyone was embarrassed. My aunt said, 'Your mother has been dead only a short time, and so we're not celebrating Christmas this year.' My grandmother saw that I was unhappy, and she was right. I can't describe how hurt I was. The pain of that day was like a second loss—and instead of being able to blot out my mother's death, my aunt's words were ringing in my ears. *Your mother has been dead only a short time. . . .* '"

John's doctor explained later that the young man had been looking for the security of a home, seeking a Christmas and family that would make everything right again. When no one had a gift for him, he felt lost and alone.

"When my grandmother saw how upset I was, she gave my uncle fifty dollars for me and said, 'John, please go out and buy something for yourself.' But I was in an emotional turmoil. I felt depleted and wounded. I felt impoverished—without a family. I left the house in a daze, telling my relatives I would call, but I didn't. I wasn't able to talk to anyone who would tell me my mother was dead and that things couldn't ever be the same again. I didn't want to see anyone who was grieving or mourning. I wanted things to be as they were before my mother died."

That New Year's Eve, John went out with strangers, as though there was no death, and drank himself into a New Year that he celebrated as an Old Year.

As the third anniversary of her mother's death approached, Mary Stellakis, living in Greece, was shocked beyond measure at the country's macabre funeral laws. She had learned that her mother's body had to be disinterred! Because of a lack of space, there were too many bodies for the grounds available.

"About half the population of Greece," Mary states, "lives in Athens. It's as though Washington, D.C. had 120 million people. For this reason, cemeteries near large, populated areas in Greece require that, after three years, families must disinter the remains and move them to a permanent lot elsewhere. The cemetery in which my mother was buried was not considered a permanent resting place!"

Mary was told that the funeral laws did give her one other option. She could choose a mortuary chapel where her mother's remains could be put into a metal box, numbered and stored with others, stacked just as crates were in a warehouse. "I couldn't stuff my mom away. The mere thought was stifling to me. So, I went to her hometown, Kyparissia, and bought a double-sized plot."

What followed was even more bizarre. Mary was appalled when she heard that sometimes the bodies were not entirely dissolved at the end of three years. "In that case, instead of covering them again, they are removed to another area and buried in a shallow grave which ensures dissolution in one year. To bypass such an abhorrent possibility, I asked advice from people at the cemetery. They suggested that I remove the marble plaque covering the grave so that it could breathe, to plant flowers in its place, and to give them plenty of water. So on weekly visits, besides burning incense which Mom so loved, and lighting the candle, I watered the flowers heavily with pails of water carried from a tap some distance away."

Since it was wintertime when the three years had passed, Mary was granted a six months' extension. What happened next was like a Kafka nightmare. "The following May, I had to bring wine for use in washing the bones free of soil. I watched as two men dug them up and I breathed a sigh of relief that they were clean of flesh. I watched as another man, wearing rubber gloves and a rubber apron, washed away the soil with the wine. Then he set my mother's bones on a marble slab with the identifying cross from the grave. He waited for the arrival of the health department's doctor who would disinfect the remains and issue a permit for their removal from the cemetery. This having been done, the remains were packed in a large paper carton and carefully wrapped. I took them home. There are no words to describe how I felt.

"The next day, my cousin and I carried my mother's bones, by train, down to the village where we were met by two other cousins. On the way to the cemetery on foot, we were joined by four women who took turns carrying Mom's remains to her final resting place, back to her native soil."

We have seen above how one daughter was able to assure final burial for her mother. We will now hear from a surviving son who was not able to secure a resting place for his parents—they were murdered in the Holocaust.

Max Glauben reflected on his first days in America. He had arrived in New York at age seventeen, after having been liberated from a concentration camp in Germany. Some kind person had taken him to see a Christmas performance at Radio City Music Hall. "I looked around and saw all the families sitting together, everybody happy, everybody enjoying the stage show. But I couldn't stay in New York after that because, in my mind, the city was synonymous with happy families.

"When I had an opportunity to be moved to another location, I thought it was going to be Atlantic City, but because of my poor understanding of English, it turned out to be Atlanta, Georgia. There I went to live with a widowed lady and her children who were about my own age. It was in that atmosphere that I first became aware of Mother's Day and Father's Day. I had not known about such things in the concentration camp. Of course, I couldn't take flowers to my parents, or even to their graves. So to show my gratitude to the widow and to make her happy, I bought flowers for her. She was very pleased with them. I got flowers for her on other occasions, too, and tried to do things that would show my appreciation of what she and her family had done for me. It was my way of compensating."

For nine years, Dan Sutherland had been wrapped up in his career. He had become a workaholic, and late hours in the office coupled with out-of-town travel prevented him from visiting his father as much as he would have liked. The first holiday after his father's death was Thanksgiving, one of the few holidays that Dan took off from work. In the past, he, his wife, and children had always spent Thanksgiving Day with his father and sister.

"That year, following his death, none of us were up to Thanksgiving but we felt we had to do something because of the kids. My wife invited my sister to our house. When I woke up that morning, my insides were churning. I dreaded getting out of bed, for I didn't want to face this day. Finally, I forced myself to get dressed. I couldn't watch my wife preparing the dinner, and so I got into the car and went for a long drive. When I reached one intersection near a road that led to a picnic area we used to go to, I thought I saw my father standing on the corner. He had on a cap that he used to wear and waved it at me. I swerved, driving onto the curb and almost hit a tree trunk." When Dan turned around, the man was gone.

Dan slowly drove home, nervous and trembling. "Was that really my father?" he wondered. "When I got back to the house," he continued, "everyone was waiting for me. I pretended that I had gone out for gas. We sat down to eat, but when I saw the stuffing on the table, which was a favorite dish of my father's, I had to get up and leave the room. Although I had my wife, my kids, and my sister, I just didn't feel that I could be thankful on that day."

Easter was the first holiday to occur after the death of Alice Figura's father. In happier times, this had been celebrated as a major holiday by her family. When Alice and her brothers were young, her mother would begin days beforehand to prepare food specialties for the occasion, such goodies as linguine with clams, baked eggplant, stuffed mushrooms, and a host of other delicacies. But none of those foods appealed to Alice now. She no longer had family members with whom to share them. Her brothers lived far away and her mother, now remarried, had moved south. Easter was not the uplifting, joyous holiday it had once been.

Alone and depressed, Alice decided to comfort herself by going to the cemetery with flowers for her father's grave. But she was unprepared for her reaction. "I don't know whether it was because Easter was the first holiday after my father's death, or because I was feeling lonely and deserted, but as soon as I saw that grave, I was beside myself. It had not been attended to as I thought it should have been, and I screamed at the caretakers for the way it looked. They said the grave was in good condition, but to me it certainly was not. It was covered with dead leaves and dead grass. I didn't want that feeling of 'dead' around my father's grave."

On Mother's Day, Alice telephoned her mother and wished her a happy day, but after the call Alice again experienced that feeling of loneliness and depression. Since she couldn't visit her mother that day, she decided to visit her father. "I took plants with me, and some garden tools, for I couldn't look at an unkempt grave again. I wanted his gravesite to be attractive to passersby, and so I made a pretty design around it of red and yellow flowers and it made me feel good when I had finished working that a thing of beauty surrounded my father's final resting place."

Margaret McAllister recalls the first and second anniversaries after her father's death. "On the first anniversary, I felt very strange at the thought that he had been dead a year. On the second anniversary, it seems as if you freeze in time. Everything seems to be in slow motion and you can't believe it's been that length of time. The first year after it happened, it felt as if it were yesterday in some respects. Now, I think, 'Gee, it's been two years and I've done a lot of things. I wonder what he'd think and wonder what he'd say.' When I graduated this year cum laude, I thought, 'How would he have felt today?' If he had lived, he would have been an invalid. But he would have crawled in order to attend my graduation. If need be, he would have started the night before. It was brutally hot on commencement day and there was no air conditioning. I was looking at all of the things that were annoyances. Then, I began to think of my father and I realized that if he had been there, he would have sat through the ceremonies with his chest bursting with pride, even if he was dying from the heat—and every moment of it would have been perfect for him. This thought made me feel better.

"The first Christmas was hard. Initially, we decided against putting up a tree, but my mother said, 'No, your father loved Christmas and we are going to have a tree.' My mother had one good cry and that seemed to let it all out. Every once in a while she would slip back into a melancholy mood, remembering how much my father enjoyed this holiday. At Christmastime, he was more like a child than I was. For him, Christmas gifts were the very best—you could give him socks and he would love them. Christmas dinner was always a big deal because he got to carve the turkey. So my mother and I put the tree up and the lights, and tried to make it a Christmas that he would have loved."

Below we see a touching dedication by a bereaved son, Walter Kaner, a newspaper columnist for the New York *Daily News*. This poignant tribute to his mother was written over twenty-five years ago and is reprinted each Mother's Day in the newspaper.

What I wouldn't give to have my mother back again.

I would give up all I have if I could turn back the clock. If, just once more, I could take her out to dinner today. Or send her flowers. Or wish her a Happy Mother's Day. But, I can't. My Mom's gone.

For me, this is the saddest day of the year. A day of heartache. A day of painful memories. I can remember it as if it were only yesterday. The hospital . . . sitting by her bedside . . . as night turned into day . . . holding her hand . . . as life ebbed from her body. And my lips, wet with tears, pleading: "Mom, don't die. Please, Mom, don't die."

Mom died 26 years ago on May 5—my birthday.

The year, the day, the hour are burned into my memory.

Regretfully, children—of all ages—take their Mom for granted. We think she'll always be there—loving, caring, worrying.

Then, one sorrowful day, she is gone.

And we're lost, bewildered, heartsick. And then it's too late. Too late to say the words you wanted to say. Too late to do the things you wanted to do. What I wouldn't give to have my Mom back again. To say the things I felt but never said.

"Thanks, Mom, for giving me life. For healing my hurts . . . for kissing away my pains . . . for the nights you nursed me through a sickness. Thanks, Mom, for teaching me right from wrong . . . to respect others . . . to recognize the real values of life.

"Thanks, Mom, for your love . . . your understanding . . . your sacrifices. Thanks, Mom, for being my Mom."

I'll say those words today. At her grave. When it's too late. And I'll wish I had said them to her when she was alive. Maybe, I'd like to think, she knew anyway.

I'll stare numbly at her grave, and ache in my heart, and try not to show the pain and tears. Mom wouldn't want that. She wanted only happiness for her children.

I'll remember how it used to be when Mom was here.

Mom used to say how she wished she could afford to give her children more. She gave us plenty. She gave us love and understanding and a happy home.

My Mom was raised in Europe. She never went to school. Yet she was educated. The school of hard knocks was her classroom; common sense was her teacher.

My Mom lived by simple golden rules. Work hard, raise your children properly, help those in need, thank God for your blessings.

My Mom didn't have electrical kitchen appliances. Or a washing machine. Or a baby-sitter. Or somebody to come in and help with the cleaning.

Mom worked hard and slaved to put her kids through school so that they would "amount to something." She wanted them to have more than she had.

I realize—now—what she gave us, the sacrifices she made for us. The way she woke at dawn to press our clothes so we'd look neat for school. How she would light the coal stove so it would be warm when her children got up. How she would scrub the floor on her knees, wash the clothes, cook the meals and clean the house.

She asked nothing for herself. Her children were her life. Our happiness was her happiness. Our pains were her pains. Our success was her success.

I remember how my Mom would put us to sleep, then stay up late and sew our clothes, starch the curtains, bake for hours and wrap the ice in newspaper.

Sometimes I'd lie in bed silently watching her. Tears would moisten my pillow and I vowed that someday I'd try to make up for the sacrifices she made for us as kids.

Once I told her: "Someday, when I'm grown up and rich, I'm gonna buy you the biggest house and the best clothes in the whole world . . ."

Mom smiled, hugged me and shook her head, saying: "A mother should give to a child, not take."

My Mom's gone now. Nothing will ever take away the wonderful memories she left me.

I remember how she smiled when I blushingly introduced her to "my girl." I was 9, the girl was 8. I remember how proud she looked when I graduated from school.

I remember the worry etched on her face and the pain in her eyes when I went off to war. And the reborn look when I returned. And worrying about me had turned her shiny black hair to gray.

I remember going shopping with her on Manhattan's East Side, though we lived in Corona, because the food was cheaper. The hot summer days at Coney Island, with Mom sitting under an umbrella, taking off her shoes and stockings and wading up to her ankles. And watching Mom cry as she listened to everybody's problems on the A.L. Alexander and John J. Anthony radio programs. I couldn't understand it, but Mom said she "enjoyed" the programs.

I wish I could talk personally to every child—no matter how old. To tell him how lucky he is to still have his Mom. To tell him to love, to appreciate, to respect his Mom.

To say it. To show it.

Not just today—Mother's Day—but every day.

Before it's too late.

Because some day, like me, and so many other children—of all ages—who have lost their Moms, you'll be standing at a grave on Mother's Day.

And your hearts will be filled with hurt and your eyes filled with tears.

And you'll be thinking over and over:

"What I wouldn't give to have my Mom back again."

CHAPTER 9

Normal Grieving

After the death of a parent, normal grief is experienced by most adult sons and daughters. Mourning in a healthy way doesn't keep us from denying what has passed, nor does it prevent us from moving forward into the future. It is a very personal matter, according to Dr. Roberta Temes.

Unless we have walked in the shoes of one who is grieving, most of us will not know what he is experiencing, or what grief is like. We may be surprised and confused at our feelings and emotions. As indicated by Dr. Earl Grollman in Chapter 2, some bereaved sons and daughters are able to express their feelings by crying. Others grieve inwardly in quiet solitude. Research has shown that patterns of emotions in grief can be identified. Understanding those *normal* patterns can help us to realize that the pain we feel and the varying emotions we experience are part of the *normal* process of healing after the loss of a parent.

"Normal grief is a depression related to a life event that is appropriate," explains psychotherapist Karen Arfin, Director of the Miller Place Family Counseling Center of Sound Beach, New York. "When it is not related to a life event in any recognizable way, it is abnormal or pathological grief.

"If someone is grieving as if the death had just happened, and in reality it happened ten or twenty years ago, that's pathological. If a person is expressing no grief at all within a reasonable time after the death—say, a period of a month to a year—that's pathological. What sometimes happens in those situations is that the grief somatizes. There will be physical symptoms as opposed to emotional expressions of grief. The son or daughter may get very sick or have physical symptoms similar to those of the deceased," Arfin states.

"There are other indications of pathological grief," she continues. "If a person's behavior changes in any drastic way, or if there are serious life-style changes. If a person who has been fairly stable suddenly becomes very flamboyant, chances are this is a kind of pathological condition that is not being expressed as grief. A big indicator would be self-destructive behavior. If the person had been stable before the death and after it is not grieving in any apparent way, and there is suddenly a tremendous increase in drinking or in the use of drugs, driving at excessive speed and seemingly is very careless about it, these can be expressions of pathological grief.

"Sometimes," Arfin points out, "you will see phobias as an indicator of abnormal grief. The person is not expressing grief in an appropriate way. They are not talking about it. They are not crying, but they are obsessed. They develop phobias about illness and death to the point that they interfere with the person's functioning. This could be grief that is not expressed. It should be stated that these patterns are not the norm. Indeed, they are rare. The most common symptom is an increase in self-destructive behavior or grieving depression not related to a life event. The others happen once in a while. In terms of the phobias, a person has a fear of illness or hospitals. Sometimes after a parent has died in a hospital, the adult child has trouble going back. That's different. I'm talking about not being able to face a hospital, an illness, or a funeral for a long time afterwards. Generally, the distinguishing factor is the amount of time that elapses. For example, a certain amount of crying is appropriate and even a great deal of crying can be appropriate after the event of the death for a period of a year or two. However, if ten years later the adult child is still crying as if it happened yesterday, that's pathological."

Below, we see an example of normal grief in a bereaved daughter's reactions to returning to the hospital where her father died.

"Two years after my dad's death, my girlfriend was brought to the same hospital where he had died. She had given birth to her baby," Margaret McAllister remembers, "but complications developed and she was moved to the same floor my father had been on. It was the other side of the building, but on the same floor. I went to visit her with another friend. But when I got to the lobby, I said, 'I can't get off at the seventh floor. I can't go up there.' My friend replied, 'You've gone too far to regress. I'm here with you, so let's go up. It will be all right.' So I agreed to go. When the elevator doors opened, I had this strange urge to go over to the other wing, to the side of the hospital where my father had been. 'To do what?' I thought. 'To look around? To go into the room and make sure the person who is in that bed is not my father?' But I resisted that urge to go and I went on to visit with my friend. Afterward, I was glad I had met the challenge of going back to the hospital."

To experience normal grief doesn't mean that we won't occasionally have a moment of sadness, a pang of regret that our parent is not here. What we may think of as a "crazy" thought may be perfectly normal. Remember, we have been told by grief specialists that abnormal grief is a state in which thoughts become obsessive and interfere with daily functions.

We may hear the words, "You have to complete the grieving process." What is meant by that statement? Counselors in grief therapy say it means not being afraid of the feelings you are experiencing. It means looking at your anger and understanding that it is not uncommon. It means facing your guilt feelings and forgiving yourself. By moving through your grief, you will be able to accept your loss and resume your life again. Your dead parent will not be in your thoughts as often and good memories will remain.

Normal grieving allows us to come to terms with the reality of our loss and to rebuild our lives. Getting on with living doesn't mean you are being disloyal to your parent's memory. Recovering doesn't mean you have to forget. You will always remember, so why not remember the good things?

In the following anecdotes, we will see examples of bereaved children who experienced normal grief.

After Peggy Griffiths' father died suddenly, she grieved inwardly. She regretted that she hadn't had a chance to say good-bye to him. But on reflection, Peggy had other thoughts. " 'It's silly for me to feel that way. The Lord who called him is in charge of life. I'm not.' I remember thinking about that and so I put those regrets right out of my mind. My whole family agreed that the Lord had been kind to my father to take him as quickly as He had; my dad was an impatient person and he would have gone out of his mind had he been a patient in a hospital for any length of time. My mother as a hospital patient could adjust. But my father had never been ill, and he would not have dealt with a long illness very well."

Peggy thinks back to the important lessons in life her parents had given her. "Of course, we had discussions, but in our family there was no such thing as arguing. My parents frowned on arguments, and all of us as children had to get along together—at least when my parents were around. We were afraid to argue in their presence. They would tell us, 'You must live with yourself first of all and understand yourself. Also, you've got to learn to work together, to play together, to love each other. However, if things get to the point where you can't agree, you must sit down and talk about your problem. But no shouting or yelling!' Of course, we used to disobey when they weren't around, or we'd go out to the backyard behind the old oak tree and have our arguments there.

"That training has helped us in later life. To this day, I make it my business to get along with people. I don't suppress my feelings, but if I have a problem I will sit down and discuss it quietly. I believe my sisters and brothers have pretty much the same philosophy. None of us felt guilty after our parents' death because we all had done the best for each other while my mother and father were here. We missed them when they died, and we miss them now. But we don't dwell on it."

Beth Landau felt lost after her father's death. There had been so many things she could discuss with him, whether it was business or things of a personal nature. "It was rough the first year because I would always turn to him. The holidays were very hard and so was his birthday. Sometimes I wondered if, at that moment on the tennis court when he had his heart attack, he knew he was dying. I wondered what his thoughts were just before it happened. Someone once told me, 'Your mother can have many husbands, but you can have only one father.' "

Beth felt she needed some guidance in understanding her emotions and decided to see a therapist. "I had to know why I was feeling as I did, and if such a feeling was normal. The therapist was able to explain many things to me and helped guide me through my grief. After a few months, I decided that the first anniversary of my father's death was a good cutoff time and I didn't need to see the therapist any longer. I knew my father would want me to live."

Carol Richardson reflects on her mother's condition during the last few weeks of her life. "She had become incontinent. Now we are talking about what had been a healthy, beautiful woman and she had come to this. I just didn't want it for her. I knew if she was taken out of this misery, it would be much better for everyone involved—everybody. And I knew that was what she wanted too toward the end. She was embarrassed about the tubes and about someone having to change her. As a matter of fact, when I would do it, she would tease me and say, 'Now you make sure you do it right. I used to do it for you.' And we would laugh about it, to try and relieve some of the tension."

Carol was concerned that her mother's pain would be prolonged and tells of her feelings about her mother's death. "This is going to sound a bit strange, but I felt *good* about her death because the doctor had sat down with me and told me what was going to happen. You would have to have seen how from October until December this woman just deteriorated from 140 pounds to 90 pounds in no time. It wasn't that she walked out on the street and was hit by a car. It was something I really wanted. And no one can understand this who has not been in the same position. A great many people would say, 'What do you mean, you wanted your mother to die?' I had learned there was no cure; she was not going to get better. Once I understood that, it was easier for me to deal with her death. Of course, I was unhappy about it, but I accepted it because of her situation.

"In the beginning after her death, I tried to cook and keep house as my mother had, as I knew this would make my father glad. My mother had been very painstaking. She would go so far as to iron curtains and make sure that each ruffle was in place. I would never do that. I only wanted to meet my father's immediate needs, not try to replace my mother."

Carol found herself doing the little things that her mother had enjoyed doing. "They were things that I hadn't enjoyed doing before she died, but now I was getting a kick out of them. By doing things that my mother had found pleasure in, I was better able to cope with my grief. It takes a while before you realize that the dead person is not coming back and until you are really able to say to yourself, 'She's not going to be back.'

"Rather than concentrate on what could not be changed, I thought to myself, 'What would my mother want me to do if she were here?' She had never pushed anything on me, although she had strong feelings about education. With this in mind, I started to do things that we used to do together, and I also did some of the things she enjoyed doing. For example, she had really liked to cook, but I couldn't stand it, so now I started cooking and it made me feel closer to her."

Carol felt there was a void that needed to be filled, and she sought ways to fill that void. "I became a foster mother and I started to be a surrogate mother to my godchildren. My mother loved children and, though I was an only child, she always had youngsters around her, while I would shout, 'Get them out of here.' Today it makes me feel good to have taken on this work as a continuation of my mother. My house looks like the one in the *Mother Goose* story of 'The Old Woman Who Lived in a Shoe,' with all the children around. On my day off, I have all the kids here, and I really love them."

• • •

The first thing David Meagher did when his mother died was to reduce the time spent on work so he could have more time with his family. As a therapist in death and dying, David tells how he needed time to himself. "If I was there for other people and if they leaned on me emotionally, I wasn't going to be able to hold them up. I needed time to do something for myself. Now, it is two weeks after her death. I am supposed to be giving some lectures but I have explained that I am not emotionally ready to talk about death and dying. 'And so,' I added, 'you will have to excuse me.'" Weeks later, David found that he was able to resume his work, after having given himself enough time to grieve.

After his mother's death, David had a strong urge to call her at the same times as he had formerly done. He tells of other roles his mother played in his activities. "There were ways she helped me in my writing," he says. "She was, you might say, my unofficial editor. She made grammatical corrections in everything I wrote, doing this for my doctoral dissertation, for my book, for articles I wrote for publication. Today, when I am writing, I feel a desire to send my manuscripts to her."

David explains how he began to cope with his mother's death. "Now, if I were denying the loss, or was reluctant to let go, I wouldn't allow anyone else to see my writing—that was her job. Instead, I must now find others to do for me the things that she did. I must engage in relationships with people who are going to fill in the time that formerly went to her. However, I must also be able to bring my memory of her to the new situation, for it is important that I don't forget. I remember her as being in my past, but not in my present or in my future."

Often we hear bereaved daughters and sons say such things as, "My father died over six months ago, but I strongly sense his presence. I even smell his pipe. But I'm afraid to say this lest people believe I'm just imagining it." David, not only a bereaved son, but a bereavement counselor as well, advises people who experience similar sensations of a dead person's presence to take pleasure in them. He relates one surviving parent's experience. "I had a client five years ago who was in his eighties. He had been married for fifty-eight years. Before his marriage, he had dated his wife for five or six years—the equivalent of what we would have called 'going steady.' The last two years of her life were spent at home in bed. He cared for her, made her meals, read to her and, when she took her nap, he stayed with her so that he'd be there when she awoke. He literally gave those two years of his life to her.

"After she died, he had two experiences of what some would call hallucinations. The first time he awoke in the middle of the night to find his wife in the room with him. After he rose, they had coffee, and she assured him that everything was all right with her, and that he mustn't worry. On another occasion, he was sitting in his apartment in the afternoon when he heard a knock on the door. He opened it to find his wife standing there. She entered and again they had coffee. Again she told him not to worry, for all was well with her. When he told this to friends and members of his family, they became concerned about his mental health. 'He's hallucinating. We've got to be careful with him. Perhaps he should be in an institution,' they said. But when the man described these experiences to me, I told him I thought they were great. He asked me, 'Isn't this wrong?' I said, 'No. If you felt good about it, enjoy it!' Whether the experiences were hallucinations or a tremendous need or memories or habit, I don't know. But they certainly weren't harming him. They weren't dangerous to himself or anyone else. So if a person says, 'I can smell the pipe smoke, or feel their presence,' I try to learn if the experience is comforting. If so, I say enjoy it!"

Responding to the question, "How long does grief *normally* take?" Dr. Meagher answered: "The one thing I will never respond to is, 'How long?' When people ask, 'How long?' I say, 'Don't ask me how long. Just tell me what you see as the consequence of what the person is doing. Look to see the impact of grieving on the person's life. If a man grieves for four years because he is working more slowly than others, and if at the end of those four years he comes out of his grief a much better person, that's great. I don't like time frames."

And so we see that everyone's clock ticks at a different speed after the death of a parent. Vivian Kessler, who was forty-one when her father died, gives us another view of how long an adult child may grieve. "After my father's death, I used to see him coming down the street, or I would see him in a dream, but after six months to a year, it became like a dull ache. The feelings didn't totally consume me to the point where I couldn't think or work."

Vivian believes that when the adult child has been living with the parent, the loss is more devastating. "In that kind of relationship, there is a severe loss because the life of the adult child had revolved around the parent. In a case like that, there are daily traumas such as going into a room where the parent slept or seeing a favorite chair that the parent sat in. This sense of loss is deepened if the relationship was one of being a caretaker to the parent, getting up every morning to take care of the parent. Then, after the parent dies, there is nothing but emptiness."

Vivian also believes that the amount of grief depends on the type of relationship that had existed between the surviving child and the parent. "If the relationship was a good one, the grieving is usually much less intense than if it had been bad. When there is a good relationship, the child is generally satisfied that the parent led a full life and nothing was left to be done. Although it may sound contra-dictory, when there was a bad relationship, too much is left unsaid, and the son or daughter grieves over not having had a good relationship."

In the following stories of two bereaved daughters, we will learn about one who craved a relationship with her parents, and of another one who enjoyed a very close rapport with her parents.

Gia Williams was one daughter who yearned for the closeness she had never had with her mother. "After her death, I was able to resume work and still relate to people, but inwardly I felt hurt that I hadn't had a more positive relationship with my mother. Then again, I had never had that because my father's mother raised me after my parents separated when I was very young. So I had always had that need of a mother and father at home. The lack of those re-lationships caused me a great deal of sadness and pain. As I became older and began to meet people who didn't know who their parents were or who had a parent who physically or mentally abused them, I could see that many people's lives were even more painful than mine. With that realization, I stopped feeling sorry for myself. At least I knew who my mother was and there had been moments when we got along."

Sandra Levine's father and mother both died at the same age but not at the same time. They were seventy-six. "They were wonderful parents and we had so many good years together. I think that is what sustains me now—the fact that I push away any of the sad memories and draw from the treasure house of joy that we built together.

"Of course I was angry—in the sense that it revolved around the whole manner of my father's death and his ultimate diagnosis. He had never been sick and suddenly he was undergoing surgery for a brain tumor. He had radiation treatment as an outpatient, but that part of the tumor that couldn't be removed began to grow like wildfire. In the final weeks, a social worker told us about a hospice program and our family realized that the hospice setting would be best for him in this terminal stage. He was put on a waiting list and remained in the hospital. Unfortunately he began to slip into a coma and by the time there was a bed for him in the hospice, he was unresponsive. But even though my father could not speak, he seemed to respond to the kind of treatment he received there. He opened his eyes and squeezed my hand. It was as if he knew where he was and that he approved.

"I think his being so beautifully treated in the hospice is another memory that sustains me. My mother, my brother, and I went to visit him frequently, as did my sister-in-law, who was a real daughter to my parents. One of us was always present, but the volunteers were also there at all times—feeding him, turning him over, cleaning him. They talked to my father as though he was able to hear and cheered him up. Everybody was wonderful. And the hospice people did so much to keep our morale up. They were so sensitive on every count. For example, we received a call from the hospice one night that my father was going to die in a few hours. They wanted to alert us so we could come and be with him at the end. When we arrived at the hospice, the doctor and nurse were there making him comfortable, talking to him, holding him. It was such a wonderful feeling to see the treatment he was receiving in his final hours.

"Not only did my father receive wonderful treatment, the hospice continued to show their concern for the surviving family. They had bereavement follow-ups for the members of the family and meetings to which we were invited. My mother received notices in the mail every few weeks with a lovely note that read, 'We're thinking about you,' and each time they informed us that a group was scheduled to meet and asked if we would care to join them. My mother was never a 'joiner,' so she never went, but she knew they were there and it was a comfort to her.

"With my mother's illness, there was some type of blockage from which she suffered heart attacks and cardiac arrest. The doctors tried to insert a pacemaker a few hours before she died, but their efforts were unsuccessful. My mother had told my brother and me that if it came to putting her on life-saving devices, she would not wish that. So when the doctor indicated that there was nothing more he could do to save her other than putting her on a resuscitator, we indicated this should not be done at my mother's request. After her death, there was some guilt about that, because we felt maybe we would have had her with us a little longer. But my brother and I knew we had respected her wishes and therefore felt exonerated.

"Once my mother was gone, we became aware of the fact that we now were the elder persons in the family, and that we were next in line, so to speak. You begin to think of what kind of death you will encounter, and you hope it will not be the brutal kind that my father experienced. But you try not to dwell too much on those thoughts. You begin to move back in time to memories that comfort you and make you glad—memories of incredibly beautiful moments with two terrific parents. The one thing that did bring me up short recently for a brief period was the death of my aunt. We went to the funeral and afterward, my cousin said to me, 'We're orphans now. We have both lost our parents.'

"I guess there will always be moments like that, when we lose another member of a loving family. But because we had them for the amount of time we did, we cherish every memory of them and it is that we learn to live with."

ꙮ CHAPTER 10

When Help Is Needed

- My friends weren't nearby to give me the support I needed after my mother died. I really had no one to talk to, no one to listen to me. Because I began to feel that I was a burden to my friends, I decided to find someone who would willingly listen. I checked around and found the name of a grief counselor.

- It wasn't that I was desperate or felt that I was going through some kind of crisis. What I did feel was that I wasn't myself. After my father died, I felt lost. I couldn't concentrate at work. I didn't sleep well. My father had died of a heart attack, and the thought that I was having one was constantly on my mind. I knew I needed help.

- I always felt depressed, tired, and lethargic. I began to drink because I thought that liquor would give me energy. I lost interest in things; nothing seemed to matter. Soon I was drinking to forget, but forgetting was impossible. When I realized that my job was in jeopardy, I knew I needed help.

- I began to quarrel with my wife, my mother, and my friends. Even at work I was antagonistic. I started to put on weight. When I found myself going into the men's room and crying during the middle of the day, I decided to go for therapy.

"The parent-child relationship is possibly the strongest bond existing," says Anne Rosberger, Executive Director of the Bereavement and Loss Center of New York. "It develops during a time of our greatest vulnerability and exists through innumerable experiences, both positive and negative. It is the testing arena for our debut into the larger world." However, she says that the parent-child bond is like all other important love relationships in which, she believes, conflicts and antagonisms are always present. At the same time, says Rosberger, in such relationships, dependency needs and the longing for approval exist. So it is with the parent-child relationship.

"At times, survivors get fixed on one aspect of the relationship instead of viewing its totality," Ms. Rosberger explains. "For many bereaved children, anger, guilt, and shame remain as a residue of the loss of the parent. They may result in dysfunctional behavior or severe emotional distress. Psychotherapeutic intervention is helpful in sorting out feelings and placing them into a more reasonable perspective. This then enables the survivor to move forward more fully invested in the present and eager for the future."

Phil Musmacker was dealing with many such emotions. His pain and anguish led him to drunken oblivion. One night he went into a blackout that lasted nineteen hours. As related in Chapter 7, this led to Phil's arrest. Through a sympathetic lawyer and judge, he spent only twenty-one days in jail and was then placed on probation. The judge warned Phil that one more drink would put him back into jail.

Phil then realized that his drinking was out of control and that he needed help. At the Plainview Rehabilitation Center, his counseling began to take hold. "It was concentrated therapy for drugs and alcohol. But a very big part of it was life-style behavior. They taught me how to live, how to deal with everything as it came, and how to clean up my past." Today, Phil is involved in sports, church activities, and volunteer work. Although he is separated from his wife and two sons, they see each other frequently and are planning a reconciliation. "They are the source of my strength," Phil says.

"Another thing I have come to realize is that my father's actions were unintentional, because he had suffered abuse in his own childhood. I later realized, too, that my sisters and brothers had been trying to cope with their own pain and that they were only human. My prayers are bearing fruit because my brothers and sisters now form a much tighter and more loving family than ever before," Phil states.

A turning point in Phil's life came when his counselor suggested he write a letter to his mother. Phil remembers his initial reaction. "I looked at the counselor and sarcastically replied, 'Sure. Where do you want me to mail it? To heaven?' I thought he was trying to make a fool out of me. Here I was half insane, half out of my mind, and this guy was telling me to write a letter to my mother. She couldn't read! The idea of sitting down and writing a letter seemed ridiculous." The counselor told Phil, "When you are ready, just write it. We don't have to talk about it. Just write it."

Probably the most important step in his counseling came when Phil finally wrote a poignant letter to his mother, asking her forgiveness. He was now able to write all the things he had wanted to say to her but never could because he was too angry and too drunk. This time, instead of being dead drunk, Phil was alive, sober, and on the road to recovering. Excerpts of Phil's touching letter to his mother follow:

Dear Momma:

Since I can't speak with you personally, I thought I would write you and express a few of my thoughts and feelings, things that have been on my mind, bothering me for a long time. These are some things I wanted to say before you left me, but I wasn't able to. I wanted to tell you how much I loved you and always will love you. . . . Mom, I'm sorry I didn't stay with you as often as you needed me. . . . You see, Mom, I couldn't take looking at you in that pain anymore. It was literally killing me, tearing and ripping my heart and insides apart. I'm sorry and I regret not giving you the love and understanding and companionship you gave to me while I was growing up. Please understand, Mom, I wanted to but I just couldn't. I only just now became aware of what was stopping me. I was lacking the courage and strength because of what cancer had been doing to the most important person in my life. I wasn't able to stop or do anything to this evil situation. I became deathly afraid of this thing called cancer. . . . Every day that I didn't come to see you, I felt a deep, horrible regret inside of me. Even if there was nothing I could do for you, but just sit and hold you, as you used to do for me when I was in need.

I felt like I was abandoning you. . . . I hope today you have forgiven me for my actions, although it would be best if you were here to tell me yourself. When you were here, everything felt so warm, so complete and comfortable. But now you are gone and I'm scared and lonely. Something inside me is missing, something I can't explain.

I have no one to blame today for my feelings of regret, guilt, and shame, but myself. . . . If I had just had the strength, I wouldn't be paying this large and painful price. I do believe you're watching over me. I know you see me trying hard to overcome my drug and alcohol problem and this lousy attitude I have. You see, Mom, I have regained my trust and belief in God, and I know you are really proud of that. So, I've decided to put my problems in His Hands. . . . I do believe good comes out of all bad. I have a beautiful wife and baby boy to prove it.

I feel many regrets that you didn't get to see and hold my son before you passed away. . . . I strongly believe you're watching over Phil Jr., along with Donna and me. In my heart, I believe you've already seen him and you've been loving him all the while. Mom, I'm feeling terribly guilty and ashamed of using alcohol and drugs and trying to escape from my problems and responsibilities. . . . I was suffering from alcohol, drugs, deep depression, tension, guilt and shame, and I just went on denying it. So I avoided you, like I did everyone else. I just got angrier and angrier over my own actions and what had happened to you. I can't redo any of this whole mess, but at least I'm wiser and experienced. . . . I hope that you and God forgive me, Mom.

I am very selfishly freed from my own inner conflict and pain now that you're finally out of pain and in heaven. I kept many loved ones and friends out of my life until I finally wrote this letter and faced up to all my grief.

Writing this letter was suggested to me by a counselor, a very special person in my life today who took the time and patience to show me how beautiful life can really be if I want it bad enough. Since I was not able to say it to you personally, I am writing it to you. I'm sure grateful to him. I'm sure you're as grateful too, Mom!

I'll see you soon, Mom, God willing. I'm sure hopeful.

Love you tremendously,
Phil

Another bereaved son, John Donnelly, began taking sleeping pills to get him through the night and phenobarbital through the day. After his doctor suggested he see a psychoanalyst, John followed this advice but he had difficulty in talking to this specialist. "The beginning was touch and go. Then I got to like the psychoanalyst, Dr. Josephine Ross, very much.

But I was embarrassed about the past as well as the present. So I would invent things, make them up, and pretend that things between my mother and me had been wonderful, that she was the greatest mother in the world, and things like that—which were not true. My grandmother had died soon after my mother, but I insisted she had no real influence on me whatsoever while I was growing up. I later discovered that in this I was totally wrong and that my grandmother had been the real rock who was my support. It was almost as if I had deluded myself about my grandmother's influence so that I could maintain the pretense about my mother." During his analysis, John was able to face his anger at his mother, his guilt, and his fears after her death. He was also able to put into perspective his grandmother's role in his life. However, the road he had to travel to gain that insight was a rocky one.

"I had never been fat in my life; in fact, I had been very thin. But I had seen my mother go down in weight to such a degree that toward the end she was like a broomstick. To conquer that fear of cancer, I began to eat. I would eat two meals every mealtime and in a period of about three months I had put on fifty or sixty pounds. To me, that was great because I didn't think I had cancer anymore.

"However, I was also embarrassed at how stout I looked. Now that I was fat, how would women view me? I was heavy for about a year. I had been 145 pounds and I went up to over 190. Eventually, Dr. Ross was able to get me to go on a diet. But as long as I was heavy, in my mind I didn't have cancer.

"I will never forget the day I went back to my medical doctor after having been in psychoanalysis for about a year. I hadn't seen her for a while. She looked at me and said, 'Oh, you've gained so much weight. That's not good.' I replied, 'But I'm not withering away from cancer.' She shook her head and said,

'You certainly aren't.' She didn't realize it, but I was the happiest person in the world. I went sailing out of that office, and yet my weight was dangerously high."

John, with the help of Dr. Ross, was finally able to get off the drugs and maintain a diet to lose weight. He began to socialize again, and knew that his analysis was beginning to work. "I finally began to get back on an even keel. Every once in a while now I will remember the death but I will just tell myself not to think about it because you can't keep dwelling on it. I push it away."

We have seen how two bereaved sons derived help from individual therapy. Let's now take a look at how two bereaved daughters sought aid from a support group.

Lisa Strahs-Lorenc was grieving and didn't want to grieve alone. "I knew I needed a support group because I wanted to be with other people who knew how I felt. But that was some time after the funeral. My process of working out the grief was to really delve into it, to go into it in a way that involved my whole self. I was trying to discover a place where I could go to get help and then I heard about this group that helps adults who have suffered a loss. I am very much interested in self-help and feel there is a definite need for self-help groups for adult children who have suffered the death of a parent.

"In my group, there was only one other person who had lost a parent, her mother. The rest were mostly widows like my mom. And I was the youngest one there. I would have liked to have had other people in my position—people at any age level who had lost a father. At first I missed people who were also adult children, who would feel as I did, but I soon discovered that we all had the same feelings of loss. I mean, we would sit there and just cry and cry."

Lisa explains some of the issues discussed at the support group meetings. "We talked about what meaning that person had in our lives. We talked about how we were and we even talked about a time frame, about how far along the road to recovery we wanted to be in three months, in six months' time, in a year. We talked about what we wanted to do, why we were waiting for certain things, what we were putting off. The process just happens and suddenly you just don't realize how you got from here to there.

"By 'process,' I mean the work of grieving, the business of sorting out in your life how the death has affected your life, how the loss of that person who was such an integral part of your life affects your existence, of trying to find meaning in your life, trying to find answers to such things as 'Why did it happen? Why was that person taken away?' We were helped and guided by our leader who was a social worker. I happen to like social workers very much. I'm an ex-teacher. But I don't call myself a teacher— one who stands in front of a room full of children. I call myself a facilitator, for I am there to facilitate the learning activities of the child. So I think of our leader as a facilitator. A self-help group or a support group is a relative thing. It is a gathering of people who get together because they are in the same situation and have the same problems, but it can be formalized with someone with experience in counseling, a social worker, for example."

Prior to her father's death, Lisa had gone for counseling on other kinds of issues. "Mostly career-type things like self-development and such things. But my therapist felt I had unresolved grief about my biological mother. Even though I didn't remember her, because I was so little, I did suffer from separation anxiety, for it's rough to lose a parent at the age of two. That's when a child is really attached to a mother and is going through all kinds of growth stages. As I said, I was going through a great deal of separation anxiety. That was always my problem as I was growing up, for I was always afraid that people would go away and not come back, like my biological mother. She had disappeared, and she was gone. I don't remember what they told me, for my father had blocked the whole thing out. It was very painful for him to lose a twenty-eight-year-old pregnant wife. I would ask him, 'What did you do with me? What did you say to me when my mother died?'

"In later years, after my father had remarried, my parents would visit me in Massachusetts. When they left, I would just go crazy. The same thing with my husband. If he left and was late or something, I would think something had happened and he wasn't going to come back. This was the case with anyone close to me. And my therapist believed this was part of the unresolved issue: I thought my mother had just left and had never come back. And at that age, too."

Lisa believes therapy is often looked down on in our society. "A lot of people feel that way. My father did. He always felt that I was a failure for having gone to counseling, which is too bad, because had he gone, I really think it could have helped him. I know my support group helped me; everything that I had projected as to where I wanted to be was exactly correct. In fact, our baby was out of this. We had started trying to have the baby a week after my father died. Ultimately, we had a little girl, named after both of my biological parents, Sari Allison. Another important change in my life was that I started my own business. My father had always encouraged me to go out on my own."

When Hilary Friedman wanted to seek help, she and her mother began checking the types of organizations available. There were groups for widows, for parents without partners, for bereaved parents who had lost a child, but it was difficult to find a support group for bereaved adult children who had lost a parent. Hilary was in her twenties and in desperate need of sharing.

"I finally learned about a support group at a nearby church. It really helped me because all of us were told *what* we were feeling, and told that we *could* feel it. And because everybody was hurting, everybody was trying to deal with everyone else's hurt. We would share things like, 'This is how I dealt with the most difficult aspect of my pain.' I wasn't angry that my father died, but I had anger at the life-style I was forced to live. My father had been an attorney and our life-style had radically changed since his illness and death. We went limping along. My mother was grieving in her way, and I felt isolated and alone in my grief.

"Just being with other adults who were grieving was a catharsis. Listening to what each person would say, what our emotions and inner feelings were, made us understand we were not alone. The sharing gave us courage and hope."

Psychotherapist Athena Drewes clarifies the differences between *grief counseling* and *grief therapy*. "It is difficult to give an absolute time to when professional help should be sought. There is no definitive date for the end of mourning. Grief counseling is differentiated from grief therapy, with grief therapy reserved for complicated mourning. Complicated mourning is when the person becomes so overwhelmed, or uses maladaptive behaviors or remains interminably in the grief state without the mourning process moving toward completion. Most people seek out professional help, or are urged to do so by friends or relatives, when they become 'stuck' in the mourning process. But for most people, grief *counseling* is supportive help that should be available and sought after early on in the grief process.

"Usually there is intensive family and community support for the first three months. Then people assume you've gotten on with your life, and that the grief is past. They withdraw their support. It is at this time that the pain and sense of loss may have their greatest impact and counseling can help continue the support that is still needed to grieve," Drewes states. "You cannot handle the emotional impact of loss until you first deal with the fact that the loss happened. In grief counseling," Drewes maintains, "the goal is to help the person so they don't carry the pain with them for life. I view mourning as a process, not a state. Consequently it is more that a person is doing 'grief work' since going through the four tasks* of mourning requires work. The four tasks being:

1. To accept the reality of the loss
2. To experience the pain of grief
3. To adjust to an environment in which the deceased is missing
4. To withdraw emotional energy and reinvest it in another relationship.

"If task two is not adequately completed, therapy later on may be needed, at which point it would be more difficult for the person to go back and work through the pain they avoided."

Drewes also believes that personal variables play an important point in determining when professional help should be sought. "The person's personality, their coping strategies, supports, the level of relationship with the deceased, circumstantial fac-

---

*Written about by J. William Worden, Ph.D., in *Grief Counseling and Grief Therapy*. New York: Springer Publishing Company, 1982.

tors [how did the person die]. Just because a person cries at the funeral does not mean they are adequately dealing with the process of grief. Sometimes it takes an 'outsider' or family member who might be able to be more 'objective' to help a person realize they are stuck in the process and need help to get beyond a particular stage."

Dan Sutherland, riddled with guilt after his father's death, felt guilty for being alive. He became frightened at his reaction to the first holidays after his father's death. In the office, he couldn't concentrate, he was making bad mistakes and not even bothering to correct them, and although he had formerly been a punctual person, he was getting to the office late almost every morning.

"The fellows I worked with thought I was a basket case. During the first week I was back, no one knew what to say to me and almost everyone avoided me. The receptionist said, 'I was sorry to hear about your father.' Then she added, 'How old was he?' I wished she had just left it that she was sorry, because how old my father was didn't matter. He was gone and even if he had been one hundred, I would have felt rotten. So I didn't know what else to say and neither did she. Even my boss just said, 'I'm glad you're back,' but he didn't say, 'I'm sorry,' or anything else. It was just as if I had taken a couple of days off and now I was ready for work again. Well, I wasn't."

At this point, Dan consulted in private with his company's doctor, who listened to his problems. The doctor was able to perceive that this was an employee who had never had difficulties at his job or with his coworkers. When Dan said he felt like "socking" his boss for giving him a new account to handle, the doctor understood that Dan's anger was an issue that needed addressing and referred him to a therapist.

While in treatment, Dan was able to express his grief. He told of his self-destructive feelings, his anger, and the tremendous guilt he felt after his father's death. He was obsessed with a fear of growing older. He felt that he, too, would develop Alzheimer's disease and that he would be punished because he had not been there to help his father as often as he felt he should.

Dan's therapist explained that one does survive pain, and that surviving grief doesn't mean you won't miss your parents after they died. By not dealing with our emotions, we can become stuck psychologically. The doctor was able to convey to Dan that mourning is a normal and natural process that allows you time to come to terms with your loss.

During the period Dan was in therapy, it developed that, as a child, he had not been able to express grief when a beloved grandfather died. At age six, he was reprimanded with the familiar "Be a big boy. Don't be a baby. Big boys don't cry." Now that his own father had died, the second loss allowed his repressed grief to surface. Dan shared his guilt with his therapist. He was able to cry, to grieve, to explain the pain of his guilt, and ultimately was able to learn self-forgiveness. "My therapist also explained to me that my fears of getting the disease were part of my guilt."

Cynthia Carter felt that she was becoming drug dependent by taking the medicines prescribed for her after her mother's death. "I was afraid I was becoming hooked on sleeping tablets, and this caused me to become even more depressed. It seemed to be a never-ending cycle of depression; medication to get out of the depression, followed by more depression because of taking the medication. I was becoming desperate. I am not a doctor or pill person. And I had lost all faith in the doctor who had prescribed the medications because I felt he never followed up properly on me. He never called to find out how the increased medication was working or if my blood pressure might be affected, or anything.

"But at this time, my husband and I learned about a rehabilitation center that treated people as outpatients. So I decided to go there, where I was treated for my drug dependency." Before long, Cynthia became aware that the underlying cause of her problem was her mother's death. She identified closely with one of the counselors. "He had lost his father and could understand how I felt. He put me in contact with a nearby bereavement group for those who had suffered a loss of a loved one. The group met once a week. The facilitator of the meeting would begin by having each of us say whom we had lost and how we had reacted. One person would say her husband had died, another that her boyfriend had died, another that her cousin died, and some, including myself, had lost parents. There were eight of us."

After becoming part of a group in which others expressed their feelings of grief, Cynthia realized she was not alone. "One woman said she smelled her father's tobacco smoke in the house after he died, and we understood how she felt. Another woman said she kept dreaming of how her husband died; she had found him dead on the bathroom floor in the morning, and we felt her pain. One bereaved woman, whose cousin was like a sister to her, said she kept seeing her cousin on the street, in restaurants, and on the beach. And we felt her pain, too. Although there was a great deal of concentrated pain at the meetings, it was good because we all shared it. Strange as this may sound, I felt better after the meetings. At first I was a bit worried about them because I didn't know what to expect. But later on, we were able to joke with one another. We knew we were not alone in our grief, and we began to heal."

Dr. David Meagher explains how to recognize symptoms of delayed mourning or unresolved grief. "There are a number of symptoms," he says. "When you begin to see that the person is either making very big, or very drastic, life changes and decisions about his life, where he lives, what he does, these are signs of unresolved grief. Or they begin to either become reckless or they begin to withdraw completely, breaking long-term relationships with friends or relatives. Or they become reclusive and don mourning apparel, in both the literal sense and the symbolic sense and become the grieving individuals for the rest of their lives."

Dr. Meagher believes that *normal bereavement* is not a disease and therefore the process does not require the intervention of a therapist. "Then, what one wants, if one needs assistance, is a counselor who functions as a family surrogate, doing the things that family members did for us when we had extended families and a number of relatives living close by and being with us during this process.

"There are many clinical psychologists and social workers who have gone beyond their training and look at bereavement counseling as a separate process of support. Whomever the bereaved person chooses, be it a psychologist, psychiatrist, a social worker, or other mental health counselor, the question should be, 'Has this individual done work in the area of bereavement counseling and examined bereavement processes? Has he studied the process doing bereavement counseling?' Just because a professional is a psychologist, psychiatrist, a social worker, or a mental health counselor doesn't mean that he has automatically spent time in this area."

As to where to find the best help, Dr. Meagher suggests that referrals may be had from such persons as the clergy or funeral directors. "There has been a recognition also on the part of religious groups that there is a real need in the area of bereavement counseling and they are beginning to bring in people. So ask the clergyperson, 'Do you know of any service that is available?' Speak to your funeral director who can be very helpful in this area. If there is a hospice nearby, even if the person who died wasn't a patient there, give it a call. Speak to the bereavement coordinator and ask:

1. Do they provide bereavement services to other than families of hospice patients?
2. If they don't, can they refer to you bereavement counselors in your vicinity?"

Dr. Meagher stresses that when you lose someone you love, such as a parent or spouse, and you don't change your life at all, you may be suffering from unresolved grief. He adds, "The contrary may also be true. If the bereaved person lives as though the deceased person had never existed, that, too, may indicate the possible presence of an unresolved issue."

Unresolved guilt is a basic problem of bereavement, says Dr. Roberta Temes. To hide from the anger or guilt you feel toward the deceased is to risk developing symptoms at a later date, she maintains. These symptoms may be far more complex and difficult to deal with than the original anger or guilt. "Your feelings of anger are proof that you are human." As to guilt, Dr. Temes states, "It is perfectly appropriate to feel relieved at the same time that you are feeling devastated." Dr. Temes suggests that you examine if you have begun the bereavement process yet: "There are predictable stages of the bereavement process. Not everyone experiences the same feelings at the same points in time, but grief does typically include three distinct stages. These stages may be called *numbness, disorganization,* and *reorganization.*"*

Dr. Temes stresses the need for "a helper" to assist the mourner during each stage of grief. "During stage one of the mourning process, the helper is there to be leaned upon and give concrete assistance with managing necessary chores. During stage two the helper must provide sanction to ventilate emotions, all emotions, and must tirelessly listen to the repeated stories about the life and death of the loved one. . . . In the last stage of mourning, the helper must be there to expand a social network and encourage involvement and interest in life."**

Some bereaved sons and daughters find the pain of mourning too excruciating to bear and postpone facing their feelings. They become involved with frantic activities to occupy every hour of every day and night. Then, according to Dr. Temes, months, or even years later, a seemingly unimportant loss will set off an "inappropriate" grief reaction. "The person can panic and not understand what is happening. The answer, of course," concludes Dr. Temes, "is that the mourning process is just beginning."

We have now learned through the experiences of many of the adult children's stories that if you cannot make it on your own, by all means seek help. We have also seen that help comes in many forms. Positive steps can be taken to work through grief, as the sons and daughters in this book delineate: Keep busy . . . go back to work as soon as possible . . . avoid making major decisions during the

*Temes, R., *Living with an Empty Chair,* New York: Irvington Publishers, 1984.
**Temes, R., *Living with an Empty Chair,* New York: Irvington Publishers, 1984.

mourning period . . . try new hobbies or learn to meditate . . . take a class in something you have always wanted to pursue . . . take walks or participate in a sport . . . swimming can be relaxing, as can be gardening or getting a massage. Little things can help.

The one big step is "taking it" rather than "saying it." Above all, don't keep your feelings locked in—get them out, be it in support groups, with a grief therapist, or with friends, relatives, or other confidantes. The title of this chapter is "When Help Is Needed." Its shadow is "When Help Is *Wanted.*" It is then we reach out for help.

♪ CHAPTER 11

Differing Attitudes Toward Death and Religion

An enormous service is performed by the clergy in officiating at wakes and funerals of the dead parent. The comfort of ceremonies, the support of the structure of the institution, and the wisdom of the traditional religions are an aid to bereaved sons and daughters, especially those who believe in them. Many agnostics have indicated that they envy those who utilize their faith as a help for coping with grief.

However, as this chapter will reveal, there are many adult children who are so angry they cannot utilize their religious faith. In families where there are more than one surviving child, there can be a division of feeling about God. One bereaved son said, "I feel closer to God because I believe there is an afterworld and I will see my mother again. But my sister is very angry and believes there can't be a God if He let this happen. People told my sister that our mother had been such a wonderful person and had done so much good helping others that God wanted her. My sister was furious at that."

One daughter who has a very strong belief in an afterlife is Peggy Griffiths. "I absolutely believe in an afterlife," she says. "I am convinced that, at the time of death, someone—a loved one who has passed on ahead of you—greets you. I feel strongly about this, and I have no fear of death whatsoever. My parents were very devout Episcopalians. They went to the Church of England School as children. That was the only type of education they received, a parochial education within the Episcopal Church, and religion was ingrained in them. They, in turn, instilled it in us. When we were living in Poughkeepsie, they used to look up at the sky and say, 'Never have any fear of death because it is the entry to a happy time for everyone.' Thus I have never had any fear of it.

"I think people who believe in the afterlife have an easier time handling their grief. One thing that helped me enormously after my mother died was that I knew I would see her again and my father, too. Of this, I had no doubt. If I hadn't felt that way, I don't know how I would have survived such a traumatic period. You must have faith."

Mary Stellakis, a Greek Orthodox whose mother died ten years ago, has found salvation and strength in her firm belief in God. Mary has five *Te Deums* said every year on specific anniversaries of her mother's life. She also visits her mother's graveside five times each year. Such trips take Mary from Athens to Kyparissia, Greece, a journey of more than three hundred miles over tortuous, mountainous roads. "When my time comes, I look forward to being placed next to my mother and my brother in that cemetery. I find peace in my religion and in God. I bear my cross of sorrow within my heart and show love to all. I smile."

One bereaved son, Andrew Rezin, although a believer in God, was less than pleased when someone told him his father had gone to a better place. "Many people told me that my father was going on to a better life. I believe in Christ and the Church, but I can't see creating a world where people go through suffering and pain. I know the suffering has been going on for a long time, and perhaps it's a test of the strength of human beings, to see what kind of sacrifice they can make. I don't know what could be worse than losing someone you love, having someone close to you taken away. I never damned God or turned my back on Him, the Creator. My cousin, a priest, tried to help me. But those people who said my father had gone to a better place annoyed me. It was like saying they had made a trip there recently and had come back and could assure you how good it was. How could you accept that?"

After Max Glauben woke up to discover his father had been murdered in the concentration camp where they both had been incarcerated, he didn't know to whom to turn for comfort. "How could such a thing happen? How could one man like Hitler do this to so many innocent and good people? My father never did anything wrong. No answers to those questions were forthcoming. I remember just moving to a corner and talking to God and asking for His wisdom and guidance in helping me to understand and to overcome.

"Whenever I needed answers where there were no answers, I would go back to that corner and talk to God." In later years, Max took comfort in being able to say Kaddish [the Jewish prayer for the dead] for both of his parents.

Carol Richardson tells how the Church helped her cope with her mother's death: "The Church was extremely supportive in helping me get through this, particularly in the first few weeks after my mother's death. Just by hearing the explanation that God does not have to answer to anyone made things easier for me. I also believe there may have been a reason for her being taken from us. It felt good to know so many people—those who attended the funeral services—knew my mother, and they were all very compassionate. That was comforting."

Phil Musmacker believes that if you want to live life to the fullest, you need to have faith in God. "I can't stress enough to have faith in God and a personal relationship with Jesus Christ. Even those who don't have bad problems should have that faith."

Phil says when he started to believe again, he made big strides in coping with his grief. His belief brought him out of the depth of despair and allowed him to face his guilt and anger. His faith let him sleep in peace and he could look forward to the next morning. It washed away all the years of rage and regret. "No matter how far you stray away from God, you can always come back—it is the only way you will find peace. I tried every way before coming back and I just found more misery and unhappiness. Mankind may let you down and disappoint you, but God won't. People are not perfect, only God is. When you understand this—and accept it—you don't let people hurt you anymore.

"Nobody can push religion down your throat. The seeds that were planted in you when you were young will grow and you will accept them when you are ready and not before. Through God, all things are possible. Through God I learned to stop thinking of myself and to start thinking of other people's feelings."

We have read above how religion has helped some bereaved children. But there are those grieving children who have little or no faith in conventional religion. One of these is John Donnelly. At an early age, his father died. His mother's remarriage to a Protestant caused him much anguish at the Catholic school he attended.

"The nuns insisted my mother wasn't married. This was a subject the sisters brought up in class. It wasn't the kids who tormented me, it was the nuns. So I turned bitterly against the Church, at first emotionally and then intellectually. The more I began to read about comparative religion, the more I turned against the Catholic Church. I could no longer accept the Catholic Church as the true religion. So after my mother's death, I had no religion to fall back on. It couldn't be my crutch, but for those people who are devoutly religious, who really believe in God and in a life after death, it is a wonderful thing that religion is a help, especially in times of bereavement."

John says he never turned against God or blamed Him for his mother's death because he didn't really believe in that kind of a God. "Certainly not a God who interferes in people's lives or does good and bad and to whom you can pray. So it makes it hard, because then you're on your own, which is a difficult situation, especially when you are suffering grief."

As far as his own belief is concerned, John says he doesn't exactly believe in the Hindu form of reincarnation, but he does think that energy never dies. "I believe the energy our body gives off after our death remains and that this energy can live again. It doesn't die—so it's going to live. And if the energy takes the forms of thoughts and so on, it's like the consciousness of mankind which exists for all time, and you are part of it.

"After death, your thoughts and energies will be reborn in someone else. That helps now. But even though I believed in that, it didn't help when my mother died. I wasn't even thinking of such things. I believed them, but I didn't think about them. It wasn't anything I could lean on."

Andrea Fodor Litkei, whose father, Dr. Nandor Fodor, died after suffering a heart attack, expresses her belief in life after death emotionally, but finds that intellectually it is not a simple matter. "Emotionally, I believe in life after death because it probably suits my unconscious purposes, and one wants to believe because one doesn't want to think this is the end. Intellectually, I have trouble believing because the factors involved stun the human mind. We are using such a limited amount of our capabilities that it is a sin we live our lives the way we do.

"However, looking at it from an intellectual level and having the work of physicists who have probed some of the secrets of the universe, there does seem to be reason to support the theory of some kind of survival. The main question is, does the personality survive along with the human being or not?

"Scientists have looked into the macrocosm and found no end to the universe. They have also looked into the microcosm and found no end. We are born and we started from somewhere and changed our form. Therefore, I would have to postulate that we are going somewhere and we will change our form. So if we forget about the personality, it is very hard not to believe in survival. If you think about the human personality with all its silly memories and a lot of neuroses that go to make up the memories, then it's intellectually a little staggering to say, 'Yes, there is life after death.'

"Emotionally, I definitely believe in it and there are too many instances, not one at a time taken separately, but taking the conglomerate of so many legends and instances through the ages plus the sheer weight of happenstances that have occurred, should make us at least take a good look, and a good chance for intellectually believing as well."

Lisa Strahs-Lorenc is a rationalist and believes in those things she can see. She shares her views on religion. "As to God, I'm a very rational person and I guess if there's something I can't see—well, I don't know. I do believe in fate, but I don't know why or how things happen as they do. But I can't think in terms of a Supreme Being at all. I was confirmed and took part in other rites, but I never found any meaning to them. I found more of a meaning in ethics and morals and being a good human being. But I never found meaning in believing in something that has control over you. I believe in self-determination. I believe in day-to-day living. I don't know how I came to be this way, but my husband is exactly the same way and he was raised as a Catholic while I was raised in the Jewish religion." Lisa explains that she doesn't have "this thing about anger at God." But she also tells us that part of her rationalization in trying to accept her father's death was that she began to believe in fate.

"There were some things that happened before he died that were very freaky, almost like it was meant to be, like it was planned." Lisa goes on to explain that feeling. "Dr. Elisabeth Kübler-Ross says that people often die within a month of their birthdays. Well, my biological mother did and so did my father. They say there is a biological clock in all of us. The last weekend before his death, we celebrated Mother's Day, but we also celebrated my father's birthday.

"At the festivities, I got an unbelievable urge to see old family movies. We spent the whole weekend together, and Fred and I slept at my parents' home. We hadn't looked at those movies in years. We were looking at myself when I was born, and it was almost as if we were viewing the whole story, our entire lives together, and then my father went off and died. But it was very strange, because everything was so sudden. That's why I feel that it must have been his time. I guess that's my way of coping with it. Almost as if you have to believe in destiny."

Lisa wishes she believed in a soul. But she does feel that the memory of people lives on and that we keep them alive by remembering things we shared with them. "The situation becomes so uncontrollable and unexplainable that you have to find some kind of meaning in it. If you don't, it's very hard. And so you find some kind of rationalization that allows you to go on."

Eddie Gintz says he is a realist and a firm believer that life is for the living. "When my parents died, there was nothing I could do about it. But I'm against going to cemeteries or anything like that. I want to be cremated because I don't want anybody to be bothered with me after I'm dead. If they want to be good to me while I'm alive, that's what counts. That's what I tried to do for my parents—to do for them while they were alive. I don't want anybody coming to the cemetery when I die because I won't know about it. So who needs it?

"I don't believe in a hereafter. I know people who are miserable to their parents when they are living and then after they die they run to the cemetery every week and cry. They find solace by going to the cemetery. But this is bull to me. They should have been decent to their parents when they were living. That's part of why I feel the way I do, I guess. If someone wants to be good to me, do it when I'm living, not after I'm dead. A lot of people try to tell me that energy lives on and that there is a life after death in another form. But I tell them, 'We eat animals and all that's left is bones. So does their energy live on?'"

Another bereaved son, David Meagher, believes in some form of afterlife. "I just can't see the human spirit ending after so few years. I can understand the body not being able to function more than eighty, ninety, or one hundred years, or whatever amount of time we want to put as a limit to the bodily machine. But I feel that when humans are born, they have almost unlimited potential and the short amount of eighty or ninety years is not enough for that potential to be fully realized. So I think there is a spirit, the essence of humanness that goes beyond the physical structure of the body in a lifetime. As to its form, I am open to anything at this point. Whether that spiritual essence stays within the physical realm, I don't know.

"In our lifetime, we go beyond our bodies. We are not really restricted to the body. We are able to project outward. We are able to empathize with others. To say that the spirit and the essence that makes us human ends when the body ends is ridiculous. It places us in a realm of no better than plants, and I don't think that is so."

One bereaved daughter changed her religion because she had not resolved the differences with her mother when she died. Gia Williams was a Christian, but later became a Buddhist. At one time, she had attended church services every now and then, but in time she gave up following Christian practices. "It was not that I condemned everything, but, in my opinion, life was not fulfilled by Christianity. I felt that sitting and just asking or praying for something and then waiting for it to happen just wasn't for me. It didn't hold the answer to what I was seeking—more peace of mind, more self-satisfaction. Like, for example, our having to die and go to heaven, when I feel that heaven and hell are right here.

"I did not feel that I had resolved many issues with my mother prior to her death. Buddhism taught me not to regret my mother's death and not to live in the past or regret things that have already been done. So many times, you go through life feeling guilty about things. I didn't have that wisdom then and I felt uneasy about it for a very long time. But I don't feel that way now."

Gia was upset when attending the Christian Church she had gone to for many years. "I thought that many people in the Church seemed unhappy. Others, when in church, went through the motions and then, when they went out, put everything on ice until they attended again. It didn't seem that the people were really part of the community and trying to help others find happiness. So, for me, it left a lot to be desired.

"To me, Buddhism is daily life. We go out among the people and try to reach everybody, especially those who are in total despair. We reach out and touch those who are in pain and are really struggling to turn their lives around so that they'd be happy. We go out and chant for world peace."

Joan Urbas doesn't think of her mother as dead. In fact she felt very comforted after her mother's "death"—her mother was no longer in pain. "My mother and I both believed in reincarnation. Years ago, a friend of mine introduced me to the works of Edgar Cayce. I was so moved by it, I shared it with Mother. It began a common interest that the two of us shared from that time on for a period of about thirty years.

"We both felt that it didn't make sense that some people would have a life experience of two months, two years, or a hundred years, and be judged according to what had transpired in that period—short or long. We thought the idea of Karma, which was that we needed to experience many different settings which couldn't possibly occur in one lifetime, to round out our life experience, our personality, made so much more sense.

"I knew that my mother and I were on the same wavelength when it came to the idea of our reincarnations. It made us both feel very positive about our seeing each other again in the future."

Paul Vento thinks there is an afterlife. This has helped him accept his father's death. "Sometimes, for example, I go to a place in which I've never been in my life. Yet I feel I have been there before. This has happened to me a few times. For example, when I ran routes in New Jersey, there was one town especially which I felt I'd been to before, but in reality I had never been there.

"So maybe I was there in another life. Or maybe I will see my father again in a different life. I don't believe we're going to come back as a dog or cat or some other form of life, but I feel certain there is an afterlife. What we don't know about, we shouldn't be too doubtful about."

Patricia Tremont believes in a "great architect" but not in a specific religion. She observes certain days of prayer and lights a candle for her mother in her own home. "I don't have to be in a church to light a candle. But sometimes if I pass a church or synagogue that is open I will go in and say a prayer. I live in a big city and I can take my pick of houses of worship on any given day.

"I can't say I believe in any one religion, but it does comfort me to know that there is a place where I can say a prayer for my mother when I want to. I believe strongly that religion should be under one umbrella—that of humanity. You hear about so many wars, all in the name of religion, and you see factions among the same religion having disagreements. I just wish all people would be peaceful and able to pray as they please."

Patricia also recalls hearing that "the wisest caterpillar does not know that it will turn into a butterfly, yet it does." She believes that energy does not die. "Many scientists say energy doesn't die. If so, we possibly shed our physical overcoat, meaning our body, but our energies move on to a different state of existence. I don't say it's the same type of energy, but just take a look at what happens when a blade of grass pushes its way through a concrete sidewalk. We may not know where that energy comes from, just as we may not know where the energies we generate go after our body dies.

"I think it is a lot easier to believe that your energy doesn't die than to have morbid thoughts that once your physical body is gone, there is nothing left of you. I can feel my mother's presence, and it pleases me to think her energy lives on."

Patricia recalls hearing a talk by the late Olga Worrall, a highly respected healer. "She had very, very strong beliefs about human survival beyond the grave and not only felt the knowledge would encourage and comfort the bereaved, but that it would offer meaning and purpose to those who live. She stressed that no matter what the cause of death might be, no matter what your religious beliefs might be, the spirit lives on and no soul is ever lost.

"Mrs. Worrall explained that we are here for a brief spell," said Patricia, "that we begin our existence here, and then in fifty, sixty, seventy, eighty, or maybe a hundred years, we are ready to go into the higher life, which is an octave higher. She said the keys on a piano are divided into octaves, and you may go from one octave to the other as you move along the keyboard. But it is still one piano."

"As in the piano, life is lived in one universe, but in different octaves, she explained. Then, when we go to the next dimension, Olga said, we leave physical things behind because we're departing from a physical world. She was very explicit in her belief that God does not create to destroy and those whom we love will continue to be with us when we join each other."

This thought gives Patricia comfort. "To believe that my mother's spirit lives on has made it a lot easier to accept her death."

Sandra Ames is saddened by the idea that many people cannot derive comfort from their religion. "In my own family, some members attended an Orthodox synagogue and others a Reform temple. Nevertheless, we all gathered together in family celebrations, such as Hanukkah or Passover. These holidays were traditional just as the sitting of Shiva for my mother after she died was a part of our background, our culture.

"I feel sad that so many people look down their noses at religious 'trappings.' Time and time again I have heard people who are not Jewish say, 'Jews tend to deny their religion,' and I point out that this happens in many religions, but that many others warmly embrace their religion in all quarters of the world among all types of people.

"One thing that really disturbs me is to hear a survivor say, after a death, 'Why did God take her or him?' In my opinion, God doesn't 'take'—death just happens and it isn't that God takes an individual as punishment or because He loves no person more, or less, than the other. Dying is part of living I've come to accept, and I was glad that I had my rabbi to talk to and a synagogue to go to where I could say Yiskor (a remembrance prayer) for my mother at the high holiday days. Lighting a Yohrzite (memorial) candle on the anniversary of my mother's death was also comforting. Rituals that we are brought up with are the rock that supports us in time of adversity, and certainly after the loss of a parent."

Regardless of a person's religious beliefs, one important fact stands out: Faith is a powerful force in helping people recover their balance, peace of mind, and hope. Many people feel that the power of a simple faith can be more important than all the medical or psychological knowledge known to humankind.

❧ CHAPTER 12

Coping with the Surviving Parent

Loneliness is one of the saddest feelings that a surviving parent has to contend with. It is also a problem that often affects the bereaved son or daughter.

Earl Daniels shares with us the impact of his mother's loneliness on his life: "My father and mother lived nearby and I used to go there frequently to visit. Now that my father has gone, my mother feels offended if I don't make it over there every day. I don't have any brothers or sisters, but I often think how great it would be to have a brother or sister to help with my mother. Let's say I had a married sister with a nice home in the suburbs and children. Then my mother could go and visit her, be with her grandchildren. It would be a place my mother could go to and stay for a little while. But she is confined to the house because of her physical condition, and can't go out unless she has someone to accompany her.

"Another part of the problem is that while my father was ill, I had to take him here and take him there, and sometimes I'd be at my parents' house three times a day. I think my mother felt I would continue this afterward. But, for both our sakes, I had to be there less. Not a separation; I still go there often, and I've seen to it she is taken care of. But I have to break away a little so she won't think of me

155

as a substitute for my father. I've tried to take care
of my mother without getting totally swept into it
myself."

Psychotherapist Athena Drewes tells of some of
the issues bereaved adult children encounter with a
surviving parent. "When the surviving parent is
healthy, self-sufficient, and financially secure, the
death of a spouse is not as devastating. New relationships and bonds can emerge, with both the surviving parent and the surviving child having
weathered through a rough experience together and
growing closer as a result. They each realize time is
of the essence and use the remaining time to enjoy
life and each other and their families.

"However, the complications come in when the
surviving parent is physically ill, with either a pro-
gressive disease or chronic ill health. Then the surviving parent complicates the grief process for the
children. Rather than be able to go through the grief
stages, which includes anger, the child is thrust into
the role of taking care of a dependent parent and the
anger is fanned. The pain of loss is kept fresh by
watching the deterioration of the next parent and
wondering how much time is left. The wishing and
fantasizing for the second parent's death adds a burden to the already unresolved grief and guilt over the
first parent's death."

In her own situation, Athena believes the relationship with her mother has improved. She tells of the
events that led to this relationship. "I know for myself it was difficult dealing with my father's death.
The hardest part was watching his steady physical
decline from diabetes after he had a leg amputated.
Over three years his health and spirit deteriorated.
Trips in and out of the hospital, new complications,
new medical treatments that added to his pain. At

times wishing for his death, while feeling guilty for my anger at him. The burden of his care and my mother's was complicated by my older brothers living in Florida. They did not share in the emotional pain or responsibility and could not offer me any support. My father's pain limited my chance to have talks with him about things left unfinished. As a result, he died before my issues could be sorted out.

"Part of my grief was hindered by my mother's wishing not to think of any negative things about my father, as though not to speak ill of the dead. But I needed to ventilate my anger—anger over his death and the things left unresolved about him. Her not wanting to hear them, or even contradicting them by making him out to be greater than he was, made my work even harder.

"Then the burden of taking care of my mother began. My husband and I urged her not to make any moves for at least three years so as to give her time to think about what she wanted. But soon having been mugged in her apartment building led to her moving into an addition to our house. We added a four-room apartment which allowed for her to have her privacy and still be self-sufficient. But, again, my brothers do not share in the responsibility nor do we talk about my anger about this.

"It took me about two years after my father's death to really work through my grief and mourning. The one thing my father's death did was to help me re-evaluate funerals. I was against the 'show' they had become. But once having to go through the process I found them helpful. It gave me a chance to get in touch with the reality of his death, of the sadness I felt, to be surrounded and immersed in the event. And then it was over and I could begin to piece the aftermath of my life together. Without the funeral and wake, I would have been cheated of the chance to say good-bye and let go.

"Another thing it did for me was to requestion my belief in survival. Life suddenly became complicated. Everything became turned around and I had to sort through what *did* I believe about life, living, and death. It allowed me to realize I could not always be in control. Some things were beyond that. And it freed me to enjoy the present, to make the most of it, live each day to the fullest and not to keep putting off things to the future that may never come.

"Because of this, my relationship with my mother improved. We try not to let time go by without resolving our conflicts so that we can enjoy each other before she dies. She had to rely on me and we've had to make the relationship work, living under the same physical structure. She not being able to drive, and living in the country with no public transportation, has made her dependent on me. We have also been brought closer by the birth of my two sons, Scott and Seth. The saddest part is that my father never had the chance to know them, but through them a part of him lives."

A problem that many bereaved sons and daughters encounter after the death of a parent is the renewal of dating by the surviving parent. Beth Landau tells how she felt when her mother began to see another man. "My mother is a widow now and she is dating a widower she met through friends at their pool club. I have mixed emotions about the possibility of her remarrying and selling the house. He has been good company for her and has helped her through rough times. She is very fond of this man but it is hard for me to accept the relationship. I'm glad that she is going out, that she is not sitting and staring into space or carrying on. She is not that kind of person. But I haven't brought myself to say, 'Okay, I'd like to have dinner with both of you to get to know him.'

It's my own thing. For example, I didn't see her at Thanksgiving because I didn't want to have dinner with him. So I went to my best friend's home in New Jersey.

"I have nothing personal against him. He's a lovely person, and I've heard only good things about him. I met him briefly at the pool club, but only because he is a member. But I didn't want to spend a long period of time with him. I don't blame him for my father's death, but it's hard to see my mother with another man. After a year, then maybe okay. Perhaps I will soften up, but it will always be tough."

Beth also understands that there is a fine line between wanting a surviving parent to be happy and not being selfish. "You don't want to be selfish and you want your mother to be happy. Also, you don't want the surviving parent to be a drain and say, 'Well, you have a week's vacation. Spend it with me.' That would be selfish of the parent. But my mother is not like that. So I am happy for her that she is not drowning in her sorrows. It doesn't take her feelings away from my father."

In contrast to Beth's outgoing mother, Hilary Friedman found it difficult to cope with her mother's feelings of guilt. After Hilary's father died, she had many clashes with her mother. "I guess the main thing was that my mother was trying to deal with her bereavement. She was going through the 'I should have . . . I could have . . . If only . . . I meant to . . .' My mother had many regrets. And she was resentful of being left alone—in the sense that my father was not with her. My mother needed someone to lean on and since both she and I were grieving, neither of us could lean on the other because we were too sore to be leaned on. So that was an additional problem.

"Even when you don't mean to hurt another, you

do because the wound is too raw, too tender. The issue with my mother is still unresolved. The problem is that I have no more desire to live by myself than she has a desire to live by herself. Yet we are literally living apart in the same house, each of us grieving in her own way."

After his mother died in a drowning accident, Tom Andrews had to come to terms about his feelings toward his surviving parent. His parents had been separated, and Tom could not forgive his father for having left his mother. He blamed his father for her death. If they had not parted, Tom thought, his mother would have never met the man with whom she went on the boat and so she would never have drowned. Prior to meeting the new man in her life, who loved sailing, his mother had never even been on a boat.

Tom, who was bitter, had no wish to see his father, but his two sisters who lived in another state felt differently. "At the time my parents split, both my sisters were sympathetic toward my father. They were always closer to him than I was. Sometimes it happens that way between fathers and daughters. But I felt he had walked out on my mother. She was left alone and unhappy. All their friends were couples and she no longer felt comfortable with them. She said she felt like a 'fifth wheel.'" Tom's father had met another woman he was interested in and had moved in with her. When the news of his mother's death came, Tom called his younger sister, and told her he would not get in touch with their father.

At the funeral, Tom sat with his wife and sisters. He insisted that his father sit in a separate section. "Although I have dealt with my anger at my mother for going on the boat, I still cannot forgive my father. Maybe one day, but I don't see it."

• • •

Lisa Strahs-Lorenc tells of the physical problems she and her mother encountered after her father died of a sudden heart attack. "Sometimes I would hear my heart pounding and that kind of thing, but it happened to my mother more than to me. With every little thing, she thought she was having a heart attack. It was a big help when I got her to go back to her job. Before that, I was going to her house every day—a drive of almost an hour—because I didn't want her to be alone. The first week, I stayed there, but then I realized that I couldn't take the place of my father.

"Thank goodness she had friends who really stood by her. None of them have left her, as some couples do. In addition, she went to a widow's group at my urging. So now I see her about once a week, and since the baby arrived, she wishes that it would be more. So we will probably end up moving closer. In fact, we came home back in 1979 from Massachusetts because I wanted to be close to my parents, a move I'm very glad we made because I would not have wanted to miss out on that time with my father."

Paul Vento was another bereaved child who traveled a distance to see to his mother's needs after his father died. "We had problems then because of the distance, but we did manage to see her often and we spoke to her every week. My mother was still working at the time, and she had friends. She also loves to sew, and she made all her own clothes, in addition to things for us and our children. When she retired she took up painting and did wonders with roses in her pictures. She also began singing at the senior citizens' group she had joined, and she was very good. Although we're proud of everything she has done, we realize that she's alone. Her apartment rental didn't work out well. Because there were so many problems with that, we're going to have to get a bigger house. Anyway, I want to take care of my mother and not have to worry about her."

Paul comments on his mother's wish to be left alone for New Year's Eve. "We celebrate many holidays with my mother, but she says that New Year's Eve is hers alone. She had always celebrated that holiday with my father and she kind of wants to feel that she's with him, I guess. But we call her and wish her a Happy New Year and want her to know we are still remembering her on that day."

After his father's death, Eddie Gintz became concerned about his mother. As the years progressed, she became increasingly depressed. It had not been her nature to be less than vivacious. "She drove a car until she was eighty-three, worked on a kibbutz in Israel every summer, and was very active with friends and various organizations. She was admired by all who knew her for her tremendous energy and fighting spirit. She was in good health, but many of her friends at the same age level were beginning to fail. Some had died. Psychologically, this was destroying her. Mom felt that if her friends were in failing health and dying, then it wouldn't be long before she would suffer a similar fate."

Eddie took steps to bolster his mother's depression. "I would go over and play chess with her, or take her out to a movie. But it preyed on her mind that she was losing all her friends either because of illness or death. The depression factor was tremendous. I had never seen her so bad. So I decided to buy a condominium in Florida near where my sister lived. My mother went to live there and she loved it. I figure it added ten years to her life. I wanted to do things for her while she was alive."

• • •

After Peggy Griffiths' father died, her mother continued to live in her house in Poughkeepsie. Peggy tells of the family's concern. "We all worried about her being up in that house. You know, things like: Is she eating? Or is she going to fall down the cellar steps or anything like that. Such things are always a worry when your parents reach their late seventies. So we got her to sell the house and rented a large apartment for her in New York City where she was very happy. She knew a lot of people and would go to the theater in the afternoons. There was a lovely garden attached to her building, and she enjoyed that. She found all kinds of ways of entertaining herself in addition to working at St. James Episcopal Church and carrying on her own activities. She was out every day. I had one sister, two brothers, and many friends and relatives, so my mother did not want for companionship. She was also very active in many things including the Ellis Island Relief work to help the needy, the Red Cross and the Goodwill."

Peggy explains her mother's philosophy about not wanting her daughters to depend too much on her as the only remaining parent. "My mother had wanted to work part-time but a mild heart attack put the kibosch on that. Every summer thereafter she visited her family in England and there she would spend May, June, July, and August, returning home in September. It added variety to her life and made my sister and me less dependent on our mother. She did not want us leaning heavily on her as the one surviving parent. I thought that was very intelligent."

Margaret McAllister was concerned about her mother's health after her father died. "My mother started to have physical signs of his illness. She became very congested and would say, 'Now I know how your father felt. I feel like I can't breathe.' In the next few months, she was worried that she was going to die the same way he did.

"My mother had always been very strong, stronger than my father. She had more resolve. My father was more of a feeler—he *felt* things, while my mother was a thinker. So after his death she took on a lot of responsibility that was his before he died. Although she was very strong, she didn't realize how big a role he played in our lives. She told me she never realized how much she would miss him.

"My mother and I have always had a good relationship, but I think it has undergone a subtle change because I have become a stronger person. Now I am a grown woman and we look at each other on a different level. If people were to observe us and didn't know we were mother and daughter, they would believe we were two women who were very good friends. We have a great deal of respect for each other and for one another's achievements in life. When you are young you grow up thinking that you will never do things the way your parents did them. But now I think, 'I hope I can do them as well as they did.' "

Norman James was concerned about his mother's depression after his father's death. "She became a recluse. She felt as if the world had come to an end, for she and my father had been very close. My mother was also concerned about money—my father's illness had depleted most of their savings, and this was the money they had wanted to leave to their grandchildren. She no longer wanted to see any of their old friends with the exception of one person who had been close to them. She told me that she had tried to go along with other couples for a while, but that the friendships were not the same as they had been when my father was alive. Furthermore, she wasn't ready to start rebuilding a life with new people, so she stayed home most of the time.

"She didn't even want to come to our house for Thanksgiving. We insisted, but she didn't want any celebrations. Even two years after my father's death, she doesn't want Christmas presents, and she just sends envelopes with some money in it for the kids. Her close friend will be moving to Florida soon and that won't help matters because she is the only one my mother really talks to."

Norman began to resent his mother's refusal to resume a normal life. "Because she wouldn't go out anywhere or go to see anyone, I felt responsible. I felt she needed me and so I began to try to fill the void. I would go over there nights after work and stay a few hours. This made my wife angry because she felt this wasn't fair to our life. I was really torn, for I felt my mother was so alone. But as the months went on, it was increasingly difficult to continue going to my mother's with any great frequency. My job changed and I had to work later hours. This didn't give me much time other than catching a late train home. Since I could no longer see my mother during the week, I felt I owed it to her to see her weekends.

"The strain between my wife and me became very rough on both of us. We seemed to be fighting so much of the time, usually about my time away from home with my mother. My wife felt cheated of time with me and also felt that my mother was very selfish not to recognize our need to have more time together. Frankly, I was beginning to feel the same way, and became annoyed each time I headed toward my mother's house. When I was with my mother, I was angry that she couldn't see the inconvenience and hardship it was to me to come there on the weekends. When I left her, I felt tired and resentful.

"My anger kept increasing and one day I just exploded—at the wrong person. A friend of mine suggested I talk to a counselor. I used to think that going for help was a sign of weakness, but it was soon clear to me that it was a lifeline for me."

Norman let his mother understand his resentment at her not finding ways to reach out to try to rejoin the world. "I explained that it was hurting both of us. Finally, I convinced her that other women often felt as she did and that many surviving spouses attended a nearby group for widows. I was astounded when she agreed to go, but I was even more astonished at the effect this group had on my mother. It was wonderful to see the change in her. Where formerly she had never been able to get dressed or to go out for a holiday, now she was dressing nicely again, and while I wouldn't say she is exactly eager for holidays, she doesn't seem to begrudge them to others.

"She is now facing up to her grief and is again part of the human race. As soon as she met other women who felt as she did, and who were experiencing the same kind of loneliness and fears, she began to make contact with the outside world. Several of the women call her, and they play bridge together once a week. I never thought I would see the day that my mother would have guests in her home again. I can't tell you how much that group has helped her, and me, too. Where I previously felt obligated to see her every week, it was now established that I did not have to be there every weekend as a penance. I visit her now because I enjoy being with her, and, because it doesn't demand every free moment of my time, I no longer resent it. If on some weekends I can't make it, I don't feel guilty. I know that when I can manage to be with my mother, I'll do it, but not at the cost of my marriage and time with my family."

One of the major problems faced by bereaved adult children is how to find help for a surviving parent. Support groups are often an excellent route. One such mutual-help program, Widow To Widow, is the subject of a book with the same title by Dr. Phyllis R. Silverman, whose views are given below. Surviving sons and daughters will find them valuable in determining how to help a widowed mother, and thereby helping one's own situation in dealing with the surviving parent.

Dr. Silverman believes mutual-help groups create an environment that minimizes barriers between people. Such an environment, she holds, confirms people's need for each other and their ability to use their experience on each other's behalf. She questions the role of professionals in helping the bereaved widow and is concerned that many professionals may not be qualified to help because, as she says, "The plight of the bereaved is heightened by the death-denying attitudes prevalent in American society. Grievers are expected to be circumspect and act . . . as if nothing has happened. Professionals emphasize 'recovery'—and often look for it in six months."

Dr. Silverman challenges those who classify bereavement as an illness that requires intervention by professionals: "To seek a cure for one's responses to an irretrievable and real loss—the end of life for a person one had loved and still loves—seems inconsistent with the nature of the event. Defined as a natural reaction to death, an inevitable human experience with which everyone must cope, grief would be expected to bring stress and pain, which in turn would be seen as legitimate and appropriate." Dr. Silverman initiated a widow-to-widow project which was carried out for six years by the Harvard Medical School. In speaking to widows and caregivers, she determined that the widow's needs are not greatest at the time of the death or immediately thereafter, but months later when friends and family have returned to their own lives.

"For some widows, two or three years later may be the best time to offer assistance, new opportunities for friendship, and a chance to expand the social network," Dr. Silverman states. She gives no timetables, recognizing that there are too many variables, both within and outside the griever, to make any timetable acceptable. She observes that although mental-health professionals can answer some of the widow's needs, mutual help is possibly the best solution.

Dr. Silverman's conclusions support the idea that the most effective helper for a widow is another widow, one who can say, 'Yes, I understand. I have been there.' Silverman's concern is whether professionals are able to respond to emergencies, such as those occurring on weekends—an area where, on the other hand, mutual-help interveners respond immediately. Another concern she expresses is whether a professional may reinforce the widow's sense of inadequacy and defectiveness at the very time she needs to have her sense of self and independence reinforced.

"Most widowed people need a variety of help. Initially one to one may be most meaningful; later on, people may find group discussions useful. Many people enjoy socializing with friends they may have met in these groups," says Dr. Silverman.

Efforts to help widowers are the focus of a book, *Men Alone*, by Scott Campbell with Phyllis Silverman.

Dr. David Meagher, coauthor with R. D. Shapiro of *Death: The Experience*, explains his view on a surviving parent making a new life. "When I work with people who are concerned about continuing on, I try to get them to realize the reward of making a new life, the ability to share again, the personal satisfaction that comes from sharing. I also try to make them see how great it is to accept and be accepted by others. When I can get them to go back into their lives and remember how good it felt to have fulfilling relationships and to do things, and to be able to love, they lose some of the fear of doing such things."

Anne Rosberger, a social worker who with her psychiatrist husband, Dr. Henry Rosberger, works with people trying to cope with bereavement, notes that another compounding factor is that someone who is retired or who has been a homemaker for most of his/her life, has more time to dwell on a loss. When couples have been married for many years, Mrs. Rosberger points out, there is no one with whom the surviving parent can share confidences, no one to show physical or emotional frailties.

"We see this very often, too, in high-ranking executives who have lost wives after long marriages— the loneliness of command, the increasing isolation, ill health, self-doubt," says Rosberger. "It is not uncommon for a strong man to become despondent at the loss of a wife on whom he had depended for emotional support for many years. Such men are generally reluctant to seek professional help, but when they do, the results are often positive." Mrs. Rosberger told of a corporate vice-president in his sixties. "The man had been away on a business trip at the time of his wife's death and his guilt was great. He was trying to use the same bravado he used in business to deal with his feelings, and of course, it wasn't working," she said. "He had loved his wife and had always seen her as dependent on him. Then, as he experienced her loss, he realized how much he had relied upon her. Once he understood that it was okay not to be 'Mr. Macho' he was able to deal with his feelings of guilt and of remorse."

Bereaved adult children are often concerned about the physical condition as well as the mental state of their surviving parent. And with good reason. Widowers in general represent a high-risk group. A twelve-year study by Johns Hopkins University researchers of more than 4,000 widowed men and women revealed that men were much more likely to die within several years after the death of a spouse than are people of the same age whose spouses are alive. One theory is that men do not expect to outlive their wives and so are psychologically ill-prepared to cope with the death. Another theory holds that a woman feels at ease in her home, whereas a man may feel disoriented. Yet another idea suggests that since men have been used to hiding their feelings, they often do not allow themselves to go through the necessary grieving process. Often a surviving parent, be it father or mother, will suffer from a broken heart—or from sheer loneliness in missing the spouse. In other instances, a parent who has suffered from a physical illness may be especially vulnerable to the death of a spouse.

In the case of a murder or suicide of a spouse, there are other issues to deal with by the surviving mate as well as the surviving child. Carol Tyler tells of the suicide of her father: "My dad was used to holding down a job. He had worked all his life and suddenly he was told he had to retire. He was home all day and didn't know what to do with himself. Now he and my mother were together twenty-four hours a day, and my mother couldn't get used to it. 'He is always underfoot,' she would say. 'I wish he would play golf or find some buddies to be with during the day.' Then he became morose and despondent. He had never had any real hobbies, and he felt useless with no job. Although his health began to decline, we never had any indication that he would kill himself. We knew he was depressed but never in a million years did we think he would take his life.

"It was horrible. Not only the shock of losing him, but the imprint it left on all of us. We felt so guilty. It was as if everyone was pointing a finger at us. When my own guilt became really severe, I knew I had to get help. I needed to sort out the feelings of anger and guilt. I was especially angry at my mother for picking on him so much. In many ways, I feel she was responsible, that she drove him to it and our relationship is now very strained. I can't stand being in a room with her alone."

Carol was stunned when she received word that her father had committed suicide. She couldn't believe it. "Other than a general lethargy, there were no signs, no indication that he had planned to do this. At the funeral, my brother and I sat there while all of our relatives went to offer my mother comfort. A couple of them hugged me and quickly moved on to my mother. No one made any motion to comfort my brother other than to squeeze his shoulder. No one seemed to feel that we were in need of solace. At the cemetery, I could hardly walk to the plot. My husband and my best friend had to hold me up, but no one else came over to me as we walked away. Everyone hovered over my mother. I don't know why I resented this so much. Perhaps I felt my mother should have seen this coming, or found a way to prevent it. Somehow I felt that I was grieving more than she was."

When Carol returned to her mother's home after the funeral, she was unable to talk to anyone. "I felt as if my tongue was made of cotton. I just couldn't speak. I don't know whether I wanted to talk or not, but I do know that I was simply unable to utter a sound. I think I was moaning, but I'm sure that if I had opened my mouth, I would have screamed. I remember I didn't want to go into the house. I wanted to stay in the car, but my husband gently insisted we had to go into the house. I guess I was fighting going into a home that my father would no longer be in and where my mother still was."

Later, when Carol went back to work, her coworkers looked away and didn't know what to say. "It was bad enough to know that person's father or someone else in the family had died a normal death, but when it's a suicide, no one knows what to say to you. So they would ask me, 'How is your mother doing?' Lunch hour was terrible for me. I used to sit with a crowd and yak it up. But after the first day back, I gave up having lunch with others. Believe it or not, I ate my sandwich in the ladies' room just to avoid facing anyone or to chance running into them in the local restaurants."

What Carol resented most was the advice of family friends or relatives who would say to her, "You have to be strong for your mother." Carol was enraged. "I don't have to be strong for anyone but me!" Secretly, she wished she could have been strong for her father. "I kept thinking maybe there was something I could have done. Could I have relieved him of some burden that was too heavy? Was there anything he would have wanted to tell me if I had been there more often? I used to wish we had more time together, and now there will never be more time together. I feel like screaming because I can't tell him all the things I want to. I just can't understand why he did it and why he didn't talk to us first or something. But I feel my mother should have been able to see this coming. She was there."

In this instance, the relationship with the surviving parent was put to the test after the death of one parent by suicide. Adult children who feel that they, too, were in some way responsible for not preventing the death, seek explanations. Dr. Pamela Cantor, a clinical psychologist and professor at Boston University, is also on the board of directors of The American Association of Suicidology. She states that suicide is a sign of depression that can afflict anyone. Depression is not particular in picking a target—it strikes rich and poor alike.

Roslyn Marcus, Bereavement Director of Transition Bereavement Program in Centerport, New York, explains that suicide survivorship is different from survival after other losses. "The social stigma and the accompanying feelings of powerlessness can cause the survivors to blame themselves for not being able to prevent the death. The sharing of these feelings with a trained professional can help not only the individual but the family to gain insight and understanding. Bereavement counseling can help explore the feelings of shock, anger, guilt, and depression and help move through the isolation that often accompanies this loss. With time and understanding, counseling can help surviving sons and daughters, as well as the surviving parent, explore the questions and help relieve the pain and anguish that remains after the death of a loved one."

☙ CHAPTER 13

A Nursing Home Trauma

For some reason, we tend to think that when we are adults we will be able to cope with "adult matters". And, certainly, losing a parent is an adult matter. Or, is it?

No matter what age we are when a parent dies, be it in our thirties, forties, fifties, or sixties, we are still the child who has lost our parent—and we experience the emotions of a child whose parent has died.

One such adult child—who is both a mother and grandmother herself—shares with us some of the memories of her parents. She also shares some of the trauma and devastation she experienced when her father died suddenly at age 84 and, later, when her mother was placed in a nursing home.

Gladys Halpern Schnitzer never deluded herself that her parents could live forever. To the contrary, even when she was very young she was dreading the day when she would have to face their demise. "I was so close to both of my parents. I always said that when the time came for my parents to go, I would not take it very well, and that I would probably have a breakdown.

Taking a walk down memory lane, Gladys describes what it was like to have the kind of mother and father that every child dreams of having. "My

174

father was such a gentleman, in the old-world sense of the word. Very soft spoken, gentle, and very handsome with a little moustache. He was so dapper, he looked like an actor. Everybody adored him. He was generous and extremely kind—to everyone. He was also very intelligent. My father always read two or three newspapers every day and was up on what was happening in the world. I could sit with him for long periods of time and discuss very many things.

"I was the apple of his eye and I luxuriated in the warmth of that caring person who was always there for me. And, he was so thoughtful of others. I remember once when I was about 10, a friend of mine was with me when I asked my Dad for some spending money. He reached into his pocket and gave me a dollar. Then, he smiled, turned to my friend, and gave her a dollar too. He was so special.

"My mom was very special too. She was always looking after our needs, our clothes, our health, making sure we ate right. She taught me to be a good homemaker and I later had a lot in common with my mother on different levels. I spoke to her every day when I was raising my children about how they were. She imbued in us the basic skills and ideals that would make us good parents. My father and my mother both made us better people, I think. The woman who later took care of them said, 'To have had parents like your parents is the greatest legacy anyone could have.'"

Gladys' father and mother were living in an adult center when her father contracted pneumonia and died at age 84. Although Gladys was expecting it to happen, it was a shock when a call came in the early morning hours telling her that her father had died. Her pain was and still is severe. "I have a lot of friends who have lost parents, but none of them seem to have gone through it as painfully as I did. My husband lost his parents. My parents lost their parents, but I don't remember seeing this kind of pain. I know it's part of life and that you are supposed to be able to to move on, but I can't seem to get past this terrible feeling of loss. I do think, however, that my father really felt he had lived long enough. He was starting to lose it mentally and that was bothering him.

"Knowing him, he didn't want to cause any discomfort to the family. So I think he just let go. It was so much like him—to go fast, without a lot of fuss."

After her father's death, financial considerations required placing Gladys' mother in a skilled nursing home. This took a toll on Gladys in many ways. In attempting to care for her mother, the role reversal was acute and Gladys was shattered at the thought that perhaps she was not doing the best thing for her surviving parent. She tells what it felt like when she went to see the nursing facility for the first time.

"My brother, Herb, went with me. The social worker showed us the first two floors of the nursing home. They looked okay. I wasn't happy about the idea of her being there, but I realized we didn't have too many options open to us. The only alternative would have been for me to stop working to stay home and care for my mother, but that wasn't feasible. So it was agreed this would be the next best thing. We then had to wait for an opening at the nursing home. When they called advising they had a bed for my mother and told me to bring her in, I didn't want to ask anyone to go with me because I knew everyone was so busy and I didn't want to impose. And, in my mind, I was trying to calm myself, telling myself that it wasn't going to be very traumatic, that I would just go there and do what I had to do. I was trying to psyche myself up not to become too emotional and just to do it matter-of-factly."

Realizing what a huge task it would be to get all

of her mother's clothes packed and move her physically to the nursing home, Gladys decided to call her cousin. "She's like a daughter to my parents and is my father's niece. She and her husband both came to help me pack and take my mother to the nursing home, but it was very hard on them too. I saw that."

Gladys describes that day in June. "It was a very humid, hot 98-degree day in early summer. We were dragging four suitcases with us containing my mother's clothes for every season. When we got to the nursing home, things didn't get off to a good start. They told me that all of her clothing had to be labelled, which was not told to us beforehand—otherwise we would have done it leisurely in advance. And now, we had to stop and label every undergarment, every gown, every sweater, every piece of clothing she owned, or it would be stolen. So we were given magic markers and started scribbling her name on everything. Afterwards, they took us up to the third floor—not the first or second floor they had shown us earlier. The third floor was an absolute snake pit and I was literally in shock."

Unprepared for the condition of the patients she encountered, Gladys recoiled at what she saw. "I had never seen anything like it. All of these people were either sitting in wheelchairs or lying on stretchers in the halls. And they were crying out, 'Help me; move me; take me out of here; are you my daughter?' I saw this scene and I broke down. I turned to my cousins and shook my head, 'I can't leave my mother here. What should I do? I just can't leave her here. I'm taking her back with me.' My cousins were also shaken. They saw the torture I was going through, but they were rendered speechless."

In the middle of Gladys' quandary, she heard a voice call out, "Doris! Doris Halpern—is that you?" "I looked up and a tiny woman, a nurse's aide, was speaking. I asked her, 'How do you know my mother?' She answered, 'I know her from the adult home when I used to work there. Everyone loved Doris, she was everybody's favorite, such a wonderful lady, so good-natured. She never had an unkind word for anybody.'"

Although this woman seemed to know a great deal about her mother, Gladys could not contain her anguish. "It was the lowest point of my life seeing my mother in those surroundings. The woman was sympathetic to what was happening to me, and tried to make things easier. She confided, 'I have a lady here that I take care of as a private companion. I have a friend who may be available to do the same thing for your mother, and I know they would love each other. If you like, I'll speak to her and ask her to meet you tomorrow morning here.' It was the first ray of hope I saw in struggling through this dark tunnel. I left on the note that maybe there was a way—if I could leave my mother in loving hands. But I was very shaken by the traumatic events of the day, and was far from being convinced that I was doing the right thing."

Gladys returned to her place of business that afternoon. Overcome with remorse about her mother, she was unprepared for a wrenching physical reaction. "When I got back to the office, it was 5 p.m. Everyone had just left except one woman, Helen, who is my assistant. I came in, went right into my office and sat down. Helen followed me and asked, 'Are you alright? Herb has been trying to reach you all day.' I nodded and said, 'I just need to be alone for a few minutes and then I'll call him.' I took a few breaths and then dialed Herb, who was upstate. He was very concerned. 'I've been so worried. I didn't hear from you all day.' I couldn't respond. The only thing I could say was, 'I did something so terrible today. I can't talk to you right now.'" I hung up the phone and I began to throw up.

"Herb got so nervous at how I sounded, he called Helen back and suggested I be taken to the hospital. I said, 'I don't want to go to the hospital. It's just that I did something so awful leaving my mother in that place, that I'm sick to my stomach over it.' I couldn't stop throwing up—all over the walls, the desk, everything. Helen called my husband, who was 50 miles away, and he came. He was very supportive. Without him, I probably would have landed in the hospital. I had to take a tranquilizer, I was so upset."

After a while, the tranquilizer helped, and Gladys managed to get through the night until the next morning, when she met the nurse's aide. Happily, the meeting with her mother's prospective companion went well. "The woman fell in love with my mother. I suppose her friend had also given her some background of how she knew Mom at the adult home. So, it helped make my decision knowing there would be two people there who cared about my mother and what happened to her. Another saving grace is that the nursing home is right on the ocean and in a very beautiful setting. From the outside, it looks like a country club. But once inside, it is a different story. I had asked about changing my mother to a different floor, but was told it was not possible because of her condition. She had been diagnosed three years ago as having Alzheimer's Disease, but I really think it's just senility."

Many months have passed since Gladys' mother first arrived at the nursing home. During those months, Gladys has been able to make certain observations about her mother's astuteness and perception even at the age of 88. "My mom has a tremendous sense of humor. But, apart from that, she is really so smart. And she is always doing or saying things to make other people feel good, to make certain that she never hurts anyone's feelings—ever. For example, one day, I happened to ask if she knew what day of the week it was. Sometimes when she hears questions that require her to stop and think a minute, she gets a little annoyed at herself for not remembering. But her true personality wins out, as it did on this occasion, and she responded to my question with, 'Well, it's the best day of the week because you're here.'

"My sister lives 1500 miles away. My mother will often ask for her, 'Where's Rozie?' I explain that Rozie lives in Florida and can't be here right now, but that I am here. When I ask her if she knows who I am, she will pause and look at me quizically. And I say to her, 'Mom, you gave me a happy name. You always told me it was a happy name. It starts with . . . ' And then she will remember 'glad' and she will smile and say, 'Of course! You're Gladys and glad is such a happy name.' So, that's a special little thing between us. On other days when she cannot remember 'glad' she will say, 'What's the difference what your name is? You're the perfect one, because you are here.' "

Gladys tells of the compassion her mother shows. "One night, something she said really threw me because it required a lot of thought on her part. She said, 'I think it's time for me to go upstairs.' I asked if she was getting tired and she said, 'I'm not. You know I never get tired, but sometimes you have to be aware that your company is getting tired and that's why I am going to go up now.' I smiled and said to her, 'Ma, I can't believe how smart you are.' At different times, I remind her that she raised five children, that she has 12 grandchildren and five great-grandchildren. Every once in a while, she will say, 'So, where are they? Why don't they come to visit me?' And then, she will catch herself and say, 'Oh, I know they are all so busy. It's okay.' Then I sometimes say, 'Well, you did a good job with your family. They are all very productive and everybody's working and keeping busy.' One night, she turned to me and said, 'Well, that's how it's supposed to be and even if they don't come, it's okay.' "

Gladys explains that her mother seems to be happy at the nursing home for the most part. "As heartbreaking as it is for me to see her there, I would say she enjoys the visits. We sit and sing and laugh. This is her reality. Every once in a while she will ask where Dad is and I will say he is taking a nap, and she will say, 'That's nice.' She hasn't realized he isn't here anymore. That is the best defense mechanism that nature could have given her to protect her from the reality."

Very recently, however, Gladys was taken aback by her mother's breakthrough into the true reality of her situation. "I came in one night and she was completely different. She was very serious and seemed very down, rather than her bright, bubbly self. Suddenly, she began to ask, 'What am I doing here? Who are all these old people? They're so sick. I don't belong here. What kind of place is this? Who put me here? How did I get here? And then she looked up and saw how distraught I was, as much as I tried to hide it and disguise my anguish. She quickly caught herself and said, 'Oh, it's not so bad,' and then she did something strange. I knew that she was completely aware of her surroundings, but she held my hand, and looked me right in the eyes and said, 'This is your time now. Make the most of it. Remember, it's an important time for you, and do what you have to do.' And then, after that she seemed to float back to the way she had been before. The reality was too harsh. I have to say that she's in a better place in her own mind. And, its better for us too because it's an easier visit. That was the only time she broke through the veil. And, I'm grateful for that because it's better to see her happy than unhappy."

Now, when Gladys leaves the nursing home, she

goes to visit her three grandchildren. "It's the oppo-
site end of the spectrum. I go from the nursing home
to my daughter's home, where she has these three
little dolls. It is the complete antithesis. If something
good can come out of something bad, I've learned to
treasure every moment of every day. I've learned to
express my feelings, because if I had suppressed
them, I'm sure it would have come out in other
ways."

CHAPTER 14

Sibling Conflicts

Family feuds can erupt after the death of a parent when siblings are left to cope with each other's feelings. Often, there are short fuses and tempers may flare, with adult children finding themselves reliving roles they had played earlier in family pecking orders. "A battle between siblings can also be a way of blocking out grief," says Dr. Roberta Temes. "Bereaved sons and daughters may let off steam to avoid dealing with their sense of abandonment and may prefer to be angry at a sibling who can retaliate rather than at a deceased parent."

Emily J. Marlin tells of issues encountered by brothers and sisters after the death of a parent: "You hear many horror stories about wills or struggles over which possessions go to whom. Old sibling rivalries may resurface, and those emotions are replayed after a parent dies. When fights and arguments take place, siblings generally move into the same roles in the family they held as children. They have disagreements like those they had as youngsters, and whatever jealous feelings they had in childhood emerge again. Even things with little monetary value can be the basis of intense squabbling. Hostilities are rekindled when old grievances enter the picture."

In order to protect confidentiality, the names of the adult children in this chapter are not given. And because some brothers and sisters may find ways to reopen lines of communication or reconcile their differences, that anonymity is offered to them.

Each person has his or her own calendar when it comes to grieving. Every family history has a different theme woven through it. Arguing may be the theme for some. In others, brothers and sisters may struggle to establish authority. After the death of a parent, the members of close-knit families become more cohesive, while the less loving may split. Whatever the theme of the family may have been, it will surface after the death of a parent. The family members will do what they are comfortable with.

The following experiences are shared with us by bereaved adult children who found themselves in the midst of sibling conflicts.

One daughter told of the tremendous hostility that resulted because she and her sister disagreed on the course of treatment for their terminally ill mother. "Rather than leave my mother in the hospital to die, I thought we should bring her home and hire a convalescent helper to stay with her. That way, we would be home in the morning before leaving for work and again at night. As a further help, my sister and I could rotate vacations. Neither of us was married or had other responsibilities, but because my sister was older she felt she had the right to make the final decision. Every time we had to come to an important choice about a problem—such as what house repairs were needed or where to take a vacation—my sister had the final say. It was always a matter of giving in to keep the peace; I hate arguments.

"After my mother died, I had serious pangs of guilt. I regretted not having stood up to my sister and made her agree to bring my mother home from the hospital. Our relationship has not been the same since then. In fact, my sister has become even more overbearing. After I come home from work, I stay in my room upstairs most of the time, and I try to have breakfast and dinner before she does, just to avoid scenes. It's all so different since my mother died. I guess it was she who held us together. Now we are just two strangers living in the same house."

Two brothers who had been rivals since childhood found themselves vying for their father's watch. It was not the material worth of the watch they fought over—only its ownership. "We were ready to do battle over that watch," said the elder son. "I know my father wanted me to have it. I was the oldest son and my father's father had given it to my dad as the oldest son. But my brother was livid. He insisted my father had never designated to whom that watch was to go and that he had just as much right to it as I did. My sister took the watch and said she was going to hold it until we simmered down."

When there is no will left by a parent, children are cautioned to wait a few weeks or months to let emotions cool before deciding who gets what. Therapists and counselors urge bereaved sons and daughters not to confuse objects as a substitute for the parent who owned them. After the death of his mother, one bereaved son broke off all relationships with his sister and her children. "My nieces and nephews were like vultures at my mother's home," he said. "I had bought the house for my mother and it never occurred to me that my sister would think the house was half hers.

"My mother had life-insurance policies with beneficiaries designated, but she hadn't made a will. When the time came for my sister and me to discuss the contents of the house, she and her children had already drawn lines. They brought boxes and put into them the things they wanted. It meant I would have had to sort through all of that stuff to see if there was anything I would have liked to keep. It was ludicrous. Then when my sister asked me if I wanted to sell the house, I indicated that I did. But I was really shocked when she asked me what price I thought 'we' could get. I explained to her that Mom had always understood I bought the house for her, but that it would revert to me. My sister and I fought about this and many other things. Now I won't speak to her. I think their conduct was unconscionable. I don't think we will ever get back together again as a family."

Although a parent's death can create a stronger bond of closeness between siblings, in other instances brothers and sisters may drift away from each other. Their life-styles may be different. Distances also may play a role, and the holidays that brought the families together are no longer predominant after parents are gone. A bereaved son describes how distance affected family unity. "There were five of us children. My father had died several years before, but my mother still maintained her own home. Every Thanksgiving and Christmas we would all go to my mother's house. It was the only time we all got to see each other, except when a business trip would bring us in proximity to the hometown of one of the others. But after my mother died, there was a different type of feeling among us. It was my mother we had all gone to see for those holidays, rather than one another. And now that she is gone, there isn't any central place for us to be.

"At first," he continued, "we had Thanksgiving at my sister's in Cleveland, but it seemed more of a struggle for us to get there at Christmas. The result was that two of us went and the others stayed home with their families for the holidays. It wasn't that they didn't want to be with us; it's just that it was no longer the same. The driving need to be with our mother was missing. She was the glue holding the family together."

In another family, the surviving children had made lives of their own and seldom saw their father who had remarried. Then, after their father died, the sister and brother found themselves divided about maintaining contact with their father's wife, who had borne him two children. "My brother and I were divided in our thoughts concerning my father's wife. We had two half brothers and didn't want to lose touch with them, but we felt cheated by my father's will. Almost everything had been left to his sons by his second marriage. One was ten and one twelve, and we realize our father probably wanted to make sure of their future, their schooling, and all that. But I'm twenty-eight and my brother is twenty-six. And we both feel that we're stepchildren. Perhaps my father thought he would live to be very old, and by that time my brother and I would be firmly established and making money. We tried making excuses like that in the beginning, but they didn't work. If my father thought he would live to be very old, for example, then his other two children would also be older and perhaps in a position to make money, too. My brother and I were both very hurt by our father's will.

"It's hard to visit our father's wife when we see her living in his house and enjoying everything he left her," the daughter continues. "My husband says to forget it, that we don't need any of that money, but it gets to me. Not the money itself, but that he didn't think it necessary to secure our future in the same way as his other children. My brother won't even visit there. He thinks she should have offered to let us take some things from the house. He is very bitter in general and feels he has no obligation to visit her. As to our half brothers, he says he has no reason to take it out on them. They didn't do anything wrong, but he will see them only if they are visiting at my house. He will not go to their home. It doesn't make for very happy holidays."

One surviving daughter told of her resentment at her brothers and sisters. "When Mother was well, they all lived far away. When it was discovered that she had a malignant tumor, the doctor felt it was best to operate. My mother had told me beforehand that she would go along with whatever this doctor recommended. She liked him and had faith in him, but after the surgery, I was held accountable by my brothers and sisters. 'Do you think that was the right thing to do?' 'Shouldn't you have gotten another opinion?' 'Was he the best doctor to have performed the operation?' I was boiling mad. Who were they to ask me questions? Where were they when the biopsy was taken? Where were they when the doctor asked, 'What do you wish me to do?'

"I know it must have been painful for them to think of Mother undergoing surgery and I realized their questions were caused by their wishing this had never happened. I felt the same way, and I took their comments personally. I still wince at the memory of having to respond to them. Instead of being of any comfort and understanding what I was going through, they put me through the Inquisition."

Another bereaved daughter complained of her bitterness toward her brothers who lived out of state. "Many times Mother would feel sad that no one had called or remembered her, especially at birthday time or holidays. When I saw that she was feeling down, I'd take steps to make things better for her, but she never knew it. I would call my brothers, for example, and caution each of them, 'Don't tell Mother I've spoken to you, but why don't you give her a phone call. She's feeling a little blue.' In the next few minutes the phone would ring and Mother's face would light up at hearing the voices of her other children and grandchildren.

"I did this with all three of my brothers, but I was annoyed with my nieces and nephews, who were all adults. They never called, either. And, whenever they came to see her, they never thought to bring a small gift or some token of appreciation. It really galled me, and after Mother died I felt an even deeper bitterness. I knew she set a great store by little remembrances and it hurt her when the grandchildren never brought her anything. I know I shouldn't harbor resentment, and I try to forget it as my mother would have wanted me to do. However, it isn't easy to forget. You can forgive, but you don't easily forget."

One bereaved daughter had a fight with her brother at the cemetery where their father had just been buried. The daughter tells us: "In our family plot, there were spaces left for two graves. As we were leaving the cemetery, my brother made the comment that he and his wife were to be buried there. I was outraged. First of all, who in his right mind would talk about such a thing at a funeral? My aunt asked me to excuse him, adding that he was overwrought by our father's death. When my brother heard my aunt he really went berserk. He insisted he was entitled to be buried there because he was the oldest child. I couldn't believe it—and here at the cemetery! I shouted at him and called him all kinds of names. He just stood there thunderstruck, as if he couldn't understand what I was shouting about. Later I found out he had no right to be buried there unless he should die before me, or unless I should transfer my right over to him. We argued a lot over that. Finally I told him it wasn't in our hands. Whoever dies first goes there. First come, first served, but I would like to be near my mother and father, too, when my time comes. It's just a terrible situation."

"Although we are aware that we shall probably be pre-deceased by our parents, we never feel ready to lose a loved mother or father—those who gave us our earliest warmth and nurturing, those who lived our history with us," says Anne Rosberger, Executive Director of the Bereavement and Loss Center of New York. "The death of a parent is often viewed as a rejection of the survivor—an abandonment by the parent, God, and fate." One bereaved daughter tells of her brother's inability to cope with their mother's death:

"We all knew it was just a matter of time, but when the doctor told us she was gone, my brother refused to believe it and began to yell at the doctor, 'It's not true.' We tried to calm him, but he broke away and ran down the hospital corridor. Two orderlies subdued him and he was given a sedative. He called the doctor a murderer. The whole thing was very embarrassing to me and my husband. Perhaps because I'm much older than my brother, I was able to take our mother's death more philosophically. My brother had been a change-of-life baby, and is only twenty-six, while I am forty-eight. He and I are really of different generations. I was at a loss to know how to get through to him."

Although she had invited her brother to live with her and her husband, he refused. "He wanted to continue living at home, in the house where he had lived with my mother. My father was still living there, but he and my brother don't get along too well. My father had never been a talker and when my mother died, perhaps my brother just followed in our father's steps by not talking. I felt like I had lost a father and a brother as well as a mother, for no one was communicating, no one knew what the other was feeling.

"A year later my brother had a nervous breakdown and was unable to work," she reflected. "He would stay home two days and work one. Finally, his boss read him the riot act and told him that if he didn't shape up, he would have to fire him. My brother's girlfriend lost patience with him. She couldn't bring him out of his tailspin and eventually she broke off with him. All these misfortunes were too much for him to handle and he stayed in bed, with no desire to do anything. Our family doctor referred him to a therapist.

"After about seven months, we saw a definite change for the better in my brother. He moved out of the house and got an apartment of his own. He was less moody, less withdrawn. I could see a real difference in him for the first time since my mother's death. I began to meet him for lunch occasionally, and we were able to get much closer and to offer each other comfort. I think he saw me as a sister for the first time. Up until now, he said, he thought I was a second mother."

When his father died, one grieving son refused to speak to his sister. The father, during his lifetime, had worked long hours driving a taxi to support his family. "He was an immigrant and had always stressed education to us as children. He sent my sister and me to the best schools. He was as close to me as a father can be to a son, but I always felt he had a stronger attachment to my sister. He couldn't do enough for her, but she never appreciated it.

"When she got married," the son recalled, "she put on all kinds of fancy airs. She moved to an exclusive part of Connecticut and joined a country club.

Whenever my father said he was going to visit her, she told him to be sure to park his cab at least ten blocks away. He never said anything, but I know it hurt him. My sister didn't want anyone to know her father drove a taxi, but it was his driving a taxi that had put her in the house she was living in now and in the life-style that she was enjoying. This grated on me, and I told her off more than once about it, but it didn't make a dent. She knew she had my father wound around her little finger."

In time, the young man's father was taken to the hospital, where he was put into a semi-private room. When the sister went to visit her father, she insisted that he be put into a private room, but none was available. "She was miserable. It wasn't my father's comfort or welfare she was thinking about. Her only concern was that some of her fine friends might visit my father and find him in a semi-private room! In addition, she thought the man who shared the room was 'slovenly' and she made no bones about letting the poor guy know that she didn't care for him as a human being. The man's hair was messed up one day because he had perspired a lot during a sleepless night. My sister went down and bought him a comb—not because she wanted to be kind to the man, but because she was embarrassed by his appearance.

"The thing that finally disgusted me," the brother said, "to the point at which I stopped talking to her, occurred when my father died. She didn't tell her friends that our father had passed away, because she didn't want them to come to the wake and meet our family members and friends, many of whom still spoke with slight accents, something she was always trying to correct in my father's speech. Only my sister and her husband came to the funeral. I wouldn't even sit with her when she came, but got up and walked out of the room. As far as I was concerned, I didn't have a sister."

We have now seen how the death of a parent places strains on the surviving siblings, and even more, how that death can split the family, making further contact almost impossible. At this point, it is refreshing to relate how one family pulled together after the death of their parents and became much closer.

David Meagher says, "I have several brothers and sisters. Many of us were there when our mother died, and during her last days, we spent a great deal of time around her hospital bed with her and with each other. We came together as a very large family at the funeral and after the funeral. There has been a concentrated effort on the part of all of us, even though we may be physically distant, to remain close so that we can share. The biggest thing is sharing the remembrance of my mother, the things that we as individuals had with her, with each other, and with her as a group. And it is a very important time for us."

❧ CHAPTER 15

Friends and Relatives

Well-meaning friends may wish to lessen the pain of loss, but they are not always capable of doing so. Insensitive or unthinking statements may add to the pain of the bereaved, while angry reactions may cause rifts in friendships. However, those who have themselves endured the despair of bereavement after the death of a parent are capable of relating to the sufferer. Such people qualify as "friend" to the son or daughter who has newly come to such grief. It follows that friends who do not meet that prerequisite face the difficult and sometimes impossible task of trying to console one who is bereaved. It is primarily at this time that friendships, even those of long standing, are tested. Many do not survive the strain.

Friends often don't know what to say to the bereaved, especially if the parent died at a fairly young age. Hilary Friedman's friends didn't help much because Hilary's father had died so young. "None of my friends had experienced the loss of a parent. Their mothers and fathers were still young, and so they really couldn't relate to my sorrow. Yes, they cared. Yes, they expressed their sympathy and some actually showed up at the funeral and for the sitting of Shiva, but during the year, no one asked how I was doing.

"If people had kept in touch," she reflected, "it would have helped. In fact, there was absolute silence for about six months. The phone didn't ring for me. There was no mail for me, although I had been hoping my friends at school would write me. I needed for them to write first because I didn't have the energy. I didn't have the cheeriness to say, 'Hi, how are you?' I felt very isolated and alone." The pain caused by her friends' seeming lack of care and interest struck deep at Hilary's feeling of self-esteem and at her morale, which was already at a low ebb. "It was one of my biggest hurts."

The problem of having no friends who had experienced a similar loss affected two other bereaved adult children. Paul Vento and Peggy Griffiths were both in their twenties when their fathers died.

"You see, when my father died—he being sixty-three and I twenty-one—most of my friends had parents who were much younger than mine," Peggy Griffiths recalls. "As a result, not many of my friends had lost a parent at the time of my father's death. When my mother died twenty years later, it was a different story. By that time, many of my friends had suffered this experience and so were far more understanding."

Peggy remembers one friend in particular who was of help to her. "At the time my mother died, my very best friend, who had lost her mother through cancer, told me, 'Peggy, I want you to do something for me. I want you to put this whole thing about your mother and her illness and death out of your mind. I want you to keep as busy as you possibly can and then take a look at it. You'll be able to handle it much better then than you can now.' Well, that is exactly what I did. It was difficult, but I did it, and it helped enormously. I kept busy both in my personal life and at my job. When I returned to work after my mother's death, I said to my employer, 'I want you to do me an enormous favor—keep me busier than you have ever done before.'"

Paul Vento had no one to talk to after his father died. "None of the friends I hung out with had experienced that kind of a loss. Neither had my wife. She still had both her parents. A lot of my friends had been rummies, too. And when you quit drinking, you don't see them anymore. They forget they ever knew you. It's better that way, too, but as a result, I had no one to talk to, absolutely no one."

John Donnelly feels much the same as Paul about not seeing old friends. "I had friends who were good and others who were bad. New friends who hadn't known my mother were very good for me. They would listen to me talk about the good times I'd had with my mother. I started doing that about seven or eight months after she died, but my old friends, the ones who had known her, especially from college, I didn't see at all. Certain things they would say, such as 'She was too young to die. She should never have died. She was such a nice person,' drove me crazy. I didn't want to listen to stuff like that, so I stayed away from them.

"I know some of my friends were hurt because they felt I was ignoring them," John says. "But my pain was so great that I couldn't be around them. I couldn't chance my reactions to what they would say. My new friends were unable to remind me of things about my mother because they never knew her. Only one new friend was able to really reach out to me because she had lost both of her parents and knew how I felt."

• • •

Sandra Ames felt nurtured by her friends after her mother's death. The community she lived in was a close-knit one, with many of her friends living nearby. After the funeral, when Sandra and her family had returned home, several of her friends served a large buffet table of food they had prepared. There was chicken, turkey, meat loaf, tuna fish, and a lot of salads, plus pies, cakes, and cookies. Sandra's friends had also set out paper cups for sodas or coffee and had brought in folding chairs for the many visitors who streamed in and out of the house.

"I knew my friends would be there for me. I'll give you an example of the kind of people they are. Before I moved to this area, I lived about forty miles away in a neighboring town. Many of my friends were happy I was moving near them. On the actual day of moving, I wondered how on earth I was going to manage everything. The movers went on ahead of me, and I was seeing to last-minute details to make sure nothing was left behind. When I arrived at my new house hours later, there were my friends. One had agreed to be there when the movers arrived. But I was really surprised when I found so many of my friends unpacking all of the sheets and pillowcases, putting the dishes away, setting up the kitchen chairs, and doing a hundred other things.

"And that is just the way they were when my mother died. When we came home from the funeral, I knew they would be there to make things easier for us and to comfort us."

One friend in particular spent many evening hours with Sandra. "She was there when the house emptied out, for her mother had died two years earlier and she knew what I was feeling. She had known my mother, and had shared a lot with us. She had visited my mother in the hospital and came to see her often when she returned home. This good friend knew what I had gone through with my mother, how ex-

hausted I had been, and how irritable I was. After
my mother's death, I would often put my head down
on the table and cry. Joan would then reach out her
hand and touch my head and remind me of the good
things I had done for my mother, for I felt very guilty
after her death.

"Joan listened," Sandra remembers, "and she
would softly speak of the happy times we had with
my mother and how much my mother had enjoyed
doing things with us, like playing cards, or going for
a drive to the beach. Joan kept my head above water
during those first months. She was very supportive
and kept me from falling back to thinking I should
have done more for my mother. She would point out
that I drove my mother to the doctors, to the hospital, to the dentist, to see her friends. While I can't say
I am totally rid of guilt, Joan certainly did everything
humanly possible as a friend to see me through a
really rough period in my life."

Some bereaved sons and daughters don't want to
talk, while others appreciate the opportunity to talk.
It is the grieving person who should give us the clue,
therapists advise. If he or she indicates a wish to talk,
then we can listen and respond. It is unfair to urge
bereaved persons to talk about the death if they prefer not to do so. Friends can usually discern this re-
luctance to discuss the loss by the abrupt response
given. In many instances, bereaved children wish to
talk at a later date. One such bereaved daughter tells
of this in the following anecdote:

Margaret McAllister tells about her inability to talk
to anyone except a dear friend—until an unusual
meeting on a train with a man who knew her father.
"With my closest friend, I started talking about my
father's death almost immediately. With her I could
say anything and she wouldn't judge. It wasn't as if

I were sorting out my feelings. I would make a comment and she would say, 'Yes,' or 'No,' and there it would lie. But she always gave me the impression that if I wanted to talk about it more, she would be glad to listen with understanding, because she had lost her dad, something with which she is still dealing. Although I always felt comfortable with this friend, I wasn't comfortable talking to other people about my father until many months later. He had died at the end of my spring semester at college, and I was grateful that I didn't have to go back to school and face my classmates right away."

Then an incident occurred that enabled Margaret to begin to talk about her loss: She bumped into a friend of her father's on a train. "He was a pleasant man, but he had always struck me as being a bit odd. I was to change my opinion that day. We were exchanging a few words when, all of a sudden, the train stopped. We were stuck in the tunnel. That wasn't bad enough, I thought, but to make it worse I was stuck with a man who would talk my head off. I kept thinking, 'This is not my day.' As we sat waiting, I could see that he wanted to discuss my father—and nothing else. Before this, when anyone had started talking to me about my father, I immediately changed the subject—even with my mother. Up to that point, I had dealt with my guilt by not dealing with it, but this man wanted to talk only about my father. I was trapped. There was no graceful way to change the subject because we had nothing else in common. I couldn't be rude and there was no way to leave. As a result, whether I wanted to or not, the subject of our conversation was going to be my father."

The man continued talking to Margaret. "He said to me, 'Your father was the greatest person I have ever known,' to which I replied, 'Yes, he was a very good person.' Then the man would go on and I would just say, 'Yes. Yes,' hoping he would get to some point that would open the door to another subject. Then he turned to me and said, 'You know, he loved you very much.' I just stared at him as he continued, 'Your father talked about nothing but you. To him, the smallest thing you did was important. Not only was he proud of you, but he also knew you well.' The man then gave me accounts of little incidents that I hadn't been aware my father knew about. Then he said to me, 'Your father always felt you would develop into a strong personality because you were just like him.' What a joy it was to hear that my father felt I was 'just like him'!"

Margaret began to soften and replied, "But I caused him a great deal of grief." "Don't worry about it," the man said. "He adored you and nothing you could do would make him love you any less." "Yes," Margaret replied, "but there are many things that I should have said and done." Again, the man reassured her: "Don't worry about it. Don't live in the past. Your father never would have, and if he were alive right now and you said to him, 'Dad, remember the time I did this to you or said that to you,' he would say, 'What? I don't remember that. If it happened, it happened *then*. This is *now*.' "

Margaret continues: "The man went on and said, 'Don't remember all the things that were wrong. Just remember your father and what he was.' Right after he said that, the train began to move. I was grateful for having run into this kindly man and after that meeting, I began to talk to other people about my father."

Friends can convey a sense of caring in many ways. Be available to help with any special needs—such as going to the supermarket, doing the laundry, watching young children, or helping with anything else that will give relief. Most important, just be there to listen.

Psychotherapist Emily Marlin suggests, "Encourage, but don't force, your friends to give vent to any grief they are feeling and to talk as much and as frequently as they wish. Avoid making any comment which might imply that the care given to the parent at home or at the hospital was inadequate." Bereaved children are often guilt-ridden enough without any assistance from friends or relatives.

Many friends, having visited or telephoned the bereaved son or daughter, believe they should wait for a reply. If your friend does not seem ready to talk now, make known that you are available and will keep in touch. Often the bereaved may keep friends at arm's length until they wade through feelings of numbness, anger, and guilt. At other times, they will want friends at their elbow to lean on. Either way, it is a help to the bereaved to know that friends care enough to be available or to call during the next weeks and months.

Lisa Strahs-Lorenc tells of her disappointment in her friends' failure to call. "It was different for my friends because all their parents were in the same age bracket as mine. I guess they wanted to avoid thinking of their parents as being mortal, too. As a result, I didn't hear from them, although I had expected they would call to find out how I was doing. They were there for me at the funeral. Everybody came then. But after that they disappeared into the woodwork until I felt better and was more verbal, at which time they were available again. I suppose I had been too depressed for them. When I was finally ready to start reaching out again, I made some phone calls. I then got the feeling that since I was sounding happier, they were ready to resume friendship, for all of a sudden they'd say, 'Let's get together,' where before they weren't saying that at all."

Lisa was especially disappointed in two special friends, both of whom had lost a parent. She had expected that they, at least, would understand her situation. "The ironic thing was that two friends, a husband and wife, who I really felt would be there for me, weren't, although they had experienced what I was now going through. Her mother had died about four years before, and he had lost his mother about ten years before. Perhaps for each, my loss brought back their terrible memories. Perhaps they didn't want to cope with that again. It could very well be they had a lot of unresolved grief and my father's death brought their grief back again. Maybe they didn't want to have to deal with that."

When Lisa returned to work she was equally disappointed. "My expectations there were very high, too. In my office we dealt daily with very sensitive issues, and perhaps I expected my coworkers would be more caring about my need to verbalize. Well, none of them wanted me to talk about it. It was as if they had put up a wall."

The person who offered the most support to Lisa was her husband, Fred. "He had also lost his father when he was about fifteen. His father's death was handled very differently, though. He never really took part in the business of death or burial, and so he never fully grieved. He had been much closer to my father than he was to his own father. When my father died, Fred was really grief-stricken. The problem was that he took on the role of 'the rock'—of being the strong member of the family. Because my mother was falling apart, I was trying to help her. He, in turn, was trying to help me. He was there helping both of us, trying to be our 'support network.'"

Another bereaved daughter explained that she felt quite annoyed with friends and family members who tried to distract her from her grief by persistent talk about trivia. "They talked about travel, football and baseball, the weather. Maybe they thought if I got my mind off my loss, I'd feel better. But I really resented this tactic, if that's what it was. If it wasn't, it was in poor taste. Another thing that really irked me was people telling me how I felt. For example, 'You must be relieved that she isn't suffering anymore.' Others would say, 'I know how you feel.' How does anyone presume to say that to another person? Unless they have experienced a loss like mine, how do they dare to imply they know how I feel? It infuriated me when someone would say that to me. I would have preferred they said nothing. I remember hearing someone say 'Silence is golden and talk is silver,' and it couldn't be more true when talking adds to the bereaved person's suffering."

Alice Figura was angry at her brother for the way he acted after her father's funeral. "It was unbelievable and I was truly shocked. He wanted to check out every item in the house for its value. He even wanted to know how many Green Stamp books my father had saved, for he felt those should be divided up between the three surviving children, too. Some of our cousins who had been more friendly with my brother were also like vultures. They would pick up a piece of china and say things like, 'Who is this earmarked for?' These are the same cousins who said to me, 'You must be glad now that it's all over.' I was disgusted with them on every count. They made me sick. I loved my father dearly, and, no, I was not relieved. Yes, I was glad his pain was over, but, no, I did not feel any sense of relief or gladness, just anguish that he was no longer here. How dare they come and finger his possessions. Is that all they came for?"

Alice was very grateful for friends who stood by

her. "I don't know what I would have done without Louise and Paul. They stayed with me, tried to ease my pain, and felt my hurt and embarrassment at my cousins' and my brother's greediness in taking stock of the household property. There really wasn't much money to speak of—my father was not a wealthy man. In my heart, I felt there were things from our home he would have wanted me to keep, but I didn't feel like fighting my brother for them. My friends listened to my anguish, not only at the death of my father, but at the death of my relationships with so many family members."

Bereaved sons and daughters should seek out environments where they can grieve comfortably, say grief specialists. Friends, inside or outside the family unit, are of the utmost importance in the healing process. We need the caring and nurturing of other people who will stand by us, understand us, support us and help us to survive. A true friend is one who allows us space, and yet is there when we want them to be part of that space.

☙ CHAPTER 16

Returning to the Workplace

When Earl Daniels returned to work, he didn't tell anyone of his father's death. He explains this now: "I was glad it happened between semesters, leaving me some time before I had to return to my teaching job. I didn't want anyone to know, for I was sure they'd be uncomfortable in whatever they'd say to me and that I'd be uncomfortable hearing it. That is why I didn't say anything to anyone."

Like Earl, many bereaved adult children experience some apprehension of what coworkers or associates will say to them after the loss of a loved one. Returning to the workplace can be extremely painful and even traumatic. The bereaved person may be able to make it easier for an employer or coworker by going to each individual and thanking him for his notes or flowers: "Thank you. It meant a great deal to me. Of course, I'll miss my mother, but it feels good to be back with my friends again, and it's nice to know so many people cared about me."

However, one bereaved daughter tells about walking into the company cafeteria and being avoided by people she had known for years. "It was as if I'd had some communicable disease. My mother had died of cancer and it seemed that no one knew what to say, so they just stayed away. But I was very hurt by their actions."

In greeting a person who has had a loss, there are many things one can do to make the bereaved feel better. One of them is to simply go to that person, appropriately touching his or her shoulder or arm, and simply pausing. That silence lets the person know everything. It is also quite proper to say, "I'm sorry to hear about your loss." If you are fairly close to the person, it would be helpful to say, "If you need to listen, I will be here to talk. If you need to talk, I will be here to listen, but please know that I am here."

Coworkers as well as friends often make the mistake—usually when a parent or older relative has died—of asking how old he or she was. The implication is that the death of an elderly person won't be as bad on the surviving child as the death of someone younger would be. Asking questions of the bereaved can be unsettling for most people because they don't really know what is appropriate. "We don't go through practice sessions of this type of behavior," says Dr. David Meagher.

"As we grow up, we practice going to a dance, or a party, or we ask how we should act when visiting—but no one tells us how to talk to one who has lost a family member. As a society we require verbal communication," Dr. Meagher continues. "Because we are not comfortable with nonverbal communication, we feel that when encountering another, we must say something." After we say, "I'm sorry to hear about the loss, and if there is anything I can do for you, let me know," we are stuck and search for something else to say.

Remarks by coworkers may be innocent, but they can be painful to a bereaved son or daughter. It is generally not good to say, "It was a blessing," because a person who has suffered may not want to hear his pain was caused by a blessing. Because of the standoffish approach to mourning in our society, the coworker who wants to say something but is afraid of the bereaved person's reaction may think the proper thing is to distract the mourner from his or her grief.

Even such professionals as doctors, nurses, and the clergy may be unable to help the bereaved through grief. They may feel helpless in the face of such suffering and be unable to provide the support needed by the bereaved. They may remain silent rather than say something that could increase the grieving person's pain or evoke his anger. Nevertheless, bereaved employees have to cope with the loss, and coworkers and management can help them to do this without making them feel ostracized or alone.

One of the worst things a coworker can say is, "Shouldn't you be over this already?" Or "Shouldn't you be better by now?" "Shoulds" are not words the bereaved feel comfortable with because everyone's clock ticks at a different speed when it comes to recovering from the loss of a loved one. There is no time limit, just an adjustment and a moving toward "recovering."

A bereaved daughter explained her dread of going to work each day. "After a month or so, everyone in my office took it for granted I was fine again. They didn't know that I couldn't concentrate. I would get so angry at everyone's indifference that I'd want to pick up an ashtray and hurl it against the wall. I couldn't accept that the world was going on as if everything was the same, when it wasn't the same at all. I felt disoriented and miserable, with terrible feelings of guilt about my mother's illness and death, wondering if I'd done everything for her that I could.

I was trying to cope with those emotions and to work at the same time."

After the death of a parent, the intensity of the loss may be a determining factor in the employee's ability to function well at work. Some problems that have been noted at the workplace include tardiness, crying spells, and a lack of concentration. In addition, there may be such physical reactions as loss of appetite or overeating, sleeplessness, and even symptoms that the deceased suffered before they died. The grief, or the inability to express that grief, can affect the bereaved son or daughter's morale and carry over to coworkers and management. If, for example, an employee is unable to function well on the job, coworkers often "cover" for the bereaved person, thinking it will be just a matter of time until the worker will return to normalcy. But coworkers willing to take on the extra work will eventually want to relinquish it. At that point, the bereaved person can become an office "problem."

One of the difficulties that grieving adult children may encounter upon returning to work is an over-reaction to any further loss. It doesn't have to be a death. It can be the loss of a desk, an office, the transfer of a friend, or the death of someone in the organization whom the bereaved barely knows. Although the bereaved may react inappropriately to the "second loss," such reactions are normal, says Dr. Roberta Temes.

Some psychologists and grief specialists caution about getting well *too soon* and putting on the air of "professionalism" at work. The paradox, they warn, is that the scab on the wound may start to heal, but the wound itself is still festering. A bereaved son or daughter who may appear to be getting over a loss very quickly will often suffer severe setbacks at a later time. This appears to be especially true of professional men and women who believe they have to maintain an image of "being in control."

The grief process lasts much longer than most people think. Time—and help with going through the grief period—are the healers. One bereaved man expressed his view: "Personnel and management should familiarize themselves with the growing number of support groups for the bereaved in their community and become aware of the many good books now available on helping the bereaved to adjust." He also felt that more employee-assistance programs should include help for the bereaved similar to those for rehabilitating alcoholic employees. "I really resent it when companies assume that because you are a man you don't have feelings, that you don't bleed the same way a woman does after the death of someone you love."

Another man said, "I think most men are afraid of expressing their true feelings at work. When my mother died, I wasn't back at work two days when I laid my head on the desk and wept. A couple of the guys I work with every day walked by, but neither of them said a word to me. I know they couldn't handle it. It wasn't so much that they couldn't handle my grief, they couldn't handle their own reactions." And yet another bereaved man had this to say: "If men would realize that other men feel pain and grief, they would feel more free to express their own emotions, and that these are normal feelings."

A bereaved woman observed, "The bottom line is that employers and coworkers may want to help ease your pain but may not know how to approach you. It is really up to you to show them how to help you, especially if it is an anniversary date of the death. You're going to have good days and you're going to have bad days. Just watch your temper and if you're having too many short fuses, see if your company can help you with a referral to someone who works in grief counseling. Or check with a pastoral person or your family doctor about a referral." Sometimes just a short period with a therapist can help put a bereaved employee back on the right track.

There are some tips to help the bereaved when returning to work after the loss of a parent. They include the following:

- Coworkers and associates may want to help ease your pain but may not know how to approach you. It is often helpful to take the initiative and help them in their efforts to be supportive.

- You will have good days and bad days. As anniversary dates, birthdays, and other special occasions come along, you may find help by sharing with others in a group atmosphere or talking to a close friend or coworker.

- You may have very little energy, an inability to concentrate, or physical reactions such as loss of appetite, overeating, sexual difficulties, or inability to sleep. Try to maintain a good diet, get enough rest, and exercise moderately.

- Medication should be taken sparingly, and under the supervision of your doctor. Many substances can lead to chemical dependence.

- It is generally wise to hold off, when possible, on any immediate major decisions, such as changing jobs or residences.

- If you find yourself crying at the office, excuse yourself and take a break for a few minutes. (Therapists and counselors have suggested—in order to prevent crying in inappropriate places—to give yourself a prescribed time and place to cry. Call a friend or relative at, say 7 P.M. in the evenings, or find a quiet place to cry at home. Tears occur because thoughts and feelings have to be expressed, say psychologists. The more these can be expressed verbally, the less you will need to express them in tears.)

There are also *Shoulds* and *Shouldn'ts* for those who wish to help the bereaved:

You should . . .
- Let your real concern show.

- Say you are sorry about what happened.

- Urge them to be patient with themselves and not to press too hard or expect too much.

- Let them share any grief they are feeling if they wish to do so.

- Indicate you are available to listen or to talk.

You shouldn't . . .
- Say, "I know how you feel." Unless you have walked in their shoes and shared a similar loss, nothing irritates bereaved people more.

- Look the other way or change the subject if they mention their parent.

- Be judgmental and say, "Shouldn't you be feeling better by now?"

- Suggest that the care given to their loved one, whether at home or in the hospital, was in any way inadequate.

- Stay away from them. The "pariah" syndrome becomes a painful addition to an already devastating experience.

❧ CHAPTER 17

The Road Back

Months after the death, when its reality starts to set in, bereaved children begin to cope with the outside world. They literally pick up the pieces of their lives and return to their daily routines. We have seen the initial shock after the loss of a parent, the anger and guilt that go with the realization that the parent is dead, the difficulties of facing first anniversaries and holidays. We have also observed how the bereaved face relationships with a surviving parent, and with siblings, friends, and relatives. We have also seen how those who need help in handling their grief go about obtaining outside support.

We shall now see how some bereaved adult children started on the road back.

Beth Landau reflects on how she began to travel that road. "The beginning was really tough. About a month after my father died, I went away to Club Med, hoping to relax. Later, I began to go to a therapist, but I stopped seeing her right after the unveiling which was about six months after he died. That seemed a good time to cut the visits, but I say Kaddish every day. In this whole year that I have been mourning, I have gone through changes. My responsibilities at my job changed, and I am trying to do

212

new things in my personal life.

"For example, I redid my whole apartment, and I have lost weight. I feel that I am ready for whatever will come next, that I am now ready to get married. I feel that I am getting older and it's my turn to become a parent. I would like to name a child after my father and perpetuate his memory that way. After this whole year of change, I felt the urge to speak to my therapist. Because I had not seen her since September, I went to her office to summarize everything. She was impressed by my improvement, by how I was handling a variety of matters. For example, when things got too frustrating at work, I knew that I didn't have my father to turn to and that everything was on my shoulders. I soon learned to handle things alone, for my mother could only deal with so much. It was certainly an arduous year for me."

Carol Richardson took a big step when she made a decision about her mother's clothing and personal items. Carol had kept her mother's belongings for quite some time and then one day decided that everything, excepting the jewelry, but including the clothing, was going. "I realized it was the best thing to do. If you throw out something you want, you can go to the store and buy another one like it. I found that just having my mother's things was very depressing, and so I decided to hold onto only those items that would remind me of pleasant days. The first things to go were items she had taken to the hospital. I don't even know why I brought them home. I should have dumped them into the garbage can when I left, but hospitals give you a big box filled with the deceased's possessions, and you are in such a state of shock that you don't think clearly."

In one way Carol was fortunate. She had been at the job she then held for only a short time, and none of her coworkers had known her mother. As a result,

Carol didn't have to acknowledge solicitous comments or words of sympathy. "No one at work was a part of me. No one there had been associated with my mother. As a matter of fact, the people didn't even know me very well, for I was a new employee, and my troubles were of no major concern to them. I was working with the program director at the time of my mother's death, and I just went about my daily schedule." This allowed Carol literally to recoup her strength.

David Meagher was struggling with his feelings after his father died, but he didn't know why. "So I began to question and check things out. One day when I was teaching a class on the philosophy of health, I thought, 'I am going to bring up the issue of death and how I view it.' When I raised the issue, the classroom became absolutely silent. I had never experienced that kind of one-hundred-percent response in any group before. No matter how good I might be, I always knew that the thoughts of five percent of the people were somewhere else. But this class became so quiet that a pin being dropped would have sounded like an atom bomb. I said to myself, '*That* is interesting—and it is important. It's important *because* it is so interesting.' Anything that could bring that kind of universal response—complete withdrawal, silence, and absolute fear—is something that has to be dealt with. So I began reading. I wrote to some of the people mentioned in journals and got information back from them. I was then ready to start my doctoral work, and I concentrated on the area of death and dying."

As a counselor on death and dying, David had to put aside his immediate commitments when his mother died. "The first thing I did after my mother's death was to forget what I was doing to help other people because I couldn't be there for them. If I was there for them and if they leaned on me, I wasn't going to be able to support them emotionally. I needed to do something with myself. Two weeks after her death, I was supposed to have some presentations, but I told those who had engaged me that I was not emotionally prepared to get up and do justice to the subjects I had planned to discuss. I said, 'I'm just not there yet, so you will have to excuse me.'" Soon thereafter, David was able to return to helping others with bereavement problems, but first he had to help himself. "You must work out your own issues first and regain the strength you need, so that others can lean on you and find support. If I put my issues aside and never focus on them, I am not being very good to myself or anyone else." David provides an illustration. "If you see a man drowning, and you are weak and tired and unable to swim, don't jump in and try to save him, for there would then be two losses—you and the other person."

Marjorie Martin and her twin sister, Ellen, wanted to move out of their home after their father's death, but it was not financially possible at the time. To try to obliterate the memory of the scene of the crime from their minds, the two women began to avoid the house as much as possible, using it strictly as a place to sleep. "For about a year and a half after his death, the thought of our father and what had happened to him was constantly on our minds. We always had to face memories when we went back to that house. My sister returned to work and I was working, too, but at the end of each day, we didn't want to go back to our apartment. We stayed out until all hours of the night to avoid returning there. We went to the movies, sat in coffee houses, or did anything to keep us busy. When it was late enough to return, we would walk into the apartment as if we wore blinders. We didn't look left or right, but went straight through to the bedroom and directly to bed."

Their goal was to save enough money to move into a neighborhood some distance from where the crime had occurred. After they achieved this goal, Marjorie and Ellen slowly returned to the life they had known before their father's death. They began to travel to expand their interests and they made new friends. The sisters became more involved in community work and slowly resumed their literary pursuits. Today, ten years later, they live a comfortable and active life. They doubt that they will ever forget the way their father died, but they have learned to live with their bitterness and the sorry fact that the robbers were never caught. "That doesn't mean we do not find good things to enjoy in life. Our father would not have wanted us to brood. We also remember the beautiful times we spent with him and we shall never forget his greatness as a human being."

Coincidentally, Harry Finnegan had lost his job and was home when his mother became ill and needed him. "In one way, you could say it was destiny. I always thought that perhaps fate arranged things so I could be there when my mother needed me." But following his mother's death, Harry felt there was too much time to think while he was still at home. He realized that prolonged inactivity allowed him to replay his depression over and over again in his mind. He said to himself, "I've got to get back to a regular schedule of work as soon as I can."

Two months after his mother died, he found a job that seemed to be what he wanted. "I threw myself into the work. In a way, I was lucky because it required many hours of working late, six nights a week. People thought I was overdoing it, but for me, it was probably a salvation. I would go home, eat, and go right to bed. In the morning, I would get up, have breakfast, and go to work. I continued this for about a year. At the end of that time, I had moved out of my depression and was able to handle my mother's death more realistically."

One of the profound effects of her father's death on Hilary Friedman was that she had to give up her plans to go to law school. Since her father had been an attorney, she felt she would be involved in something that was "too much a part of him and I wouldn't have his guidance." Meanwhile, she would seek employment, but Hilary found it difficult to prepare a résumé to submit to possible employers. At that point, she decided to work for an agency through which she could get temporary jobs. "It was a good choice because office work allowed me to be with people again, and to keep moving and meeting with people and handling new job assignments. Then, when I would not be given assignments for a few weeks, I would see the difference between the life-style of being out in the world among the living or staying home and dying. When you don't know that a difference exists, you can't get out of your morass, but when you learn that such a difference really does exist and then you recognize it, you can start to change it. When you don't know there's anything wrong with the way you are living, you can't change it. So a good part of my problem was worked out just by being in another atmosphere."

In her beginning days on the job, Hilary would work for a couple of days and then feel totally drained. "I would stop for a while, but as the agency kept sending me to more and more jobs, I found I could do more and more at each place. I could feel myself wanting to do so, whereas, originally, I would feel depleted and exhausted, with normal effort being too much effort. It was like having muscles that are out of shape, but I was emotionally out of shape.

I felt I could absorb only a limited amount, that any little thing was overpowering. Even TV was overpowering. To use an analogy—I was in neutral. I was idle in the state of neutral, and that was the most I could do. The next step after getting out of the house was to shift gears, to go to second, third, fourth. Then, after a bereaved person shifts gears to go forward, she can't go back. It's just not possible. I had gone forward, and after working initially just for days, then weeks, and working up to taking a job for a month at a time, I was ready for a permanent job. My social life is better, too. I've been seeing people whom I haven't seen for several years. I have more of a feeling of who my long-term friends are, which is nice. The girl who was my best friend was away at school and so I saw her only occasionally, but she came home this past summer and I was with her all through the fall. That helps a lot."

Sandra Ames found therapeutic value in creative hobbies. She has an artistic bent and decided to apply it to making costume jewelry for her friends and family. It also helped relieve some of the long hours at night after coming home from work. "At first I bought some small tiles and made them into magnets to affix to such surfaces as refrigerator doors. I decorated them with a variety of designs. On one of the tiles, I designed the face of a clock, with two arrows pointing to the hours. After I looked at it, I realized I was telling myself I had too much time on my hands, and much of it was given to thinking about my mother's death. So I decided to expand into making jewelry. I made a great variety of necklaces, earrings, brooches—work of which I knew my mother would have approved. She would have liked the pretty things I was creating. So it comforted me to know I was making new and pretty jewelry instead of thinking about past and dead matters. You probably could say it was a road back."

Patricia Tremont was brought up short in her grief by the death of a friend's child. "When my best friend's daughter was killed in an accident, I was at her side mourning her loss. I knew that she had lost the future. I had lost the past. My mother had lived a long life. While there had been some rough periods for her, she had had the love of her children and grandchildren, and she had enjoyed the company of many good friends. Yes, I was very unhappy when she died. To make it worse, I did not get to see her before she died, or to say good-bye. The sudden death of my friend's daughter was so tragic and my friend, too, did not get to say good-bye to her child.

"I am still missing my mother in some ways, especially on my birthday, or Mother's Day, but I no longer feel the guilt weighing heavily upon me. I know my mother would have forgiven me. But, now, when I see Sally mourning for Lisa, I can't compare my loss to the tragedy of losing a teenage daughter. My mother lived her life. Lisa was just beginning hers."

From talking with others who have lost parents, Patricia has come to feel that many of the difficulties are the result of issues that were not resolved before the death of a parent. "But I have also seen people who feel they have to continue mourning out of loyalty," Patricia comments. "Sometimes it's almost a question of saying, 'Cut the shit and in memory of your loved one, move on.' In the interest of the bereaved, it's important to be hard-nosed, so as to make sure we aren't mired in our grief. Without wishing to be insensitive to anyone's loss, I suggest that the depth of some adult children's reactions seems to indicate that the bereaved have a great need to be in the trenches of grief. Something about that kind of reaction is distressing, and it does an injustice to the memory of the dead parent.

"We have dealt with a tragedy and if we can take it and make the experience meaningful—and not only superficial—we have achieved something that can affect our personal growth. If we can walk outside and smell the flowers and see the birds after our parent had died, and if, recognizing how brief a time we have on earth, we develop a deeper appreciation of life, then we don't become 'stuck' in the loss and find ourselves unable to deal with unresolved grief. Coping with grief is turning something negative into something positive. We have the ingredients; it is merely a matter of putting them together.

"A lot depends on what we brought to the grief, what kind of baggage, and on our need to focus on the grief to get reactions from other people. Sometimes we see surviving sons and daughters who want to wallow in self-pity, and we want to say to them, 'Enough already.'"

Alex Tanous, who lost both of his parents by the time he was twenty-four, also comments on self-pity and on his mother's lack of it, even though she was very ill. In fact, his recollections of his mother's laughter and joy in living enabled Alex to cope with many stressful moments in his day-to-day activities. "Whenever I came up against a problem, I would remember how my mother handled hardships and how she never complained. I would also remember her laughter and how she wanted us to make the most of every moment in our lives and to make something of ourselves. In fact, my mother always told my brothers and me that she would live until we had all graduated from college—and she did. After my father's sudden death when my mother was twenty-nine, she went through great hardships to see us all through school. Two of the things which she has contributed to my moving ahead in my life were the use of her philosophy and the efforts to live as she did, making the most of it, 'doing our thing,' so to speak.

"I once wanted to write a book called *My Mother Played Shortstop*. We were eight brothers and Mother played ball with us to make a team. That's the kind of person she was. Although in the beginning, I had mourned the loss of my mother deeply, I knew I had to face the reality of her death. That little piece of love was gone from my life and I would never have it again. I had to resign myself to that void in my life—that missing piece of love. It was useless for me to think it could be replaced. And I think that was the greatest hurt, knowing that it couldn't be. So how do you adjust to that loss?" You have to fill that void with love in different ways—not as an escape but as a realization that life must go on. You go back to your work, to school, to being with old friends, meeting new people, and trying to enjoy the good things in life.

"And every once in a while, you will pause and think, 'Wouldn't it be nice if I could see my parents?' Or 'Wouldn't it be nice if they could be here to enjoy this with me?' And this is normal. We will never forget our parents and it is a natural feeling to think of them when you enjoy happy times."

Charlene Stevens was despondent after her mother's death. Her depression continued for many months until, one day, while watching television she saw a commercial advertisement for a local health spa. Because she had been having headaches and suffering from a general malaise, Charlene decided to attend the spa because it had a pool, and she felt that swimming might relax her tensions. "I had no idea that all of the exercises would offer such relief, and when I swam in the pool, I experienced a great release. I felt nothing but the water. Slowly, my feelings of tension, of guilt and despondency began to diminish. It didn't happen overnight and at first I didn't recognize how much it was helping me, but my husband saw a big change and so did my friends."

Charlene believes it is important for grieving children to find avenues of release, such as bowling or dancing, attendance at sports games, or traveling. "Anything that can offer some relief from emotional pain helps. My husband and I had been having difficulties in our sexual relationship after my mother died. I constantly felt lethargic and never had any desire to engage in the playful games we had enjoyed before her death. In fact, I was having a hard time to avoid shouting at my husband for any little thing, even things that I knew weren't his fault. All of that changed after I began my swimming and exercising. It was a tremendous outlet for me and I know it helped me out of the depression I was in."

Charlene believes that one never forgets a parent's death, but that getting on with life is a path onto which the bereaved must step. "What is originally a sharp pain gradually becomes a dull ache. That ache is there from time to time, but sometimes it is worse than others. It's similar to the physical pain of arthritis that may grow worse when it rains. Similarly, the pain of loss can be more severe at times. At other times we are more vulnerable because we hadn't been able to take all the pain at one time, and it was siphoned off in spurts so that we could handle it better. We have mental safety valves that stop the pain when it reaches a certain threshold. That explains why we sometimes feel an unexpected, sharp, painful memory when we aren't expecting it.

"We may have thought we were prepared to cope with special days, but then something hits us, perhaps at a restaurant when a woman wearing a Mother's Day corsage orders our mother's favorite dish,

THE ROAD BACK 223

or is wearing a dress similar to the one our mother wore, and it hits us in a painful way. On the other hand, you may see a calendar and remember that it is her birthday or the anniversary of her death. But don't worry. It just means you are recovering."

Chuck Akerland believes the most important aid to survival is to accept life as it is. "For some this is easy, but for others it is very difficult," he says. "If the only loss you have suffered in life has been that of a pet, it is somewhat easier to accept things as they are than if you have lost a brother or father through suicide." Chuck adds that whether or not you accept the way things are, they still are the way they are. He adds, "As a result, you can either do it the easy way or the hard way."

From our reading here of various approaches to recovery, we have seen that bereaved sons and daughters find many different ways of coping with reality. For adult children who have suffered such a loss, the best way is whatever works for them. What works for one person may not work for another. There is a story about two friends who met for coffee one day. Each had been to see a doctor concerning health problems. One woman had gone to see Dr. Jones and was told in an abrupt tone that she needed to have surgery. The doctor was very specific—there was no question about it. He urged her to have the operation as quickly as possible. The woman didn't care at all for the doctor's attitude. She didn't like his manner and felt she was being pushed into a hospital.

So she went to see Dr. Smith for another opinion. His tone was totally different. In a soft-spoken voice, he told the woman, "My dear, you must be feeling discomfort. Yes, it's possible we may have to perform some surgery, but let's wait a little while and see."

The woman felt reassured and more comfortable after visiting Dr. Smith and looked forward to telling her friend about the two doctors and how glad she was she had gone to see Dr. Smith. However, when the two women met, her friend spoke first, saying, "I must tell you of a problem I've had with some doctors." It seems she had gone to see a Dr. Jones—the same Dr. Jones—and she spoke of him with great enthusiasm. "He was straightforward, and didn't pussyfoot or beat around the bush. He leveled with me and told me exactly what was wrong, and I appreciated his truthfulness." She went on to relate how upset she had been when, to reassure herself with a second opinion, she went to see a Dr. Smith, again the same Dr. Smith her friend had seen!" All he wanted to do was stretch out the visits and say, 'Oh, you poor thing.' "

What is right for someone else is not necessarily right for you. It is right if you are comfortable with it. It is wrong if you are uncomfortable. Some may try ways and find them excellent; others may try the same ways and have a rotten experience, causing them to look further. If you're not happy when you have tried one way, don't despair that there is no other way. If you are made to feel uncomfortable, make a change. Find a way that is comfortable to you—because that way is the right road back for *you*.

☙ CHAPTER 18

Remembrances and Recollections

The writer remembers a day which should have been a happy event—my thirty-second birthday. My mother was still living at that time, but my father had died when I was five. Today, memories of my mother surface at every point of my life that is meaningful.

On more than one occasion my mother told me that she had known I would write, that I would paint and that I would express many talents. The first time she mentioned this, I asked her how she knew this in advance.

"I used to talk to you when I was pregnant," she confided. "I would sing to you so you would learn to carry a tune. And I would read to you so you would develop a taste for writing." She would rub her tummy, she said, and pour forth all of the loving and warm dreams she had for me.

During my mother's illness, I discovered her favorite color was purple. Until then, I had not known it. We talked of many things I had not known of, and it was a time for sharing all the little details we take so for granted in life. She died soon thereafter.

There were a lot of things I never knew—like knowing at the time that my father was dead. In the following article, "Recollections: I Remember What

They Looked Like," I tell about my father's death and the traumatic events which led to my frightening thirty-second birthday in the hospital:

It's a strange kind of atmosphere that pervades a home when a member of the family dies. I was not aware my father had died. Nor, at the age of five, am I sure I would have understood what dying meant. Yet there was a sense something had drastically changed.

But when my grandfather died a few months later, I was very much aware of events. He was put into a box that was laid on what looked like a long coffee table in the living room of my grandmother's home. My grandmother rushed over to me as I was led into the house, swept me up to the box and in a choked voice whispered, "Take a good look at your grandfather, child. You are never going to see him again. Be sure you remember what he looked like."

I wasn't at all sure I could remember what he looked like and was overwhelmed by the idea that I would never see him again. Nor did I understand why he was lying in a box in the living room of my grandmother's house.

In order to make sure that none of us ever forgot my father's face, my grandmother requested that a picture of him be placed on the tombstone of his grave. I can't be certain if the *impression* of being told to look at my grandfather lest I forget what he looked like—or the impression of seeing my father's picture on his grave—was the thing that created the *ultimate impression* of never forgetting what a loved one looks like. But then, is that the importance of what remains in a child's memory—is what the person was really like imbued into the actual remembrance of what they looked like?

What then do we remember at the age of five, at

ten, at eighteen or at eighty? What is it we recall about a lost loved one? Do we remember a smile, a hug, a caress, a lingering look of love? I recall when I was almost four, my grandfather used to take me to the corner grocery store and I was allowed to proudly carry back a bottle of milk. On one such day, a large dog came bounding across a nearby lawn and pounced on me, causing the milk bottle to shatter under the impact of my fall. My wrist was gashed from the pressure of the broken glass and my grandfather was horrified to see me lying in a pool of blood. He quickly grabbed me in his arms and ran to the nearest doctor's office a mile away. His face, taut and tormented with anguish as he watched the doctor sewing the stitches, was a look I remember— a look of caring. Yes, I remember what my grandfather looked like.

I remember, too, when I was almost five what my father looked like the day we went fishing and the small boat capsized. I was pitched face forward into the lake. The shock of finding myself hitting the water with such flying impact frightened me. I panicked and began to flounder, gulping large doses of water at the same time. I suddenly felt no air, felt I couldn't breathe, felt myself sinking. The next thing I remember, I was lying on the beach with my father's face hovering over me, having applied artificial respiration. I remember his smile when I looked up at him and the enormous relief that swept over his face. What is it then that takes place in a child's mind when a look of love overcomes all other thought impulses? What is it then that remains in a child's memory bank as to the way a person looked?

On the day my father died, I was told he had gone away for a while. I can't remember who told me this. I did not see my mother on that day, and was sent to visit an aunt. I remember one song I seemed to want to hear endlessly, "The March of the Wooden Soldiers." The day after my grandfather died, my young cousins and I again played the song. I tried to remember what my father looked like. I wondered if my father had become a soldier in wood like my grandfather in the wooden box. He, too, had gone away and had never come back. I could not envision my father's face. But I did envision the face of a family friend who had visited our home shortly after my father's death. I heard her saying, "How awful that he died on his birthday—his 32nd birthday—and, on the operating table!"

Some 27 years later, I found myself in the hospital awaiting surgery the next morning. My mother telephoned me from out-of-state and expressed her regret that I would be spending my birthday in the hospital. "But, Mother, this is not my birthday," I replied in an astonished voice. "Oh, yes," she said, "tomorrow is your 32nd birthday."

With full force, it suddenly hit me. A memory buried for so long: *"How awful that he died on his birthday—his 32nd birthday—and, on the operating table!"* And now, I had not even remembered that it was *my own birthday. My 32nd birthday!* And it was to be spent on an operating table! Was I to tempt the fates in this manner? Was I, too, destined to die in my 32nd year? Would my family be asked to remember what I looked like?

Once again, I recalled my father's face over his grave. I also remembered what my grandfather looked like in the wooden box. I knew I had a choice I could make. Fear should never be allowed to rule. And, certainly, prior to surgery fear should not rule supreme. I asked to see the Chief Surgeon who was to operate the next day and told him I could not be on an operating table on my 32nd birthday. Sensing the emergency that was enveloping me and the tenseness of the situation, the doctor relented and granted my request. *I was operated on the day after my 32nd birthday.*

I asked that a picture of my father and a picture of my grandfather be brought to me. I wanted their faces with me in life. I wanted to remember that I need no longer fear remembering what they looked like. No longer was my father's face over his grave. No longer was my grandfather in a wooden box. They were here with me in my hospital room—and I was remembering what they looked like.

The following eulogy tells how Vivian Kessler remembered her father. This loving expression of all the things her family appreciated about her father sustained Vivian then, as it does today:

Dear Daddy:

It's Tuesday morning. You're not here and already we miss you very much.

We miss the Daddy who told us he killed Pinnochio's Monstro The Whale, who read The Frog Prince to Joanie and Cinderella to me. The Daddy who could make all our bad dreams go away. We miss the Daddy who was never too busy for his children. The Daddy who played Hit The Penny with us, cooked us chicken soup, brought us groceries and made sure we never ran out of soap. The Daddy who would drive us anywhere anytime and smile while doing it because nothing was ever too much or too hard when it came to his family.

We miss the Daddy who would brag about us and show our pictures to anyone and everyone whether they wanted to see them or not—to show off his "Millions," his wife and children. As his family expanded, he would show off the interest on his millions—his seven grandchildren.

We miss the Daddy who quoted Shakespeare and adapted it to suit any occasion. The Daddy who loved music, gave us all lessons—piano, voice, accordion, saxophone, and bought us the finest instruments. Regardless of our ability, or lack of it, he thought we were great! We were his kids—we had to be good.

We miss the Daddy who would hear tunes on the radio and ask, "Vivela, who wrote that song?" in a sort of guessing-game way. My answer was always, "Irving Berlin, Daddy," because he was the only popular composer's name I would remember.

We miss the Daddy who bought a station wagon just so he would be able to chauffeur Harold's teenage Rock Band's instruments on their Saturday night gigs. The Daddy who called his wife and daughters gorgeous as well as brilliant—and you knew he meant it. The Daddy who taught us the value of an education, but not the cost of common sense.

The Daddy who would whistle his special tune outside the door, signalling us he was home. The Daddy who brought home pounds of our favorite foods— green peas and Hershey bars. The Daddy who would send his teenage daughters Valentine cards signed by a mysterious admirer. The Daddy who gave us security, help, compassion and tenderness. The Daddy who showed us, by example, responsibility, honesty, morality and charity. The Daddy who knew the ravages of war, the hate of anti-Semitism and the agony of loneliness. The Daddy who knew all this and yet by the limitless love he gave us taught us how to give love to others.

So Daddy, we miss you and will always miss you, but we want to say "Thank you for being our Daddy." So long, Pop, we love you.

Following are reminiscences by many of the bereaved sons and daughters who have appeared in the book. They have gone beyond the many stages of grief, beyond the anger, the guilt, the disbelief. They have all taken the road forward using the best path for them, and can now look back and remember the good times they enjoyed with their deceased parent. They are no longer looking at the sorrow, the hospital scenes, the shock. They can now remember happier moments. They will still miss their parents but fond memories now surface more than the pain.

Lisa Strahs-Lorenc remembers that from the time she was a baby, her dad was a very involved father. "Because he owned his own business, he was home in the house at five o'clock. I remember we always played together before dinner and afterward we always did family things, or went out bicycling together. He taught me to ride a bicycle, how to throw a ball. We did everything together because we were a real family in the sense that it was a child-centered environment where you grow up feeling that you're important and loved. When my husband, Fred, came into the family, he couldn't believe the type of life we had. He had never experienced anything like it before. Birthdays were always very special, as were holidays. Vacations were spent together and we talked about everything."

Lisa also remembers that her father could be very difficult on occasion. "There were times, in our conversations, when he was very hard on me. He drove us crazy many times because he was stubborn. If he had an opinion and a thought, that was it. He would never waver, and that would get us really angry. He was also very hard on me in that he always expected me to do better. When I gave up teaching, he was very disappointed that I couldn't afford to go on with it. He knew how much I loved the classroom, and he wouldn't accept my assertion that right now teaching was something I couldn't afford. As a result, I took a sidetrack in my life. I became an office manager and more of a business-type person, but my father knew my primary love was children and that I wanted to open my own nursery school, which I intend to do in the future. Of course right now, in the meantime, I own my own business and I help other people decide on careers."

• • •

Beth Landau remembered a request her father had made of her about a year before he died, one that she was determined to grant after his death. "My father was the last remaining child. He was one of four children. His parents had died when he was in his twenties and in the war. He asked me if, when he went, I would take care of the maintenance of their graves. I thought it was an odd request, coming out of left field. I remembered this when he died, and I felt that it was my duty to visit the cemetery. My mother kept shouting at me, 'What are you going there for? Why are you driving yourself crazy? You don't have to pay for anything.' Well, sure enough, he had gotten a statement for the upkeep of their graves, but he died before he was able to pay it. So I paid it and I wanted the cemetery authorities to maintain it. Then I went there on Father's Day. First I went to see my grandparents' graves and then to my father's. I went alone, and that was a very emotional experience. I felt my father would know that I did this, that I had done what he had asked of me."

Paul Vento remembers a paradoxical father who was always hollering and yelling, but was always full of fun. "He was a jolly guy. I guess he had his ups and downs because of his health and it wasn't so easy to find jobs. He probably had to fight all his way. But he always took care of us, and we never worried about anything, you know. For a while we went to the cemetery, but then we felt there was nothing there anymore. You know, the body disappears. So that's why we didn't continue going.

"My father was kind of crazy, in a nice way, and I have a lot of good memories of him to think about so that's what I hold onto about him. He had a great sense of humor and had been a comic at one time in vaudeville, with Jimmy Durante and others, before he met my mother. In fact, he met my mother when he was performing at a party. You forget the bad things faster than you forget the good things. The only rough feature is that I lost two good friends in the last couple of years and that has brought back some of the memories of my father's death. But for the most part I have good thoughts about him."

Mary Stellakis, who brought her mother home to Greece from America, poignantly reflects on her mother: "She is always in my heart and she sometimes visits and talks to me in my dreams. The ocean no longer separates us. I go to visit her and my brother four to five times a year and feel that they are aware of my presence and I'm comforted. One day I'll join them and this thought, too, brings me comfort."

While John Donnelly doesn't feel despondent anymore, he regrets his mother is not alive. "Especially when something nice happens and I say to myself, 'Wouldn't it be great if my mother were here to see this?' I now remember the goodness and don't have to dwell on the badness. I can remember the times that we were happy—like going up to Greenwood Lake for the summers or our many vacations to Canada and other interesting places. I don't have to remember the unhappy moments, or sad ones, and that makes me feel good."

Gia Williams philosophizes about the role of parents in general: "I tried to think about the times we *were* happy. Let's face it, just because you're a parent doesn't mean you have all the answers, too. A lot of people think that once you become a parent, you are not supposed to make mistakes. Parents are only human beings. Then, too, my mother had me at a very young age. Looking back at it now, it must have been kind of hard for her to cope, too."

Harry Finnegan lived with his mother until her death. While there are memories that emerge in looking around their home, Harry feels this is a normal reaction and deals with it as the feelings surface. There are options to move if he wishes, but he is comfortable to remain in the surroundings of the house they shared. The family dog, Ruby, adds a comforting ingredient—an extension almost of family life, because Ruby shared the same home with Harry and his mother. Harry believes it is best not to linger on death, but to remember the happy times with a parent and the knowledge that a child has done everything possible to aid, comfort, and care for an ailing parent.

Peggy Griffiths feels that as much as you grieve internally at the loss of a parent, you treasure them even more when you don't have them. "The things they taught you never leave you. You may stray, but you remember the basics of their teachings—of being courageous, of being honest, of telling the truth, to always look your best, neat and well groomed, and not only look that way but keep your home and your surroundings that way and to do the best you can every day, to try never to hurt anyone. They are simple principles, but they are things that stay with you.

"After your parents are gone, I think they become even more ingrained in you. I think you realize that now you don't have anyone who is going to listen to you, to your side of the story as you go through life. This is what parents do. They always listen to a child's side of the story before they make a decision, and very few other people you are going to meet in life are going to be that kind to you. Your good friends will, but not always. After your parents go, you grow up in a hurry if you haven't grown up at that point."

Patricia Tremont has moments when the old sorrows return and she feels them mostly when she is under stress. "Many times I would think, 'Oh, great. I'm really out from under now and I'm through with the grief.' Then something would happen that would knock the pegs out from under me and I would feel as if my mother had died yesterday." Patricia understands that this is not unusual in grief. "I have a good friend who said she has also felt this way. Her father died about seven years ago. My friend had gone to a therapist who told her that painful experiences can take a long time to run their course, but that it is normal to have moments of vulnerability. The only time this type of temporary setback is serious, she said, is if you couldn't continue with your everyday life."

Sad feelings can also emerge during a very happy time of life, Patricia believes. "Six months after my mother died, my niece became engaged. Two months after that, she was married. At the wedding, I thought, 'If only Mother were here to see this.' She loved my niece very much and would have been happy to see her take her vows. Then, for a little while, I felt sad and depressed at this festive occasion, while at the same time feeling happy for my niece, her husband, and my sister."

❧ CHAPTER 19

Messages of Hope

Worry, fear, and despair can turn to self-pity, which, in turn, leads to depression. The bereaved are helped when they take steps to give their lives purpose and meaning—to live one day at a time, and, more importantly, to live and let live

In Harold Arlen and John Mercer's classic song, "Accentuate the Positive and Eliminate the Negative," we are given the key to recovering. Negative thoughts never help—they only destroy. By pushing them aside and allowing positive thoughts to take over, we can make life worthwhile.

After a parent's death, adult bereaved children become concerned about their own mortality. By making every hour of each day truly meaningful to us, *we defy death* simply by not concerning ourselves with it. *By focusing on life*, we improve the quality of that life for all the days and hours we are allotted.

Because individuals are different, their reaction to fear, mental pain, guilt, and anger are different. Each person deals with those emotions in his unique way. In this chapter we will read messages from many of the sons and daughters who have shared their stories with us in this book and who have gone through the process of grief, whether it took six months, a year, ten years, or more. They now offer their words of encouragement and hope to those who are looking for ways out of their pain.

From Margaret McAllister, whose father died when she was twenty-two:

It's all right to feel the things you do—the guilt, the anger, the sadness. It's okay to let yourself run the gamut of emotions. I know some people who have lost a parent and then turned their grief inward and shut out the world. By the same token, I have known others who have lost a parent and for the first time suddenly had a need to express themselves. *Whatever it takes*, even if it means throwing things, do it. If you need to get frustrations out, get them out. Don't be ashamed of displaying your emotions. Don't feel it's wrong and don't make excuses to anybody.

As time passes and you get to a point where the grief is lessening, don't try to bury it. Don't say, "The death and the mourning are over, life goes on and we are going to live without looking back on this time." Don't try to live without looking back on your deceased parent, thinking it will be too painful for you. I don't believe you should feel that way. Some of the best times I have now are looking back on my father or talking to someone about him. I believe that helps me. I think if I were to pretend that he never existed, I would be cheating myself and certainly cheating him of what he deserves. So I say, "Don't be afraid to remember. It's normal and you need it."

From Carol Richardson, whose mother died when Carol was twenty-one and who lost her father some years later:

When this first happens, you may feel that people are being insensitive toward you because they don't understand. For this reason, I think it is a little easier if you tend to expose yourself to people who have already been through it. I know that when my mother died, there was nothing anyone with a mother could say to me because they had not been there yet and I did not want to hear them.

Another thing is just start taking care of yourself. Don't let yourself go down, keep yourself up, and you can if you just expose yourself to positive ideas. Make sure that if you feel some hostility or anger, you discuss it or talk it out with a professional person. However, that is not for everyone, and in some cases, it can add to the stress.

In one instance, a neighbor who thought of herself as being considerate sent a psychiatrist friend of hers to see me; I told him to get the hell out, that there was nothing I had to say to him. It seemed as if people couldn't understand why I wasn't jumping and screaming and crying. Everyone will accept a death in a different way. If you are the jumping and screaming and overemotional kind, then that is what you are going to do, but if you are a quiet person who can deal with things rationally, it would be unusual for you to change. I've been there and I know. You think you can't survive, but you can.

From Dr. Alex Tanous, who lost both of his parents:

In trying to come out of mourning, my advice to other bereaved children is to realize that this has happened. We cannot ask any questions or why God willed it. All the questions will put us deeper into ourselves—and there are no answers there. You have to accept the fact that the dead are no longer with us, that a void exists and that you must find a way to fill that void—*not as an escape from guilt, but as something that will make life go on.* I had to face the fact that my father would never take his lunch pail to work again and that my mother would never hug me or cook for me again. I will never see them in our old home again.

We have to get away from the past and that is not an easy thing to do. One of the most effective things that I suggest to the bereaved is to get out of the house, count the cracks in the sidewalk, or look at the different leaves on the trees. Go back to work and keep as busy as possible. The worst thing is to mope around the house and allow yourself to be depressed. I also think it is important to get rid of the souvenirs of the dead parent. Every time you look at one, it will bring back sad memories and the "Why did it happen?" syndrome, and you will become attached to their memory. It doesn't make you a slave to the dead person, but a prisoner in the sense that you are a slave to things your parent owned.

I don't mean you can't carry a picture or keep a piece of jewelry, but if you do, don't think of it as an attachment that will make them come back and cause you to relive the memory and its related heartache. Although I know that disposing of souvenirs is not easy, I think most of them should not be kept.

After a parent dies, you are bereft. It's as if the house has burned down and your home is gone. Everything you knew and loved was in it. But the house is gone and now you have to accept that fact. You must build a new house, a new life. After you have mourned, you must move on in your life. Yes, remember your parents, but don't be more attached to the past than to the future.

For example, if there is a room being kept as a shrine, clean it up and make it alive. Bereaved children have to change their attitudes. They have to become aware that their parents would understand. Otherwise, you become the slave of what you think you could or should have done. *That's the real sorrow—never releasing yourself.* You have to learn to let go. And to do just that—let go.

• • •

From Dr. David Meagher, who lost both his parents:

At groups where there are various workshops, you will often hear participants say, "I was concerned that I didn't do it better." My response: *"Well, we are only people and as people we don't always make the right decisions."* Also, as people we sometimes make mistakes—and that's great, because that only shows that we are people. That is what we have to focus on—that we are human and that humans are not perfect.

From Gia Williams, whose mother died in her early forties:

Life and death are the same in that we are born and we will die. That is just the natural law. We are born. We're here. We stay for a while and then we go on. So I think that, instead of thinking of death as a tragedy, we can use the time we are here to try to leave something for other people to follow or to use in their lives. However, when you see people who are suffering from a variety of diseases, it is very sad. But I think that while we are here in this lifetime, we should use it by creating and giving joy.

From John Donnelly, whose father died when John was a young boy and whose mother died when he was twenty-five:

If, after the death of a parent, people are functioning poorly, as I was after my mother's death, their greatest need is professional help or they run the risk of ending up in a mental hospital. But no matter how bad your situation may seem, if you have the proper help, you can come out of it, with much of your success depending upon your relationship with the lost parent. It took many years after my mother's death before I could really accept the facts as they were, but if I could, anyone can. It's a long road and a rough climb, but you can do it if you take a step at a time.

After recovery, people may wonder if they will slip back to where they were in the depths of their despair. Toward the end of my analysis, I asked my doctor that very question. Her reply was, "Yes, you can slip back, but *things will never be as bad for you as they were, for you now have the key: You know the reason why, and this knowledge will act as a life preserver. When you find yourself in treacherous waters, that life preserver will keep you afloat.*"

From Alice Figura, who took care of her father while he was dying:

There are two things that I consider to be traps after the death of a parent: 1) blaming the tragedy on God, and 2) trying to minimize other people's problems and considering our own as the heaviest burden. God doesn't cause tragedies and He doesn't stop them from happening. Harold Kushner wrote in his book, *When Bad Things Happen To Good People,* that God gives us the strength and perseverance to overcome our tragedies. I sincerely believe that. And if we can just get beyond the initial anger, and give ourselves time to return to the religion we grew up with, we will be better for it. I think the clergy make a big mistake in the early period of grief by trying to shove religion down your throat. If they would give you a little breathing space to let out the pent-up feelings, then you would be better able to hear and accept what they are saying. If they waited until you had released that anger, their words would have more meaning.

From Patricia Tremont, who lost both of her parents:

Keeping busy is the chief key to dealing with any

problem in life that is major, especially the death of someone you love. I knew that to survive I had to keep my mind and hands occupied. I think if you have an interest in sports or traveling, or have a hobby, or enjoy dancing, that you will need to immerse yourself in the activity that absorbs you. You will have less free time to think about the 'ifs' and the 'shoulds' and the 'coulds.' Nothing you can do will bring them back. By becoming involved with an activity or hobby, you give your mind a much-needed rest from the different emotions. It's like giving a prisoner a reprieve. And, eventually, you are able to resume your life.

From Max Glauben, whose parents were killed in the Holocaust:

In life, you have to realize that you must talk about living and dying. Our body matures, but many times our mind doesn't keep up with our bodily growth. When you are fifty years old, your body shows it, but if your mind has not kept up chronologically, you can still have the thoughts of a teenager who doesn't think about death and can't accept it. Yet we must accept it. Adult children have to realize that death is a part of life and that when their parent dies, it is part of living. Once you accept that death is a reality, its impact, when it strikes a loved one, will be much easier to face. Unfortunately, most people will not accept the reality of death.

Another point I would like to make is that if you have children, prepare them for the reality of the world. That will be a great act of love on your part. Prepare them to face the world on their own. When bad things happen, talk to them about it and tell them that this is life. Don't wait weeks or months to explain a bad action directed at your children—talk about it right away.

Sometimes you think things may never get better,

but I would like to tell you a story about something that happened to me. After my father, mother, and brother perished in concentration camps, I had assumed that my father's two younger sisters were also led to the gas chambers at a death camp. Then, last year, at the American Gathering of Jewish Holocaust Survivors in Philadelphia, there were computer data banks into which people were asked to put information about themselves. At first, I felt there'd be no point in my doing this, for I figured there was no one left in my family, but my wife urged me and so I did.

After I returned home to Dallas, I received a phone call—a very extraordinary phone call. My two aunts, Hanna and Irene, were alive! And they were living in Philadelphia! They had been looking for me for forty years! Like me, they had been sent to work camps. Right after liberation, someone told them I may have made it alive. They searched for me in Israel and through computers, but could find no trace, and eventually they gave up trying to find me.

Now, after these forty years, I find I am not the only surviving member of my family. I cannot tell you the euphoria I have experienced in talking to them and seeing them. My sense of loss and grief was greatly diminished by my newfound gain. So when we think we may never again know the warmth of being with those who were part of our lives, something like this can happen to uplift you, and which can turn your whole life around. This incident was important from another standpoint: I had never actually seen my mother's death and they verified it.

From Lisa Strahs-Lorenc, whose biological mother and father died, but whose adoptive mother still lives:

What I would like to say is what was said to me during the HEAL group sessions. When I first heard the name HEAL (*H*elp *E*ase *A* *L*oss), I didn't understand it and I don't know if others will. HEAL is staffed by volunteers who have already been through the sorrow of loss. We, the newly bereaved, ask them how they feel now, as it has been some years since they suffered their losses. They reply, "It does get better, and it doesn't hurt as much. Time really helps." That was their reply to my questioning, but I ignored them because I was hurting so badly. I thought to myself, "There's no way that I will ever feel good again or be happy again." *But everything they said is true. It does get better.* Now I can't really remember how it was the first year, but I guess time takes care of that. At the moment, it seems to me that it was another lifetime ago—and another person's life.

From Phil Musmacker, whose mother died of cancer:

If you isolate yourself from the world, you will never recover from your depression. After a parent's death, you must never quit. Rather, you must keep going on and never limit the areas of your search for help. Inquire about roads to recovery through a counselor, a clergyperson, the church, or organizations that help. To close up will be your finish. You must let everything out—the anger and the guilt. If you isolate yourself and keep in your hurt, you will never make it—you will self-destruct.

So keep searching, no matter how much effort it takes. Good things can begin to happen in your life when you find ways to help yourself. I am a living example of that. My wife and I now have two beautiful sons, Phillip and Bryan, and we are working toward living a meaningful and fulfilling life together.

PART TWO

Helping Hands

CHAPTER 20

Role Model for Bereavement Support Program

Karen Arfin, Director of the Miller Place Family Counseling Center of Sound Beach, New York, describes how she proceeded with a mutual support group of which she was the leader:

"A typical session starts with a warmup exercise, something that will get the group focused on the material at hand. Perhaps we will go around and share reactions to last week's session, or perhaps we will tell what the week has been like for us. In other words, we will try anything to get focused on what we have to do.

"Many things come out of this, such as remembering what we had to do while we were grieving, or going for a job interview, or getting the washing machine fixed, or any other thing that stirred emotions. I also, through that process, recognize that although it is difficult to come to these meetings, it's important for the mourner to do so, and we are glad that each one was able to be with us. That is the first part of the meeting.

"In the second part of the meeting, which really has the most content, I may do a variety of things. I may have some kind of written exercise to get the group in touch with whatever their bereavement issues are. I may ask them to write down two things that are giving them difficulty in terms of bereavement. Then, we will go around the group and discuss those difficulties. The second activity would be to write down two things with which they feel they have made some kind of progress.

"To me, it seems important to legitimize the fact that grieving is a process, and that oftentimes when we are immersed in the awful pain and anguish of grief, we lose sight of the fact that progress *has* been made. Many people think progress must be really dramatic and expect one day they will wake up feeling good. However, the reality of bereavement is that it doesn't work that way. I try to help the bereaved to see that last week or two weeks ago or six months ago, they couldn't have said the things they say now, such as 'I couldn't go into his room and clean it, but now I can.' Or 'I couldn't go to the supermarket, but now I can.' Or 'I was behaving like a robot but now I am thinking more clearly.'

"Then we move on to a point where, in the beginning, there had been numbness and disbelief. Beyond that is the reality. When it really hits, sometimes people think they have gone backward and are regressing. When the real grief hits them and suddenly they are weeping and not functioning, they believe that something terrible has happened and they have lost ground. But that is not so. Underlying the whole process of the group experience is learning and being able to conceptualize grieving, that it has a beginning and an end, that things will get better. They will never forget. Their lives will never be the same. It can never go back to what it was, but that is not to say they cannot hope to achieve some kind of meaning.

"As for me, I wouldn't do this work if I didn't feel there was some kind of hope. When people are desperate, in pain and are learning they are not going crazy, that other people go through this, and that they aren't alone and perhaps they will survive, too, that to me is the most important thing. If people can go away with some measure of hope that life can go on and have some kind of meaning, then I think we have given them a wonderful gift.

"The groups are kept small because it seems to work better that way, giving people a chance to say what they need to say. Often when people are under terrible stress such as a time of bereavement, the support of a small group is more effective than a large one, which could be overwhelming. I have volunteers whom I have trained to work with me, and in a two-session training program, I provide supervision after each group is organized as to what happens in the group.

"To provide a model of assistance to others who may wish to contemplate forming a mutual help group, I have developed a Bereavement Support Training Manual.* Portions of it are shown below."

Surviving children can also benefit from the insight of what takes place in a mutual help support group.

PROGRAM DESIGN

A six-consecutive-week, short-term crisis intervention model is utilized. The program enhances the rapid focusing on difficult material, development of trust, and importance of intervening quickly during the bereavement crisis. It also allows for sufficient time to cover the most essential areas of the grieving process in the group. In addition, more people can be accommodated over the year with a short-term group. Group size varies from six to ten new mem-

Bereavement Support Program Training Manual, prepared by Karen Arfin, M.S.W., C.S.W., Copyright © 1991.

bers per group with a maximum of twelve members to provide sufficient time for individual sharing of feelings and experiences.

A new group series starts every two months, so waiting lists are not a problem. Phone contact with the prospective new member can be maintained, if necessary, while awaiting the beginning of a new group.

All prospective new members are screened by the leader for membership. The great majority of callers are appropriate for the groups and can function adequately in the group in terms of being able to discuss their situation. If the leader feels it advisable, or the member requests it, the leader can suggest more in-depth counseling, either for bereavement or other problems affecting the member's life.

The support group is open to any adult who is experiencing the loss of a significant other adult, either a parent, family member, or friend. Weekly group sessions offer guidance and support through discussion with the program director or a team of trained volunteers.

A core of six volunteers has been trained and supervised by the leader. The volunteers have been divided into two sets allowing each set of three to rotate participation in the group. This permits the volunteers to serve two to three groups per year thereby diluting, for them, the often painful intensity of the group experience. The leader provides supervision on a weekly basis to volunteers, at the end of each group session, to interpret and process the experience. All the volunteers have been through at least one serious loss of a loved one and are able to understand and support group members because the volunteers have "been there." Some of the volunteers were group members and remained on to assist others.

NEED

The breakdown of the nuclear family and the increasing mobility of people in our society have resulted in a lack of long- or short-term support following the loss of a loved one. Community programs dealing with bereavement were unavailable to people in many areas, resulting in increased feelings of isolation and depression for community members, while attempting to cope with their bereavement.

Bereavement support groups have been formed to address this problem by providing emotional and social support, as well as information to those who grieve, to help them cope as fully as possible with their loss.

Bereavement Support Group Outline

Session I

1. Introduction
   a. Introduce leader and volunteers
   b. Brief history of the Bereavement Support Program
   c. Mechanics of group
2. Warm-up exercise
   a. Participants go around in circle and share about their situation
   b. Leader comments briefly when appropriate
3. Group expectation exercise
   a. Participants spend a few minutes thinking about what they hope to gain from the experience
   b. Participants go around in the circle and share their expectations

4. Closing
   a. Participants are directed to close their eyes and get in touch with their feelings
   b. Share feelings

Session II
1. Warm-up exercise
   a. Participants are directed to go around in the circle and share how they're feeling, reactions to last week's session, or any other comments
   b. Leader responds when appropriate
2. Presentation of material about Bereavement
   a. Kübler-Ross' five stages of grieving
   b. Roberta Temes' three stages of grief
   c. Difference between pathological and "normal" depression
   d. Discussion
3. Closing
   a. Participants are directed to close their eyes and get in touch with their feelings
   b. Share feelings

Session III
1. Warm-up exercise as in previous sessions
2. Stages of grief exercise
   a. Distribute pencils and paper
   b. Leader lists Kübler-Ross' five stages of grief on the board: denial, bargaining, depression/anger, grief, and acceptance
   c. Participants are directed to take a few minutes and think and write about how the stages apply to their own experiences and where are they currently. Where have they been?
   d. Discuss, with a focus on how participants

felt doing the exercise, as well as what they learned
3. Closing as in previous sessions

Session IV
1. Warm-up exercise as in previous sessions
2. Current concerns exercise
   a. Paper and pencil
   b. Participants are directed to list two things that they are having trouble dealing with at the present time
   c. Go around in circle and share
   d. Participants are directed to list two things that they have made progress with since the death
   e. Share
   f. Process: How participants felt doing the exercise and what was learned
3. Regrets exercise
   a. Participants are directed to think about and write down the answer to the question: "If only I was . . . "
   b. Share
   c. Participants are directed to think about and write down "What I did do . . . "
   d. Share
   e. Discussion comparing the two lists with a focus on regrets as a normal part of grieving and the importance of maintaining realistic perspective on our capabilities
4. Closing as in previous sessions

Session V
1. Warm-up exercise as in previous sessions
2. Letter to deceased exercise
   a. Pencil and paper

b. Participants are directed to write a letter to the deceased saying all the things that were left unsaid previously or anything to bring the deceased "up to date"
   Note: This is often a very painful exercise; however, most participants are able to complete the letter with emotional support.
c. Leader asks for someone to share his/her letter. It is sometimes necessary, if the participant is too overwhelmed to share the letter, that the leader read it. However, every opportunity is given for all the participants to read their own letters.
d. Continue to ask for volunteers until all letters are read
e. Process: How participants felt: 1) When asked to write the letter, 2) When actually writing it, and 3) Upon completion of the writing
f. Leader sums up by discussing both the difficulty and benefit in terms of catharsis and beginning of closure
g. Closing as in previous sessions

Session VI
1. Warm-up exercise as in previous sessions
2. "Endings exercise"
   a. Participants are directed to think about and write down two to three feelings about the group ending
   b. Share
   c. Leader discusses the importance of endings in our lives: the difficulty in "saying goodbye," the need to move on to other relationships, etc.
3. Group evaluation exercise
   a. Participants are directed to list two to three

    ways that the group has been helpful to
    them
  b. Participants are directed to list improve-
    ments and suggestions for future groups
  c. Share
4. Leader discusses referrals for more in-depth
   counseling
5. Closing as in previous sessions

❧ CHAPTER 21

Organizations that Help Bereaved Families

Helping hands come in many forms—through support groups, individual or group therapy, religion, or bibliotherapy, with many enlightening books to read. Since each family is different and each person is different, no one helping hand is necessarily the right one for everybody—but there are many helping hands! If it is good for you, then it is right. If it isn't, make a change. Try another way!

Some may be more at ease in a group setting; others may not. Some may find organizations extremely helpful, while others may find it is simply not for them. Some may prefer the intimate setting of a family doctor's office, their clergyman, or a counselor or therapist and may have a very good experience. Others may have an absolutely rotten experience and may have to look further.

It is important for bereaved sons and daughters to realize that there *are* alternatives. There are other helping hands. Find one that feels comfortable to you—because that way is the *right* way for you. If you are made to feel uncomfortable, make a change. There are other ways and you will find one that is right for you.

In seeking referrals, check with a compassionate family doctor or community clergyman to find an individual or group that focuses on grief. There are many grief centers and grief groups springing up throughout the country. Look in your local community papers. Ask the funeral director who assisted your family. Inquire at your church or synagogue or contact local pastoral counselors. Seek out information from hospitals, crisis-intervention groups, and check for private practitioners who specialize in grief therapy. But, most of all, reach out to find a way to help yourself.

Following is an alphabetical listing of some groups and organizations that may be helpful to you in your search. Again, if you are unable to find a way to help yourself, reach out to those who can aid you in doing so.

American Association for Marriage and Family Therapy

Therapists indicate that for some people their unresolved grief and mourning significantly interfere with their ability to be emotionally close to their spouse and children. Bereaved sons and daughters need to go through periods of grieving until they are able to accept what is unalterable. Much of how people react to tragedies has to do with what they experienced early in life in their family of origin and how they saw other family members deal with loss.

AAMFT is an association of well-trained individual therapists who specialize in all phases of marriage and family life. In the course of their work with individuals, couples, and families, they often have to help people deal with illness and death of family members and for this reason have experience and knowledge in how to be of help. Their 18,000 members throughout the United States and Canada include persons trained in psychology, marriage and family therapy, psychiatry, pastoral counseling, and social work—all of whom are highly trained professional therapists. The AAMFT carries on intensive educational programs to help people understand more about marriage and family problems, the role of counseling in preventing and solving these problems, as well as the dangers of unscrupulous or unqualified persons who pose as marriage and family therapists. For the public the AAMFT provides a nationwide referral service by supplying the names of qualified marriage and family therapists and general guidelines for seeking their help. To obtain most current information, it is best to write to their national office at:

American Association for Marriage and Family
   Therapy
1100 17th Street, NW
10th floor
Washington, DC 20036
(202) 452-0109

Hotline for Therapist Referral: 800–374–2638

American Association of Retired Persons (AARP) Widowed Persons Service

Adult children are often concerned about their surviving parent. To help relieve that stress, there are hundreds of groups and programs throughout the country that offer help after the loss of a spouse. A major resource, the American Association of Retired Persons, has developed a program called the "Widowed Persons Service" which has expanded to almost 200 communities. The program is comprised of volunteers who have been widowed for at least a year and a half, to insure they have a complete understanding of problems encountered by those recently widowed. WPS has been an outstanding help to many thousands of widowed men and women during this trying time in their lives. For more information, write to:

American Association of Retired Persons
Widowed Persons Service
1909 K Street, NW
Washington, DC 20049

Grief Education Institute

Many people do not know how to cope with their own grief nor how to help others who are grieving. The Grief Education Institute provides services to the bereaved, to the general public, and to professionals to counteract social stresses imposed on the bereaved by society. Services include:

1. Telephone counseling
2. Support groups for the bereaved
3. Educational programs for the public
4. Educational programs for professionals
5. A lending library of resources on grief and bereavement
6. A quarterly newsletter
7. Research on the needs of the bereaved and how to meet these needs
8. Referral to other community agencies
9. Individual counseling for adults, children, and families

The Institute states that not all bereaved persons need help coping with their grief. "Persons who are at higher risk and who are more likely to need special help include those bereaved by homicide or suicide; a sudden or unexpected death; multiple bereavements; numerous other life crises concurrent with a death; or those lacking an available support system." Although other types of losses may be as stressful as a death loss, because of limited resources the Institute focuses only on grief to a death.

In defining what a support group is, the Institute states: "The grief support group is a shared experience designed for persons who wish the support of a structured group while going through the process of grieving, or for persons who are experiencing difficulty resolving the death of a loved one. Support groups at the Institute meet weekly for ten sessions. Two facilitators lead the group. The group combines an educational and supportive approach. The focus is on healthy grieving and coping through the use of specific grief work exercises and homework assignments. Interaction with a small group of other bereaved people is one of the most valuable aspects of this process. The facilitators who guide the group are also available by telephone between sessions. This is not a therapy group. The leaders make appropriate referrals when indicated. Confidentiality is respected at all times. Day and evening groups are available.

An executive director administers the programs and services. Volunteers, who are trained and supervised, provide telephone and personal counseling, co-lead support groups, assist in program presentations and provide clerical assistance. "They may include educators, clergy, physicians, psychiatrists, nurses, businessmen, and women," states the Institute.

The Education Institute also offers a facilitator-training class twice yearly, open to anyone who wishes to receive training in leading support groups for the bereaved.

For more information, write to:

Grief Education Institute
2422 S. Downing St.
Denver, Colorado 80210
(303) 777-9324

Bereavement and Loss Center of New York

Anne Rosberger, M.S.W., C.S.W., Executive Director
Henry Rosberger, M.D., Medical Director

The Bereavement and Loss Center was founded in 1975 when the Widows Consultation Center in New York City, the first bereavement center for widows, closed for lack of funding. Anne Rosberger, M.S.W., a psychotherapist, was chief consultant and social work supervisor at the WCC. She and her husband, Henry Rosberger, M.D., a psychiatrist and psychoanalyst, founded the Bereavement and Loss Center and widened its scope to include all areas of loss and bereavement.

Those who come to the center may have experienced the death of a parent, child, spouse, sibling, or significant other, or are anticipating such a loss. The death may be the result of natural causes, accident, suicide, or homicide. Clients are seen individually or in family or group therapy. Unlike many agencies that include grief counseling as one aspect of their work, BLC's mission is exclusively in the domain of bereavement counseling. Fees are moderate.

"Many clients come to the center before or soon after the loss of a loved one. Others, such as adult children who have lost parents, frequently come many years later following a disruption in their lives which seems connected in some way to earlier parental loss," states Mrs. Rosberger. "The unique and powerful bond between these children and their parent has been described in depth over the years. The pain and suffering in breaking this bond at various ages through death has more recently become a subject of public concern and interest.

"In bereavement counseling, the range of feelings

around the death is explored—the love, the dependency, anger, shame, and guilt. The individual is guided through his often conflicting feelings about his parents, their life together, their interaction, the events and feelings that shape their relationship, circumstances surrounding the death of a parent, impact of the loss, and other factors unique to that relationship. In the process, the adult offspring is able to resolve some of the distortions, ambivalences, and dependency needs around the deceased parent and begins to reinvest his energy in relationships and events of everyday living. Though never forgetting the parent, the surviving child is able to live more fully in the present and look to the future with greater ease and confidence."

Bereavement and Loss Center of New York
170 East 83rd Street
New York, NY 10028
(212) 879-5655

Family Services America

Description:
  Family Services America is an independent, nonprofit organization supported by membership dues, industry contracts, publication sales, and government and foundation grants.
  FSA advises more than 250 counseling organizations and agencies—sectarian and nonsectarian—throughout the United States and Canada. Family Service America helps families build stronger relationships, make positive adjustments to life changes, understand the pressures of today's living, and create contentment at home and on the job. Founded in 1911, FSA's work is geared to parents, children, teens, young adults, and aging relatives.

By providing the member agencies with technical assistance and research information, FSA addresses the changing needs of the American family, in and out of crisis, by providing family counseling services, books on various issues, and innovative programs.

Family Services America publishes an annual *Directory of Member Agencies* which may be obtained by writing to:

Family Services America
11700 West Lake Park Drive
Park Place
Milwaukee, WI 53224
(414) 359-2111

Hospice Organizations and Hospice-Type Programs

Most hospices offer bereavement counseling to surviving sons and daughters. This caring help is not only extended to those whose mother or father died in the hospice, but often is offered to those whose parent may have died elsewhere, say bereavement counselors. It is suggested you call the hospice nearest you. If this help is not available, the hospice may act as a referral service for bereavement help when it is not offered on their premises.

There are more than 1850 hospices in the United States, with 1200 accredited by Medicare. Over 200,000 patients and families received hospice services last year. Overseas, there are hospices in Australia, Canada, England, New Zealand, Japan, South Africa, The Netherlands, and Thailand.

At Visiting Nurse Service Hospice Program in New York, a memorial service at the end of the year was given in honor of their deceased patients. Reverend Paul F. Morrissey, Pastoral Care Coordinator of the VNS Hospice Program, describes the memorial service and lists some of the guidelines used in planning it:

"At noon in mid-December, as the Christmas, Hanukkah and New Year holidays approached, the memorial service was conducted. Family and friends of deceased patients from the preceding 13 months were invited to join hospice team members for this touching event. It was a time to remember their deceased loved ones and patients, a time at the year's end to remember and let go. The event was a very moving experience for those attending. It included approximately 65 family members of varied religious traditions, as well as most members of the hospice team.

"The fact that it was not a dreary, depressing experience, but rather touching and uplifting—even at times humorous—was noted by many of the participants."

Below are some of the guidelines used in planning the memorial service:

Place—The beauty and warmth of the main conference room at VNS headquarters provided a perfect ambience for such a "family" event.

Music—Students from the Julliard School of Music created a gentle and inspiring mood with an ensemble of flute, cello and violin.

Story Telling—An ancient way of remembering and caressing the dead became a breakthrough from merely "attending" a service to making it oneself. Many participants shared a significant memory of their loved ones, often evoking the balm of laughter, as well as tears.

Symbols—Participants were invited to bring a small picture of the deceased. After the story telling had linked them together in a 'holding up of the lives of their loved ones,' they were asked to come forward and place the pictures on "The Tree of Life." At the same time, VNS nurses read aloud from "The Book of Life," in which the names of the deceased are inscribed.

A Social—Following the service, a time for refreshments allowed individual communication among the families and the hospice team members. Anecdotes and grief were shared and gratitude was expressed—a communal celebration of the bereavement process often missing for the families and the hospice team.

Staff Participation—Not only the Pastoral Care Department was involved in the success of this endeavor. Jeanne Dennis, VNS Hospice Administrator, provided the enthusiastic go-ahead for it and the encouragement to do it with "class," for example, the printed invitations for the families. Many of the hospice team members were involved in the preparation, as well as taking key parts in the ceremony."

Jeanne Dennis elaborates on the care of survivors: "It is important to note the hospice concept includes care to those who survive the death, up to and through the anniversary of the death. Almost all hospice programs have bereavement follow-up through the first year for the survivors. It's really much different than traditional health care where, when the patient, dies, the relationship ends between the family and the hospital or the home care agency. In hospice, that is not the case. The relationship and the support continues and is sustained throughout that first year."

To obtain details on hospice locations in your vicinity, please send a stamped, self-addressed envelope to the:

National Hospice Organization
1901 North Moore Street, Suite 901
Arlington, Virginia 22209
(800) 658-8898

National Mental Health Association

Note: The following listing does not constitute an endorsement but is provided only as another possible avenue of help. A number of these divisions and chapters conduct educational programs concerning grief and bereavement, and all their affiliates serve as referral agencies. It will be necessary to check if the particular chapter near you has an existing program or assistance available to the bereaved. You may also wish to look under "Grief Centers."

Mental Health Association in Alabama
306 Whitman Street
Montgomery, AL 36104

Alaska Mental Health Association
5401 Cordova Street, #304
Anchorage, AK 99503

Mental Health Association in Arizona
1515 E. Osborn Road
Phoenix, AZ 85014

Mental Health Association in Arkansas
3006 Meyer Building
Hot Springs, AR 71901

Mental Health Association in California
1211 "H" Street, Suite F
Sacramento, CA 95814

Mental Health Association in Colorado
252 Clayton Street, Garden #2
Denver, CO 80206

Mental Health Association in Connecticut
56 Arbor Street
Hartford, CT 06106

Mental Health Association in Delaware
1813 N. Franklin Street
Wilmington, DE 19802

D. C. Mental Health Association
2101 16th Street NW
Washington, D.C. 20009

Mental Health Association of Florida
Suite 207, Myrick Building
132 E. Colonial Drive
Orlando, FL 32801

Mental Health Association in Georgia
100 Edgewood Avenue NE, #502
Atlanta, GA 30303

Mental Health Association in Hawaii
200 N. Vineyard Boulevard, #507
Honolulu, HI 96817

Mental Health Association in Illinois
1418 S. 7th Street
Springfield, IL 62703

Mental Health Association in Indiana
1433 N. Meridian Street
Indianapolis, IN 46202

Mental Health Association in Iowa
315 E. 5th Street
Des Moines, IA 50315

Mental Health Association in Kansas
1205 Harrison Street
Topeka, KS 66612

Kentucky Association for Mental Health
310 W. Liberty Street, #106
Louisville, KY 40202

Mental Health Association in Louisiana
1528 Jackson Avenue
New Orleans, LA 70130

Mental Health Association of Maryland
325 E. 25th Street
Baltimore, MD 21218

Massachusetts Association for Mental Health
1 Walnut Street
Boston, MA 02108

Mental Health Association in Michigan
15920 W. Twelve Mile Road
Southfield, MI 48076

Mental Health Association in Minnesota
6715 Minnetonka Boulevard, #209–10
St. Louis Park, MN 55426

Mental Health Association in Mississippi
P.O. Box 5041
Jackson, MS 39216

Mental Health Association in Missouri
P. O. Box 1667
Jefferson City, MO 65102

Mental Health Association in Montana
201 S. Last Chance Gulch, #207
Helena, MT 59601

New Hampshire Association for Mental Health
11 South Main
Concord, NH 03301

Mental Health Association in New Jersey
60 S. Fullerton Avenue
Montclair, NJ 07042

Mental Health Association in North Carolina
3701 National Drive, #222
Raleigh, NC 27612

Mental Health Association in North Dakota
P.O. Box 160
Bismarck, ND 58501

Mental Health Association in Ohio
50 W. Broad Street, #2440
Columbus, OH 43215

Mental Health Association in Oklahoma
1140 North West 32
Oklahoma City, OK 73118

Mental Health Association in Oregon
718 W. Burnside, Room 301
Portland, OR 97209

Mental Health Association in Pennsylvania
1207 Chestnut Street
Philadelphia, PA 19107

Mental Health Association in Rhode Island
57 Hope Street
Providence, RI 02906

South Dakota Mental Health Association
101½ S. Pierre Street, Box 353
Pierre, SD 57501

Tennessee Mental Health Association
250 Venture Circle
Nashville, TN 37228

Texas Association for Mental Health
4600 Burnet Road
Austin, TX 78756

Utah Association for
  Mental Health
982 E. 3300 South
Salt Lake City, UT 84106

Mental Health Associa-
  tion in Virginia
1806 Chantilly Street,
  #203
Richmond, VA 23230

Mental Health Associa-
  tion in Washington
500 John Street
Seattle, WA 98109

West Virginia Association
  for Mental Health
702½ Lee Street
Charleston, WV 25301

Wisconsin Association
  for Mental Health
119 E. Mifflin, Box 1486
Madison, WI 53701

Survivors of Suicide Support Group

Description:

Survivors of Suicide (SOS) is a self-help organization offering support and understanding to bereaved persons who have lost a loved one through
suicide. When an individual dies, family and friends
begin a period of grief. The loss of a loved one
through suicide is a swift and devastating experience
for the survivor because there is no preparation time
for acceptance of the death; guilt feelings are intensified by the "if onlys"; and frustration is sharply felt
due to the unanswered question of "why." Often,
people who have lost someone by suicide are comforted most by others who have undergone the same
experience.

The SOS support group is facilitated entirely by
survivors and there is no set agenda or "steps."
Monthly meetings include informal conversations, a
sharing of experience, books, and resources. The
meetings acknowledge the pain and loss of death by
suicide, yet offer reinforcement and understanding

necessary for the healing process to occur. The self-help group encourages the ventilation of feelings which might not be shared with persons who have not lost a loved one through suicide. It offers support, understanding, and a lack of judgmental attitudes. A bond is formed through the shared experience even in the separateness of individual lives.

Survivors of Suicide maintains a listing of support groups in the United States and Canada for family and friends after a suicide death. For information on groups in your area, please send a self-addressed stamped envelope to Survivors of Suicide, P.O. Box 1393, Dayton, Ohio 45401-1393.

The Survivors of Suicide Support Group welcomes people of diverse experiences, beliefs, economic backgrounds, races, and creeds in dealing with their painful loss of a loved one through suicide. *There are no attendance or financial requirements.*

For any other information, contact;

Survivors of Suicide
Suicide Prevention Center, Inc.
184 Salem Avenue
Dayton, Ohio 45401-1393
(513) 223-9096
Note: The 24-hour crisis hotline for the bereaved to call is: (513) 223-4777.

The Bereavement Center of the Family Service Association of Nassau County, New York

Description:

A voluntary nonprofit agency that provides participation in small group sessions in which people share and learn with others as a way of coping with death. All groups are led by professionally trained social workers specializing in bereavement. Though groups are a most helpful way of coping with death, individual and family counseling is available if needed before, during, or after the group experience.

Although many experiences of bereaved adult children are part of normal grief, sometimes help is needed during the lengthy period of bereavement. The Bereavement Center was designed to help individuals and families work through this important part of living. The purpose of the Center is to help ease the transition by: coping with the death; learning to live in a world without the deceased; forming new relationships.

Group meetings are held at Family Service Association facilities and other locations convenient to group members. The fee for sessions is on a sliding scale based on ability to pay. For more information, contact:

Michael Miller, C.S.W., A.C.S.W.
Bereavement Center Director
129 Jackson Street
Hempstead, N.Y. 11550
(516) 485-4600

Salvatore Ambrosino, Ed.D., C.S.W., Executive Director; Lawrence Gumbs, M.S.W., Associate Director; Arlene Siegelwaks, A.C.S.W., Assistant Director; H. Baldwin Hamilton, Controller.

Transition Bereavement Program of Nassau and Suffolk County

Description:
Coping with death through counseling, the Transition Bereavement Program specializes in the needs of those who are experiencing feelings of depression, anger, guilt, or isolation because of the death of a parent, child, or spouse.

Often a few sessions with someone trained to guide them through this process can help not only the individual, but the family, to gain insight and understanding, which can lead to a faster return into the mainstream of life.

Since society often supports the denial of feeling during the grief process, it is sometimes necessary to direct clients, patients, friends, and relatives to a service which can help them cope and integrate the many feelings that arise during that normal grief process.

Services are provided on a sliding scale for individuals and families to help them move through this most difficult time.

For more information, contact:

Roslyn Marcus, A.C.S.W.
Bereavement Director
Transition Bereavement Program
410 East Main Street
Centerport, New York 11721
(516) 488-7697

SPECIAL NOTE:

If there are any groups or organizations dealing with bereavement that the reader believes should be included in this "Helping Hands" section, please contact the writer at the address below. We will try to put these in updated editions in future.

Katherine Fair Donnelly
Author
c/o The Berkley Publishing Group
      200 Madison Avenue
      New York, N.Y. 10016

Suggested Reading

Becker, E. *The Denial of Death.* New York: The Free Press, 1973.

Bowlby, John. *Attachment and Loss.* New York: Basic Books, 1980.

Caine, Lynn. *Widow.* New York: William Morrow and Company, Inc., 1974.

Campbell, Scott, with Silverman, Phyllis R. *Men Alone.* New York: Simon and Schuster, 1986.

Choron, J. *Death and Western Thought.* New York: Macmillan, 1963.

Corr, Charles and Corr, Donna. *Hospice Care.* New York: Springer Publishing Co., 1983.

Davidson, Glen W. *Understanding Mourning.* Minneapolis: Augsburg Publishing, 1984.

Durkheim, Emil. *Suicide.* New York: Free Press, 1951.

Dunlop, Richard. *Helping The Bereaved.* Bowie, Md.: The Charles Press, 1978.

Feifel, Herman, ed. *New Meanings of Death.* New York: McGraw-Hill Book Company, 1977.

Fulton, Robert, ed. *Death and Identity.* Bowie, Md.: The Charles Press, 1976.

Gorer, G. *Death, Grief, and Mourning.* Garden City, New York: Doubleday, 1967.

Grollman, Earl, ed. *Concerning Death.* Boston: Beacon Press, 1974.

———. *What Helped Me When My Loved One Died.* Boston: Beacon Press, 1981.

Hansen, J. C., and Frantz T. T. *Death and Grief in the Family.* Rockville, Md.: An Aspen Publication, 1984.

Jackson, Edgar N. *Coping with the Crises in Your Life.* New York: Jason Aronson, 1980.

Kübler-Ross, E. *On Death and Dying.* New York: The Macmillan Company, 1969.

———. *Death: The Final Stage of Growth.* Englewood Cliffs, N.J.: Prentice-Hall, 1975.

———. *Working It Through.* New York: Macmillan Publishing, 1982.

Kushner, Harold S. *When Bad Things Happen to Good People*. New York: Schocken Books, 1981.

Kutscher, A., and Kutscher, L. *For The Bereaved*. New York: Frederick Fell, Inc., 1971.

Lifton, Robert J. *The Broken Connection*. New York: Simon and Schuster, 1979.

Margolis, O. S., H. C. Raether, A. H. Kutscher, J. B. Powers, J. Seeland, R. DeBellis, and D. J. Cherico, eds. *Acute Grief: Counseling the Bereaved*. New York: Columbia University Press, 1981.

Meagher, D. K., and Shapiro, R. D. *Death: The Experience*. Minneapolis: Burgess Publishing Co., 1984.

Mitscherlich, A., and Mitscherlich, M. *The Inability to Mourn*. New York: Grove Press, 1975.

Parkes, Colin M., *Bereavement*. New York: International Universities Press, 1972.

Parkes, Colin M., and Weiss, Robert S. *Recovery From Bereavement*. New York: Basic Books, Inc., 1983.

Pincus, Lily. *Death and the Family: The Importance of Mourning*. New York: Vintage Books, 1976.

Raether, H.C., and Slater, R. C. *The Funeral Director and His Role As A Counselor*. Milwaukee: National Funeral Director Association, 1975.

Raphael, Beverly. *The Anatomy of Bereavement*. New York: Basic Books, 1982.

Rubin, Theodore I. *The Angry Book*. New York: The Macmillan Company, 1969.

Schoenberg, Bernard, ed. *Anticipatory Grief*. New York: Columbia University Press, 1974.

Silverman, Phyllis R. *Mutual Help Groups: Organization and Development*. Beverly Hills, CA: Sage Publishing Company, 1981.

———. *Helping Women Cope With Grief*. Beverly Hills, CA: Sage Publishing Company, 1980.

Stephenson, John S. *Death, Grief and Mourning*. New York: The Free Press, 1985.

Sterns, Ann Kaiser. *Living Through Personal Crisis*. Chicago, Ill.: The Thomas More Press, 1984.

Temes, Roberta, *Living with an Empty Chair*. New York: Irvington Publishers, Inc. 1980.

Toffler, A. *Future Shock*. New York: Random House, Inc., 1970.

Troup, S., and Greene, W., eds. *The Patient, Death and the Family*. New York: Charles Scribner's Sons, 1974.

Veatch, Robert. *Death, Dying and the Biological Revolution*. New Haven: Yale University Press, 1976.

Veninga, Robert L. *A Gift of Hope: How We Survive Our Tragedies*. New York: Ballantine Books, 1985.

Worden, W. J. *Grief Counseling and Grief Therapy*. New York: Springer Publishing Co., 1982.

Index